Janet Ashbee

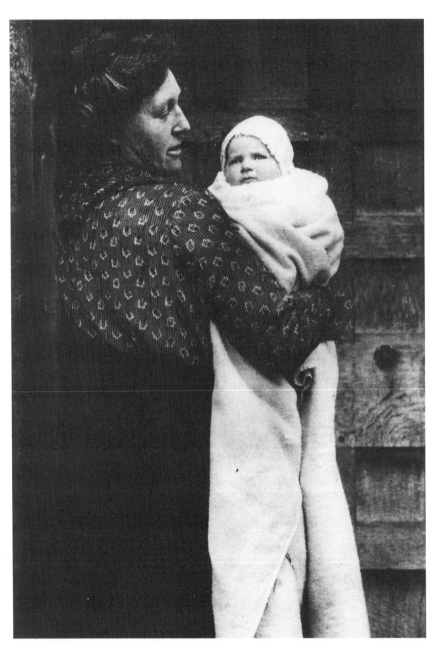

Janet Ashbee with her fourth daughter, Prudence, 1917

Janet Ashbee

*Love, Marriage, and the
Arts & Crafts Movement*

Felicity Ashbee

With an Introduction by
ALAN CRAWFORD

Syracuse University Press

First Edition 2002
02   03   04   05   06   07   6   5   4   3   2   1

Publication of this volume is made possible in part by grants from
the Guild of Handicraft Trust, Chipping Campden, and the Arts
and Crafts Society of Central New York, Syracuse.

Illustrations are courtesy of the Ashbee family, unless otherwise
attributed.

The paper used in this publication meets the minimum require-
ments of American National Standard for Information Sciences—
Permanence of Paper for Printed Library Materials, ANSI
Z39.48-1984.

LIBRARY OF CONGRESS CATALOGING-IN-PUBLICATION DATA

Ashbee, Felicity.
   Janet Ashbee : love, marriage, and the arts and crafts
movement / Felicity Ashbee ; with an introduction by Alan
Crawford.— 1st ed.
      p. cm.
   ISBN 0-8156-0731-8
   1. Ashbee, Janet E. (Janet Elizabeth) 2. Artists'
spouses—England—Biography. 3. Ashbee, C. R. (Charles
Robert), 1863–1942—Family. 4. Arts and crafts movement—
England. I. Title.
   N6797.A76 A84 2002
   745'.092—dc21   2002001378

Manufactured in the United States of America

To the Comrade Grandchildren

you are the first and only woman to whom I have felt
I could offer the same loyal reverence of affection
that I have heretofore given to my men friends.
Will not the inference be obvious to you?
There are many comrade friends,
there can only be one
comrade wife.

C. R. ASHBEE TO JANET FORBES

Felicity Ashbee was born in Gloucestershire in 1913, and was educated at various schools in Jerusalem and England. From 1932 to 1936, she studied at the Byam Shaw School of Art in London, and later exhibited at the Royal Academy. During World War II, she served in the Women's Auxiliary Air Force, where she was responsible for some memorable amateur theatricals. After the war, she worked briefly with her sister Helen in Manchester, designing textiles, and then settled in London. She was for many years a much loved teacher of art at various girls' schools.

CONTENTS

Illustrations   xiii

Acknowledgments   xv

Abbreviations   xvii

Introduction, by Alan Crawford   xix

1. Beginnings, 1877–1895   1
2. Daughter at Home, 1895–1897   11
3. Comrade Wife, 1897–1898   23
4. The House with the Copper Door, 1898–1900   34
5. The Lady of the Guild, 1898–1900   45
6. American Blossoming, 1900–1901   54
7. The Last of London, 1901–1902   67
8. Whitechapel to Camelot, 1902–1903   79
9. The First Shadows, 1903–1905   92
10. The Bulging Red Book, 1901–1908   105
11. Amputation, 1908–1910   119
12. Hope Fulfilled, 1911–1914   128
13. Family and War, 1914–1916   137
14. Campden to Jerusalem—via Cairo, 1917–1918   147
15. The Golden Bowl Filled with Scorpions, 1918   158
16. Once in Royal David's City, 1919   167
17. Administration Wife, 1920–1921   181
18. Two Houses, 1921   188
19. If I Forget Thee, O Jerusalem, 1922   197
20. Reshuffling the Pack, 1922–1929   203
21. Doves Escaping, 1929–1939   216
22. Wife to Widow, 1939–1942   226
23. Comrade-Grandmother, 1942–1961   230

Suggested Reading   239

Index   241

ILLUSTRATIONS

Janet and Prudence Ashbee   *frontispiece*

PLATES   *following page* xxxii
1. *Janet Ashbee,* William Strang, 1910
2. Sketch design for the "Procession of Fair Cities"
3. Brooch in the form of a peacock
4. *The Lady in Red,* Harriet Halhed, ca. 1898
5. Semigrand piano, a wedding present for Janet Ashbee
6. Portrait of Sid Cotton, Max Balfour
7. *Essex House Song Book*
8. The Norman Chapel garden front
9. Sketch-plan for the Rampart Walk, Jerusalem

FIGURES
1. The Forbes's house   3
2. Janet and Nevill Forbes, 1887   6
3. Janet Forbes, ca. 1895   9
4. Frank and Jessie Forbes and children   11
5. C. R. Ashbee, 1900   14
6. Mrs. H. S. Ashbee, 1900   15
7. The Magpie and Stump   18
8. Essex House   33
9. 74 and 75 Cheyne Walk   35
10. Janet Ashbee, ca. 1900   39
11. Metalworkers   45
12. Janet Ashbee, 1899   47
13. The guild river expedition   50
14. Mrs. H. S. Ashbee and Janet Ashbee   57
15. The first Roycroft Print Shop   62
16. The Hubbard family   63
17. Holidaymakers at the Court House   68
18. The music room at 74 Cheyne Walk   74

19. The High Street 76
20. The silk mill 80
21. The garden of Woolstaplers' Hall 82
22. *Alec Miller,* William Strang 84
23. Gerald Bishop 87
24. Janet riding astride, 1904 89
25. The bathing lake at Campden 97
26. Plockton 117
27. The Rolfe family 123
28. Janet Ashbee, 1910 124
29. The terrace of the Norman chapel 129
30. Mary and Janet Ashbee, 1911 130
31. Mary and Felicity Ashbee, 1915 140
32. Janet, Mary, Felicity, and Helen Ashbee, ca. 1917 144
33. Janet Ashbee's necklace 157
34. Janet Ashbee and her four children, ca. 1919 163
35. Street scene in Jerusalem 165
36. The Ashbee family, ca. 1919 167
37. House in the Wadi el Jose 170
38. Janet Ashbee, ca. 1920 171
39. C. R. Ashbee, ca. 1920 176
40. The Souk el Qattanin 178
41. The walls of Jerusalem 179
42. Janet Ashbee and her four daughters, ca. 1921 184
43. Nevill Forbes 194
44. The Ashbee children and Hélène Giadoux, ca. 1923 204
45. Janet, Mary, and Felicity Ashbee, ca. 1924 206
46. The Godden Green house 207
47. C. R., Helen, and Prue Ashbee, ca. 1924 208
48. Laurence Housman 217
49. Janet Ashbee, 1957 232

ACKNOWLEDGMENTS

THIS book has evolved into its current shape over a fairly lengthy period, and many friends and acquaintances have given me help and encouragement during this process. It was initially stimulated by Fiona MacCarthy and her book about my father and mother, *The Simple Life: C. R. Ashbee in the Cotswolds*. I have learned much from her about the lives of my parents at Chipping Campden before I was born. My conversations with the late Shirley Bury, her husband, Morley, and colleagues of hers at the Victoria and Albert Museum were crucial. At King's College, Cambridge, I would like to thank Michael Halls, then modern archivist at King's College, and his successor, Jacqueline Cox, for their readiness to help me during the periods that I spent there reading the Ashbee Journals, and Dr. Rosalind Moad, the present archivist, for her helpfulness regarding illustrations. Mary Greensted of Cheltenham Art Gallery and Museums and Frank Johnson of the Guild of Handicraft Trust in Chipping Campden have been more than generous in their support. Nita and Sinclair Budd have encouraged me and helped me to develop IT skills. Cleota Reed has been a tireless enthusiast for the book, and has done much to make its publication possible.

For permission to quote from material in copyright, I am grateful to the earl of Gainsborough (the papers of his grand-mother Lady Gainsborough), Robin Holland-Martin (the papers of Rob Martin Holland), the Society of Authors as the literary representative of the Estate of John Masefield, and Jane Wilgress (the papers of Alec Miller).

But my fullest debt of gratitude must go to Alan Crawford, author of the great monograph on my father published by Yale University Press in 1985, *C. R. Ashbee: Architect, Designer, and Romantic Socialist*. Had it not been for his profound knowledge of the subject and for his constant encouragement, the first draft would probably never have been completed. He has since then offered hours of help with editorial issues, with assembling the photographs and writing the captions, and with innumerable small details of preparing the final text for publication. I am eternally grateful to him for his constant readiness to provide me with his help, advice, and support, and for his devoted friendship, which has meant more to me than I can say during recent years.

ABBREVIATIONS

The sources most often used in the in-text citations are referred to by the following abbreviations:

AJ   Journals kept by C. R. Ashbee and Janet Ashbee, including correspondence, 1884–1941. King's College Library, Cambridge.

GMB   A folder containing typescript poems by Janet Ashbee, photographs, press cuttings, and some letters from Gerald Bishop, ca. 1903–1905. In the possession of the Ashbee family.

JJ   Journals kept by Janet Forbes (later Janet Ashbee), 1895–1906. In the possession of the Ashbee family.

EL   A collection of letters mainly between C. R. Ashbee and Janet Forbes, at the time of their engagement. In the possession of the Ashbee family.

RA   Typescript of an unpublished autobiographical novel, "Rachel," written by Janet Ashbee, 1908–1909. In the possession of the Ashbee family.

INTRODUCTION
Alan Crawford

IN the 1970s and early 1980s, I worked on a book about Janet Ashbee's husband, the architect and designer Charles Robert Ashbee, who was a leading figure in the Arts and Crafts movement in England at the end of the nineteenth century.[1] As I read through the many pages of the "Ashbee Journals," I came to know and, in a literary sort of way, to love Janet Ashbee.

I gave her emphatic letters and the difficult but somehow triumphant story of her marriage as much space as I could in my book, but I never thought of writing about her alone. Now her daughter Felicity has written her biography, quoting from her by the yard, bringing her alive, drawing on a daughter's vivid memories, and I have been asked to write an introduction that fills in the historical background. Strictly speaking, an introduction is not needed, for Felicity has written a story that explains itself, like a novel. But I have written a historical commentary, enlarging the picture here and there, and I hope that it will add to the pleasure of reading Felicity's text.

LOVE AND MARRIAGE
Janet Forbes was the daughter of a London stockbroker, and she grew up in the late 1800s in the comfort of the family home at Godden Green, outside Sevenoaks, Kent. Her future was seen to lie in marriage, and she probably saw it so herself. Since the seventeenth century at least, marriage among the middle class in England had usually included notions of love, as well as of raising children and creating and protecting wealth. The nineteenth century made this personal dimension of marriage much more important for middle-class women. The separa-

---

1. Crawford, *C. R. Ashbee: Architect, Designer, and Romantic Socialist.*

tion of domestic life from the world of work, the increasingly genteel tone of social life, and the influence of romanticism and of the religious revival created the image of a middle-class wife as a figure of perfection in the home, innocent and pure, yet full of feeling.[2] By 1895, marriage had become a magic box into which many good things were pressed: security of property, social standing, love, the safety and education of children, and personal fulfillment. But it was not clear whether the box was a gift or a trap, and matters of sexuality were veiled.

The Gothic Revival house at Godden Green in which Janet grew up was such a box, and her mother's view of things was terribly simple: "Husbands and wives vowed eternal love at the altar, and there was an end of it. Some unspeakable persons ceased to love their husbands and wives, but one did not know them."[3] Janet described herself at the time as insulated from all these matters, not full of feeling, disgusted with the marriage market. But she was the daughter of the Gothic house nevertheless. Felicity's narrative gradually reveals how much Janet owed to her upbringing, and to the nineteenth-century promise of love and security in marriage.

On 23 August 1897, Janet, aged nineteen, received a proposal of marriage from Charles Robert Ashbee, a man nearly fifteen years older than she, with whom she was not, by her own account, in love. (From now on, I shall refer to him as CRA; his friends called him that name, and so does Felicity.) By 26 August, she had decided to accept him. A week later, she received a letter in which he said that all his life his guiding star had been his love for other men. She was the first woman, he wrote, to whom he had felt able to offer such love. "Will not the inference be obvious to you?" he asked. "There are many

---

2. Leonore Davidoff, "The Family in Britain," in *The Cambridge Social History of Britain, 1750–1950,* edited by F. M. L. Thompson (Cambridge: Cambridge Univ. Press, 1990), 2:71–129.

3. See chap. 1, p. 10.

comrade friends, there can only be one comrade wife."[4] This episode is well documented, and Janet's emotional coolness at this time goes a little way toward explaining it. But the modern reader is left wondering: "How much did Janet understand? What did she feel?"

On the face of it, she should have been shocked, for late-Victorian society had a deep aversion to homosexuality, linked to the ideal of marriage described earlier. The Criminal Law Amendment Act of 1885 outlawed male homosexual behavior in private or public, in response to pressure from social reformers who saw it as a threat to the family and social purity.[5] Oscar Wilde was tried under this law in 1895, in an atmosphere of public scandal. Janet came home from Paris in May of that year, and Wilde was tried in April and May. It is hard to imagine that she was unaware of the Wilde trials. And it is equally hard to imagine how, two years later, she came to accept a proposal of marriage from a man who spoke of his lifelong love for other men—especially when that man moved, as Janet knew, in London art circles close to Wilde's.[6]

But she was not dismayed, and the reasons are straightforward. She probably had only the haziest ideas about homosexuality, for at this time she did not know what heterosexual lovemaking involved, and a patriarchal society would have kept such knowledge from her. The press reports of the Wilde trial were circumlocutory.[7] What is more, the idea of "a homosexual" was only tentative at this date. The word itself was coined in 1869 and came into English usage around 1890. Homosexual

---

4. See chap. 3, p. 25.

5. Lesley A. Hall, *Sex, Gender, and Social Change in Britain since 1880* (London: Macmillan, 2000), 39.

6. Ashbee did not know Wilde personally. He wrote, "I never knew Wilde, I could have known him but did not want to, I fancy because I was afraid of his mind" (letter to Alec Miller, 5 Mar. 1905, in the possession of the Ashbee family).

7. Hall, *Sex, Gender, and Social Change*, 54.

behavior, of course, was familiar, but the idea of a homosexual identity, of people whose sexual orientation was toward their own sex, was only beginning to gain currency.[8] Small wonder if Janet was unfamiliar with it. She would, on the other hand, have been familiar with the male bonding that was encouraged in the army, men's clubs, the colleges of Oxford and Cambridge, and public schools.[9] She probably associated what CRA told her with such things.

Janet and CRA were married in September 1898, and for thirteen years their marriage was childless. Their relationship during these years, which is the main theme of the first part of this book, moved through several phases. The first six or seven years were a time of excitement for Janet as she immersed herself in much that was not Godden Green. She met and enjoyed her husband's intellectual friends, many of whom were gay; she became part of the life of the Guild of Handicraft, as her husband's craft workshops in East London were known. In these years, she was most fully the comrade-wife that her husband asked her to be, and her affection for him was deepening all the time. In these years also, she was learning about his homosexuality, learning that he would scarcely make love to her. His touch was loving, but temperate.

In 1905, she fell in love with a friend of theirs, Gerald Bishop, and their deeply moving and wholly platonic love affair lasted three years, ending in Janet's breakdown. Over the next two or three years, she somehow drew her husband to her, and in March 1911, their first child, Mary, was born. The affair with Gerald is the pivot of this story, and the fact, so surpris-

---

8. Jeffrey Weeks, *Coming Out: Homosexual Politics in Britain from the Nineteenth Century to the Present,* 2d ed. (London and New York: Quartet, 1990), xi, 22.

9. Jeffrey Richards, "'Passing the Love of Women': Manly Love and Victorian Society," in *Manliness and Morality: Middle-Class Masculinity in Britain and America, 1800–1940,* edited by J. A. Mangan and James Walvin (Manchester: Manchester Univ. Press, 1897), 92–122.

ing to modern readers, that they would not make love is of its essence. It expressed their allegiance to the established idea of marriage. So when Janet reached out to this gentle man, she was also reaching out to Godden Green, to her husband, to the idea of marriage with which she had grown up—reaching out for what she wanted. When Mary was born, "she had only to be still in her Island of the Blest, and hug and hug and hug her wonder."[10]

Many years later, Laurence Housman wrote a comic poem about Janet in which he contrasted the liberalism of her early married years with her conservatism in motherhood. Part of it follows:

But when Janet, reproductive,
Got a family and ran it,
Then to all things reconstructive
She opposed a face of granite.[11]

The sentiment was true, but it was only half the truth. Janet as mother was still the comrade-wife. In March 1913, CRA began an affair with a young man called Chris Robson, whom he met one evening in the Strand in London. In May, he went on a holiday in France with Chris, and wrote to Janet describing his companion and their doings. Janet replied: "I confess I had a few tears this morning over the description of your lover. But I can never repay your understanding and generosity of 5 years ago, save 'in kind,' with counter-understanding when *you* want *your* romance. So bless you both."[12]

---

10. See chap 12, pp. 128–29.
11. See chap. 21, p. 218.
12. See chap. 12, p. 136.

THE ARTS AND CRAFTS MOVEMENT

Arts and Crafts was not an organized movement with definite goals, like women's suffrage or other political movements. It was more as if the world of architecture and decorative art had rolled over in its sleep around 1900 and for some years mumbled about the Middle Ages and the craftsman's touch, about nature and the deadness of machine-made things. These images belong to the late-Victorian period, like the cult of the simple life, the spread of vegetarianism, saving old buildings, the folk-song revival, dress reform, socialism before it became political—all dreams that life can somehow be more organic, more in touch with nature and the past, and it was dreamed by middle-class intellectuals, members of the class that had created so much of the modern world that made them so uneasy. The word *crank* hovers over them.

It took many forms. It could be philanthropy: craft classes in the village hall with girls doing embroidery and boys carving patterns in wood under the eye of the lady of the manor. It could be style: swag curtains and plush upholstery replaced by sturdy oak furniture, plain walls, and burnished copper, which would be swept away in their turn. It could be artists finding inspiration in the traditions and techniques of decorative art, which they could see in the growing collection at the South Kensington Museum in London (now the Victoria and Albert). Or it could be the radical notion that work, ordinary people's work, should be satisfying. In the 1840s and 1850s, the art critic John Ruskin set up the figure of the medieval craftsman, free, dignified, and happy, as an indictment of modern industry. William Morris, poet, designer, manufacturer, and revolutionary socialist, summed up Ruskin's teaching: "Art is man's expression of his joy in labour."[13]

This idea influenced much Arts and Crafts work, but the

---

13. *The Collected Works of William Morris,* edited by May Morris (London: Longmans, Green, 1910–1915), 23:173.

boldest attempt to find joy in labor for working men was CRA's Guild of Handicraft. Founded in 1888, the guild had workshops for furniture, metalwork, and jewelry, and a printing press, and CRA did most of the design work. They produced some remarkable work, but the aesthetic side of things interested CRA less than the character of his men and their experience of work. He encouraged the workshops to be self-governing and designed only sketchily, leaving scope for the workmen's initiative; he was as busy with many of his workmen in the evening or on the weekend as he was during workshop hours. And at those times, after 1898, Janet was busy with them too.

The beauty of the countryside runs like a stream through this book. How many photographs there are of Janet in bonnet and sandals, how many ecstatic descriptions of swimming and sunbathing. And it runs in the same way through all the Arts and Crafts movement: William Morris at his old stone manor house at Kelmscott by the Thames, the romantic feeling that the country was the natural home of "the crafts." Yet the movement was urban, as any modern movement in the arts would be. Most Arts and Crafts people lived and worked in cities; London was the home of many important organizations and informal networks. CRA's Guild of Handicraft was a peculiarly urban project. Started among the slums of the East End in 1888, it was an attempt to bring the Ruskinian gospel of joy in work to the urban poor: the Arts and Crafts as social work. Most architects and designers of the movement lived and worked in the center of London or in middle-class suburbs to the west. On a map of Arts and Crafts London, the Guild of Handicraft stands by itself, away to the east, a mark of CRA's radicalness.

In the late 1890s, this urban idealism was replaced in his mind by thoughts of the countryside. In 1902, he moved the workshops of the guild from Mile End to the idyllic little town of Chipping Campden in the Cotswolds. He was not planning that they live off the land—at least he took no practical steps in that direction. He was simply taking them to more pleasant and appropriate surroundings. This notion was typical of the Arts and Crafts. The movement inspired various rural settlements, but agricultural work or self-sufficiency played little part in them. Geographers have a spectrum that runs: urban-suburban-exurban-rural. *Exurban* describes settlements that are structurally dependent on cities but located in the country. The Guild of Handicraft and most other Arts and Crafts country settlements were exurban. For Janet, who had grown up in the country within easy reach of London by train, this living arrangement was nothing new. She took it, like so much else, in her stride.

In chapter 4, Felicity quotes Janet's vivid account of the masque *Beauty's Awakening,* performed in London's Guildhall in June 1899. This beautiful and slightly chaotic performance was organized by the Art Workers' Guild, a talking club for the artists, architects, and designers of the movement, and at that time an all-male organization. But when it came to making costumes and performing female roles, wives and sisters were called in. Gender relations in the Arts and Crafts movement tended to be that way. There were many women in the movement who were designers and craftswomen in their own right, and there were many more whose job was to execute men's designs. They were often wives and sisters: Jane Morris, wife of William Morris, executed his embroideries; Annie Cobden-Sanderson, wife of the bookbinder T. J. Cobden-Sanderson, stitched his books. Janet was not like any of these women. She had no particular manual skills. There were only a few Arts and Crafts people in her circle of friends. Yet she was as much involved as any embroiderer or bookbinder, for she instinctively shared her husband's sense that the Arts and Crafts was first and foremost a social movement, which meant dealing with the young men of the guild, with their growing up. Few people understood this human side of the Arts and Crafts, its role in personal development, as well as she.

Her story is interwoven with the chronology of the Arts and Crafts in a curious way, though it started before she was born. The movement grew out of the midcentury ideas of Ruskin and the example of William Morris, who set up workshops for stained glass, furniture, and textiles in 1861. But it remained a matter of a handful of people until the 1880s, when Janet was a girl. Important organizations were started then. The phrase *Arts and Crafts* was coined in 1887 in discussions that led to the establishment of the Arts and Crafts Exhibition Society, and it was this society's exhibitions that brought the movement before the London public. The breathless description that Janet, aged eighteen, gave of the 1896 exhibition—"Such tapestries, caskets, embroideries, bookbindings"—catches the atmosphere of profusion and invention.[14] New Arts and Crafts workshops were set up in the 1890s, some with fancy names such as the Guild of Handicraft, and the movement flourished in the years around 1900, which were also Janet's years of liberation. It was celebrated in the press and influential in Europe and North America, as she found when she and CRA traveled to the United States in 1900–1901. But by the time of their next visit, in 1908–1909 (the visits frame the years of her affair with Gerald Bishop), things had changed. The Guild of Handicraft had gone into liquidation, and the Arts and Crafts movement was beginning to go out of fashion, though it was far from coming to an end.

These years, around 1910, were also the years after Janet's breakdown, when she drew her husband to her. These acts of love were performed in the ruins of his hopes for the guild, and against the background of the waning Arts and Crafts movement. The subtle balance of power and attachment that made up their marriage shifted, as Janet became the mother of their children. For her at least, the Arts and Crafts was over.

---

14. See chap. 2, p. 21.

WRITING IN PRIVATE

I have referred occasionally to the rich documentation of Janet's personal life, and to her writings. They are worth attention in themselves. It was an intimate, important, and daily part of her life to pick up a pen, and the last picture in this book is wonderfully typical.

First there was her own private journal, kept from 1895 to 1908. When she married in 1898, she shared the writing of a journal with her husband. From about 1911, when she began to have children, she did not write journal entries anymore, and is represented instead by the witty, trenchant letters she wrote to her husband. Then there are collections that document special areas of her life: her engagement letters, the "bulging red book" devoted to Gerald Bishop that gives Felicity one of her chapter titles, and her commonplace books. And finally, there is the novel "Rachel," which she wrote as a kind of healing after her love affair with Gerald Bishop.

Janet's writings were personal and domestic. They served the interesting purpose of going over the day or the recent past and reexperiencing it on the page, giving it a shape. The albums and commonplace books were a way of treasuring her own past, and if they had an audience apart from herself it was her children and grandchildren. Even the novel, so much like a publishable work, was personal. She never thought of publishing it.

Publishing was not strange to her. Her husband was always writing books and articles, and her principal correspondent, Laurence Housman, was a prolific writer. Fiona MacCarthy has described her as a "natural romantic novelist." Yet she published almost nothing. At the end of her life, she chose to write her own obituary, emphasizing that the truth about her lay in her pen and in her private sphere.[15]

---

15. MacCarthy, *The Simple Life: C. R. Ashbee in the Cotswolds*, 134; *Lancaster Guardian and Observer*, 19 May 1961.

One could argue that she did not publish because she was a woman, and that the gendered structure of late-Victorian society deprived her of the audience she deserved. But that assessment would be to misconstrue the nature of her writing, which was done in and for the private sphere, where publishing would have been an intrusion. We can best understand the spirit of her writing if we see it as women's work, done for embellishment or as a gift, apart from the male, goal-oriented world of production and exchange.

Her writings were catharsis, entertainment, and communication. There is a value here much like that which runs through the Arts and Crafts movement, the value of personal creativity. In the Arts and Crafts, creativity was associated with art and making, the work of the hand. Janet had no skills of this kind, but her writing was just as creative as the Guild of Handicraft's copper bowls and silver necklaces, and of course more personal. It was the unself-conscious product of her intelligence and enthusiasm for life.

I have tried to use history not to explain or account for Janet Ashbee's actions or experiences, but to make them appear more sharply themselves. It is the uniqueness of her experience that matters. There may have been—there surely were—many women who married gay men in the years around 1900. But Janet was apparently unique in the honesty and feeling with which she wrote about it, and perhaps also in the courage and generosity with which she negotiated her love. This book is a record of a remarkable relationship.

Janet Ashbee

1 *Janet Ashbee,* William Strang, 1910. Oil on canvas. Courtesy of
Cheltenham Art Gallery and Museums.

2 Sketch design for the "Procession of Fair Cities" in the Art Workers' Guild masque, C. R.
Ashbee, 1899. His sister Agnes played Florence *(second from the left),* and Janet played Venice
(right). Pen and watercolor, ca. 3½ x 6 inches.

3 Brooch in the form of a peacock, made by the Guild of Handicraft for Janet Ashbee, C. R. Ashbee, ca. 1900. Gold, silver, pearls, diamonds, and a ruby in the peacock's eye. 5½ x 3¼ inches. On loan to the Victoria and Albert Museum from a member of the Ashbee family.

4 *The Lady in Red,* Harriet Halhed, ca. 1898. Oil on canvas.

5 Semigrand piano, made by Broadwoods and the Guild of Handicraft as a wedding present for Janet Ashbee, C. R. Ashbee, 1898–1900. Painted decoration executed by Walter Taylor. Oak, holly, and wrought iron. 40 x 59½ x 82. Purchased with grants from the Victoria and Albert Museum Purchase Grant Fund, the National Heritage Memorial Fund, the National Art Collections Fund, and the Friends of Cheltenham Art Gallery and Museums. Courtesy of Cheltenham Art Gallery and Museums.

6 Portrait of Sid Cotton, Max Balfour, 1899. Courtesy of King's College, Cambridge.

7 *Essex House Song Book,* a bound volume and some loose sheets, 1903–4.

8 The Norman Chapel garden front, Broad Campden, Gloucestershire. Repaired and enlarged by C. R. Ashbee, 1905–7. Courtesy of Alan Crawford.

9 Sketch showing C. R. Ashbee's plans for the Rampart Walk, Jerusalem.

CHAPTER I
BEGINNINGS
1877–1895

FROM his days at King's College, Cambridge, my father, Charles Robert Ashbee (*always* known as CRA), kept a journal, an intermittent but often detailed record of meetings with people, descriptions of places and events, and searchings for the formulations of ideas. He pasted in newspaper cuttings and letters from friends. When he married my mother, Janet Forbes, in 1898, the journals became a joint affair, and she added her bold, round hand to his more angular one. Anyone who delves into the unmanageably many volumes of these journals will, almost inevitably, fall in love with Janet, succumbing to the warmth, spontaneity, and humor of her entries and letters.

My mother was born on 28 December 1877, so she was only twenty when she married. It was not unusual at that time for a nicely brought-up girl from a fairly sheltered, if cultured, family to have only a vague idea about sex. Nothing in literature that even a voracious reader from such a background might come across was at all explicit, still less were there suggestions of other patterns of partnership than the accustomed one of heterosexual love, marriage, and the making of children. It is hardly surprising, therefore, that Janet did not really know that the man whom she had—with some reservations—accepted was a homosexual.

The "Ashbee Journals" bear witness to her strength and generosity. Without her rare blend of enthusiasm, and her instinctive, down-to-earth judgment, much that was accomplished in their life together might not have been, or would have foundered sooner. But in 1908, after ten years of childless marriage, she had the breakdown that anyone today would have seen coming long before. She fell by chance into the hands of the neurologist Henry Head.[1] As part of her treatment, which was short and brutal—no years of twice-weekly sessions on a psychiatrist's couch—she wrote what she called her unwritten novel, "Rachel," the biblical symbolism of whose title is "weeping for her children which are not."

In it she gives a perceptive account of her childhood and youth, and of those first ten years of marriage to CRA. She tells the story of her initiation, at his hands, into the Arts and Crafts movement and the circle of his homosexual friends, and of the platonic love affair that brought her, in her own words, to the edge of the abyss. She sent it to John Masefield, who thought it a potential masterpiece and begged her to go on with it.[2] She never did. But even in its unfinished form, her analysis of her predicament is so sure that "Rachel" provides, alongside Janet's contributions to the "Ashbee Journals," an extraordinary insight into the first half of her life. In this book, I have drawn heavily on the novel's vivid narrative and wealth of biographical detail, which have hardly appeared in print until now. The only things Janet changed in telling her story were the names of people and places. In quoting from "Rachel," I have simply reverted to the real names. The following is how she starts her own story.

In a pleasant part of Kent, which thirty years ago was unmarred by either golf course or cars, stood Godden Green, the residence of Mr. and Mrs. Frank Forbes. It was a large struc-

---

1. Dr. (later Sir) Henry Head (1861–1940), an eminent neurologist, was famous for his book *Aphasia and Kindred Disorders of Speech* (1926). His wife, Ruth, a writer and former headmistress, became a regular correspondent of Janet, particularly after Sir Henry was incapacitated by Parkinson's disease.

2. John Masefield (1878–1967), later a poet laureate, was from his first appearance in Chipping Campden in January 1903 a valued friend. CRA called him "OUR poet"; some years later, he became a confidant of Janet. Though neither she nor CRA took to his wife, Con, Masefield and Janet remained good friends until her death, six years before his.

1. The Forbes's house, Godden Green, Kent, ca. 1897

ture of the pitch-pine Gothic period, with an ecclesiastical touch about the pointed stone arches, and the irrelevant bits of stained glass.[3] Standing on a hill, surrounded by twenty-five acres of grounds, its tall slate roof and crinkly chimneys were visible to all strangers coming over the common, and it enjoyed a certain local importance. "The house had been bought for Frank Forbes by his father, a cultivated and prosperous stock-broker, who had a similar 'place' in Surrey, and wished his son well housed. . . . The establishment was in keeping with Mr Forbes's good but not vast income. He was in very comfortable circumstances, for there had been bumper years in the city, and he was laying by for years" (RA, 1–2).

---

3. The house was designed by architect Joseph Fogerty, and built in the late 1870s.

Janet's parents were untypical of their time and class. Frank, from a Scots background, was delicate and asthmatic. From fifteen to seventeen, he studied languages and music in Geneva, becoming a very good amateur violinist, and then came back to join the family stockbroking firm, in which he did well from the start. Jessie was born in St. Petersburg, of a Scots family in the timber trade with artistic and musical connections. She and Frank met by chance at a spa in Yorkshire where Frank, aged fourteen, had been sent for his asthma, while Jessie, sixteen, was on holiday from school in Edinburgh. Their ten-year courtship by correspondence ended with Frank going to Russia in 1868 to marry his bride and bring her back to Kent.

Janet describes the touch of bohemianism that her mother brought with her to Kent:

> She dressed well in the somewhat voluminous manner of her decade, performed her social duties punctiliously, ran her big house and her six servants admirably, and kept an eye on the garden. . . . She succeeded in introducing quite a number of little foreign ways into the orderly household of her husband. This, and an un-English and refreshing love for foreigners and tolerance of their ways, gave a pleasant spice of the unusual to an otherwise ordinary, and almost suburban existence. . . . [T]he couple spoke French and Russian freely together. Music also gave charm to their evenings, and to the parties they gave, for Mrs Forbes had a beautiful voice. (RA, 4)

But she was an elemental creature, with certain simple and unshakable convictions. "One of her fixed ideas was that mothers adore their children and are adored by them. Husbands and wives vowed eternal love at the altar, and there was an end of it. Some unspeakable persons ceased to love their husbands and wives, but one did not know them. Hence her dismay when she began to realise that Janet did not love her" (RA, 10). Her mother's longing for visible displays of affection grew increasingly irksome to Janet, who so often heard the words, "Janet, come and kiss me; what an unnatural child you are! you have to be begged for every caress!" (RA, 9).

And there were other things in her mother that roused in Janet a sense of a guilty feeling almost of dislike. As a child, she had a pagan delight in being naked,

> the utmost rigours of mother and nurse being unavailing to get her to be what is called "decent." It was continually: "Pull your frock down Miss Janet" or "Put that towel round you quick, someone might come in!" "What DOES it matter?" queried the stubborn Janet. Her mother would enter. "Janet! I'm surprised at you" (this was a frequent beginning). "What are you doing without your night gown on? It's not at all nice to stand like that." "I think it's VERY nice,' answered Janet unmoved" (RA, 16).

Janet maintained that from the start, her parents' inner lives were poles apart from her. To neither was she able to show the affection that both longed for, not even to her father, though he understood it better than did her mother. She had a deep respect for him, "And besides he was very handsome and very amusing. . . . [H]is gentle but inflexible uprightness and passion for truth were among her strongest influences" (RA, 9–10). Writing to her on the fourth anniversary of her marriage, Frank Forbes ended with a phrase unusable in our post-Freudian interpretation of words: "I am, my darling child, ever your debtor and lover, F. A. Forbes" (AJ, Sept. 1902).

Probably neither of the Forbes parents had clear ideas about the education of their treasured and only daughter. Both had had only brothers. Almost inevitably, as they were living in the country, they chose first a nurse, who "encompassed her ardent spirit with a sea of calm," and then, when Janet was five, a German governess, Miss Hedda Stoy (RA, 5).

> For twelve years this excellent woman gave Janet the very heart and kernel of her life, ready at all hours to play with her, to help with work or amusements, make her doll's clothes,

read to her, make music with her. She was a firm, placid, intelligent creature, sympathetic to the needs of a child, and especially a reserved and self-conscious child inclined to speculation as Janet was. . . . The chief value of the scheme lay in its splendid regularity and healthiness. Its disadvantage, and it was a grave one, was that Janet was always alone with an older and extremely conscientious woman. . . . During these years Janet appears as a stalwart little girl, tall for her age and well grown, but broadly built with large bones. She had a mane of brown hair, and beautiful grey eyes. Her mouth was large, well shaped and generous, and when amused, she had a brilliant and ringing laugh that danced all over the gamut. . . . She had CHARACTER, that mysterious spark that illumines many ugly exteriors and makes them live. And Janet was not ugly. She had a straight nose that would be beautiful in a few years; her neck was round and firm, her step springy, she streamed vitality. (RA, 5–6, 9)

2. Janet Forbes and her brother, Nevill, 1887

6

When she was five, her brother, Nevill, was born. He was a delicate child, with fairy-tale white skin and long golden hair, and very musical. By the time he was four, they were spending a good deal of time together, though it was only many years later that she came to appreciate him and they became truest friends. He, on the other hand, adored her and looked up to her as a kind of goddess. "In years to come, through all her adventures, he never lost the conviction, that she was better and more beautiful than other women" (RA, 14). But then he was sent away to school, and Janet missed him horribly: "Lessons seemed dreadfully dull without the quaint little pale face opposite to tease and telegraph to. She read of children running away from school, and seriously thought of running to one" (RA, 15).

Although her education with Miss Stoy was totally lacking in any of the sciences, she had a good general grounding in other fields. Miss Stoy could instruct in Greek mythology, standard English literature, history, and geography—at party games Janet remained infallible on capital cities and the world's major rivers! As well as her native German, she had good French and basic Latin skills. The Forbes parents took it for granted that any educated person should be familiar with more than one foreign language, and Nevill, to his mother's joy, made Russian his lifework.

When Janet was fifteen, it was judged safe to send her, with Miss Stoy as chaperone, for a year to Berlin. She was soon reveling in the stimulus of the Musik Hochschule. "Her personal affection and *Schwärmerei* for her piano-master, a beautiful, gentle character, in appearance like a gold haired Viking, caused her to work herself to the bone to achieve success. She practised four hours daily, besides many classes in harmony, composition, orchestration and choir. She also went twice a week to a *Gymnasium*" (RA, 19).

Her weekly letter home, which to her parents' chagrin showed no trace of homesickness, described rapturously every one of these lessons, as well as concerts, operas, and occasional visits to museums and galleries. She reported on the Sunday sermon at the English church, which at her parents' wish she regularly attended. The fact that there was no other social activity in the very humble boardinghouse where they were lodged bothered Janet not at all. Music filled her waking hours.

The pattern was repeated the following year in Paris, though there, surprisingly, the place picked for her and Miss Stoy to stay was the exciting bohemian pension of the de Padilla family. Signor de Padilla and his wife, Desirée Artôt, were former opera singers who took in paying guests, and they had two "thrilling daughters" of eighteen and nineteen, both of whom later became opera singers (RA, 21).

Paris soon began to give Janet something that Berlin had not: an appreciation of art. Berlin had made her into a budding musician and opera lover, but it had not offered much else by way of cultural stimulus.

> [Now] a brilliant and handsome young *Professeur* came daily to instruct her in European History and Literature, French Grammar, style, composition, and history of art. He inspired Janet with great respect, and she worked hard and zealously. He took her (and Miss Stoy) to all the Galleries, talking exquisite Parisian, and doing much to form her taste. They also went to many classical plays, and read reams of French poetry old and new, Villon and Ronsard, to Verlaine and Gautier. Janet loved to hear those ivory phrases from his lips. (RA, 23)

Every Thursday, in the big studio room at the top of the house, the de Padillas were "At Home" to all kinds of unusual people. Fascinating games were played and innocent flirtations indulged in. The Forbeses do not seem to have found it at all disturbing. Miss Stoy, after all, was always there, in the corner with her crochet. "Janet loved these little whirls of social gaiety and badinage. Whiffs of coquetry came in the train of young married women fresh from the hands of Parisian *modistes;* pleasant looking men seemed to think it worth while to draw

3. Janet Forbes with her hair in Parisian style, ca. 1895

her out in conversation, and she often found herself a centre of laughter and talk" (RA, 24).

In the midst of these activities, she remained completely innocent, and was unawakened enough not to be inquisitive. Her fellow students took her in hand about her appearance, and one of them offered to do her hair in a more becoming way, in secret, in her bedroom.

> Janet was at first indignant. The neatly drawn-back locks, twisted into a tight little plait which crawled up the back of her head, had hitherto seemed to her an adequate and permanent arrangement, like breakfast and dinner. At last she relented, and accused herself of being silly. And she felt a thrill of pleasure when the transformation was shown her in the hand-glass.
>
> Her clothes, partly German, mostly from her pre-German period, let down and altered, were next attacked. Her shoes

9

were condemned. A veil was suggested as almost indispensable to decency. The name of a "little dress-maker" (insidious diminutive!) was given her, and after writing home for permission Janet tremblingly chose a material, and submitted herself to the fitter.

The result was astonishing. A chorus of applause greeted her entry into the drawing-room.

Attempts were next made to reform her night gowns, which were of hygienic flannel, by means of lace and the insertion of blue ribbon. But here Janet was adamant. It seemed to her "frivolous" to spend so much time every week threading it in, and besides, as she very sensibly said: "Who sees it at night?" The reply was a peal of good-natured laughter, which had in it however, an irritating note of superiority. (RA, 24–25)

By the time she left Paris in May 1895, the shy, solid seventeen year old was emerging into a statuesque near beauty, more than ready for a new chapter in her life. "She got home in a ringing green and white spring tide, and was amazed as the train sped up from Dover, that she had never before noticed how marvellously beautiful English fields in April are. . . . She was the cherished only daughter coming home. . . . [T]here were going to be more experiences. Her favourite word was 'interesting.' How tremendously 'interesting' it all was!" (RA, 26–27).

OPPOSITE: 4. Frank and Jessie
Forbes with their children, 1897

CHAPTER 2
DAUGHTER AT HOME
1895–1897

YOUNG, educated, and handsome, Janet now entered a phase of her life that she had been long prepared and educated for, yet contained no obvious routines or plans, a time full of opportunity that was somehow also dedicated to the outcome that she get married. At first, she was not daunted by its ambiguities.

> Her old nursery had been converted into a bedroom, papered with a virgin and yet somehow slightly sensuous pink; and she took possession of it with delight. The roses on the curtains, and the masses of little shelves on which she could arrange all her photographs of opera heroes, pleased her as these things had not before. . . .

Then she had her Parisian clothes to show off, and she had to be very firm about her hair, of which Godden Green tended to disapprove. Cleo de Merode was supreme in Paris in those days, and Janet's *bandeaux* were a copy of the famous dancer's—tho' this was of course not divulged. . . . Janet continued, as she had always been, a contrast to all the flannel-shirted, tennis-playing, sailor-hatted young ladies of the neighbourhood.

The girls in Paris had all kept journals, enormous bulging *cahiers* in black American cloth, stuffed out with programmes of plays and dances and illustrated with countless *croquis*. Janet had never been allowed to read them, or even look at the pictures. The girls were fearful of Miss Stoy's judgements on the indelicacies they contained. But Janet had seen them scribbling away at all hours, and thought it must be great fun.

On getting home she at once bought out of her new allowance, a huge blank book, and for two years she wrote in it arduously the conventional chronicle of her actions, and an occasional, a very occasional, breath of reflection. (RA, 27)

This journal became the close friend she now needed more than ever. She accompanied her father on business trips and tried to learn to play golf. She carried on as best she could with her music, but felt aimless without the discipline of regular instruction. Even the weekly quartet playing with her father and his musician friends did not help much. Amateur dramatics, flower shows, and bazaars were hardly a substitute for the stimulus of a great city. Her main occupation was paying calls in the brougham with her mother, leaving the ritual calling cards (different sizes for mother and daughter) with the correct corners turned down—or not—according to a mystical and prescribed code. The cards were to be picked over in the flat dish that reposed on every correct hall table. There were balls, of course, in the private houses of acquaintances, but they were not an unmixed pleasure for her. She began to think "that there was 'something dreadful' about dancing. . . . Godden Green found it natural and beautiful for a young girl to spend an evening in the arms of a dozen unknown young men, who swung her around in sensual gyrations with every artificial aid to vice, scented flowers, candle-light and champagne. . . . Her feeling must have gone back to some excessive Puritan ancestor, some covenanting great-great grandfather" (RA, 29).

The actual dancing she found almost too exciting, throwing herself into it with a passionate, almost guilty enjoyment. But "the waiting in a group, like sheep at a market for selection, powerless to attract or repel, was also torture to her. It was horrible to feel the damp gloved hand of an utter stranger round her waist, and to apprehend his nearness and the various scents, tobacco, drink and personality. Yes, IT WAS DISGUSTING" (ibid.).

The only other occupation was riding. She had had her own pony from childhood, and she went on long rides alone, galloping through the glades of nearby Knole Park, and trotting along the quiet country lanes.

It was into this emotional vacuum that CRA now, disturbingly, came. Janet's father had become one of the benefactors of CRA's School and Guild of Handicraft, soon after its beginning in 1888. Janet was only eleven at that time, and if she reacted to him at all, it was with dislike: "He had a way of touching her hair which incensed her" (RA, 38). Berlin and Paris had more or less wiped him from her mind, but for one thing. On her sixteenth birthday, in Berlin, she received, through her parents, in a registered packet,

> a little bracelet, a charming trinket in chrysoprase and blue enamel, made in Mr. Ashbee's experimental workshop. She had never been allowed to wear jewelry, save a string of round corals, and the gold cross, and this little piece of dainty colour was a joy and a revelation to her. How extraordinary, she thought, that HE should think of sending her a present. And she wrote him a neat little letter of thanks, and was not parted from the bracelet day or night. (ibid.)

Mr. Forbes's patronage of the guild meant that CRA had

5. C. R. Ashbee, photographed by Frank Lloyd Wright, 1900

been visiting Godden Green on occasional Sundays, to enjoy, a little condescendingly, the comfortable abundance of the Forbeses' hospitality. Now is the time to say something about him, to give an idea of the impact he made.

He was born in London in 1863 of a Hamburg Jewish

6. Mrs. H. S. Ashbee, photographed by Frank Lloyd Wright, 1900

mother, Elizabeth Lavy, and an English father, Henry Spencer Ashbee, whose business success allowed him to indulge a passion for books, languages, travel, and pornography, the last for which he is best known.[1]

---

1. For a full account of the life and book-collecting activities of Henry Spencer Ashbee (1834–1900), see Ian Gibson, *The Erotomaniac: The Secret Life of Henry Spencer Ashbee* (London: Faber and Faber, 2001).

CRA was the only son, and he had three younger sisters. He went from prep school to Wellington College, and hated it, as Janet wrote in "Rachel": "He never forgave Destiny for those five bitter years. . . . He loathed the routine and the stupidities, the brutalities and the perpetual physical competition at the public school" (RA, 40). On leaving he demanded to be sent to Cambridge, but his father dug in his heels. "Well, he would give him £1000 to finish his precious education, and that was the last penny he was to expect, the last penny, did he hear? CRA as cold as any stone, heard, and took the £1000, and went to King's . . . and the gates of Paradise opened before him" (RA, 41).

Probably it was only after he got to Cambridge that CRA faced the reality of his homosexual tendencies. "College life developed as school had fostered, this side of his nature though it is probable that he was born with such a strong bias in this direction, that no amount of feminine influence would have pulled the balance true" (ibid.). Janet was also shrewd enough to observe that his nearness in age to his mother gave him an abnormal hold on her affections, and that she "with her German training and blood tended always to venerate 'den Mann' beyond his intrinsic deserts" (RA, 39–40). At Cambridge, CRA also became an idealistic socialist, for one of the most formative influences on him at that time, apart from his fellow students, was Edward Carpenter, a Communist, homosexual, and simple lifer.[2]

On graduating in 1886 with a degree in history, CRA chose to work in the office of the architect G. F. Bodley and to live not at home, but at Toynbee Hall, in Whitechapel, in East London.[3] Toynbee was founded in 1884 by the Reverend

---

2. Edward Carpenter (1844–1929) was a philosopher, poet, writer, musician, Socialist, and homosexual. He was a potent and permanent influence on CRA's ideas regarding comradeship in work, and with his workmen and boys.

3. George Frederick Bodley (1827–1907) was a great Victorian Gothic architect. CRA was an articled pupil in his office from 1886 to about 1890.

Samuel Barnett as the first of the university settlements where young graduates could live and share their privileged education with the poor. Here CRA was able to try out his fledgling ideas. He was soon launching into a great many other fields besides his work as an architectural pupil, lecturing on Ruskin to workingmen's clubs, learning about jewelry and metalwork, and then, crucially, setting up his own School and Guild of Handicraft in 1888, in Whitechapel. Here he developed the vital blend of aesthetics, teaching, and caring that was the hallmark of his venture. "I have to confess," he wrote later in a key phrase, "that I have never had any use for 'philanthropy' unless it came to me through some work of the human hand." And to Ruskin's ideas was added Edward Carpenter's belief in the redeeming social power of love between men. CRA's chosen name for this love was "comradeship."

When Janet returned from Paris in 1895, CRA was thirty-two, and with his growing awareness of her as an adult, and an unusual and attractive one, his visits to Godden Green became more frequent. Her description of him in "Rachel," though written in 1908, can be accepted as a valid portrait at this time, for he changed very little, either in physical appearance or in his youthful approach to many things.

> Tall and very loosely put together, unathletic but wiry, he had enormous vitality. You saw it gleaming in his very beautiful eyes, hazel-brown, flecked with green; in his brilliant smile. You felt the power of work in his large and rather clumsy hands. For the rest he had a big domed brow, and a somewhat aggressive and disapproving manner. . . . And CRA was at twenty five, still very young, very zealous, and a hero-worshipper. His heroes were William Morris, John Ruskin, and Edward Carpenter, and his creed was a blend of their teachings, with his own particular fire added.
>
> His intimate friends loved him devotedly, for he had recesses of great beauty in his character. But he was not popular amongst his acquaintances who accused him of conceit and arrogance.

To Mr. and Mrs Forbes he represented merely the other side of things, that strange outer world of Bohemia, where people wore soft felt hats, and turned down collars, and ambiguous ties, and often did not go to Church. It was whispered that some were even not baptised. (RA, 37)

Eventually, the two mothers exchanged calls, though they had little in common apart from unmarried daughters. CRA's parents had legally separated in 1893, and a certain coolness remained, for Mrs. Forbes did not really approve of people whose marriages ended before death did them part.

But there were CRA's two youngest sisters, Agnes and Elsa. They were about eight and five years older than Janet, intelligent, artistic, and as yet unattached, so they seemed suitable companions for a somewhat restive "daughter at home." The Ashbees lived at 37 Cheyne Walk, Chelsea, a house designed

7. The Magpie and Stump, 37 Cheyne Walk, London. From *Neubauten in London* (Berlin 1900), pl. 7. Courtesy of Chelsea Public Library, London.

by her son at the time of the separation and known as the Magpie and Stump. CRA had his architectural office in the house, and it was important enough to be the subject of a long article in the *Studio*, which appeared just at the time when Janet first saw the house.

> She felt at once, "This is right. This is really beautiful." The proportion of the grey oak door, the modelling on the little bronze handles, the touch of blue enamel behind the bronze, they were just what was wanted.
>
> The door opened and she found herself in a bare reddish room. There was hardly any furniture, and the fireplace was surmounted by a chessboard of copper tiles, some with strange flaming discs and patterns, and letters upon them. . . . She felt a wave of satisfaction, of contentment, almost of home-coming, sweep over her. And this warm wave, which was much more intellectual than emotional, drowned her finer more accurate instincts. If she had not been so led by her brain and her love of beauty, she would have apprehended that, in spite of the perfect taste, the house was quite dead; dead and full of ghosts; cold and merciless ghosts. . . . She was herself however so young, so brimming with life and ob- jectivity, that she noticed nothing but the lovely colour, and the absence of ugliness and complexity. (RA, 35–36)

When it came to lunch, they sat down at

> a long, narrow table, so narrow that it was awkward to look into the eyes of your *vis-à-vis*. The place opposite Janet how- ever was empty—CRA was late. . . . To his mother this late- ness indicated his frantic industry, so she never corrected him. It was one of her maxims that the fingers should be in perpet- ual motion, and between helping the soup and the meat she laboured at a granulated grey crossover that hung in a bag to the back of her chair.
>
> The two daughters were friendly and talkative, well- dressed and full of vitality. The younger who had been at Girton, was now going through a revulsion in favour of fri- volity and sport; the elder, who was almost beautiful, had a quieter dignity, not untinged with melancholy. (RA, 43)

CRA eventually appeared,

> awaking in Janet a feeling of interest. She was, however,
> dimly aware of a suppressed indignation among the sisters,
> and a plastic gesture of conciliation from Mrs Ashbee. The
> conversation was still-born, and CRA ate in a rather august
> way he had, asking Janet now and then a question about her
> reading. . . . After lunch . . . she was invited to come into his
> office, and rout among his docketed letters for autographs,
> which at that time she collected in an irrelevant manner. . . .
> She followed him rather timidly through doors and narrow
> stairways. She felt dreadfully conscious that her gown was not
> at all in keeping with the severity of her surroundings, and
> feared they might think her ordinary. At last they came to a
> little, chilly room, hung with cold chaste blue linen. It all
> smelt of London smuts, mitigated by the perpetual soap and
> water with which Mrs Ashbee, after the manner of her race,
> waged a hopeless war against the dirt. (RA, 44)

For Janet, that smell, ever after, stood for "the soul of that house in all its grim sense of duty. The aestheticism was a superimposition; the proof of CRA's power over his mother" (ibid.).

She started seeing quite a lot of the two girls, going to art galleries with Agnes, who was a very creditable watercolorist, and concerts with Elsa, who was studying the piano at the Royal College of Music. When it came to Janet's coming-out dance that December of 1895, both Agnes and Elsa were invited and stayed for several days afterward. Agnes brought a book of Keats's poems as a present from her brother, whereas Janet's father's gift, apart from the dance itself, was "three packets of *charming* bookplates, designed by 'V.V.'" (JJ, 28 Dec. 1895). These initials were Janet's (unexplained) code name for CRA.

In October 1896, there was a large Arts and Crafts exhibition in London, in which CRA's Guild of Handicraft figured prominently. Janet was invited to choose a gift.

[She] took a hansom to the Magpie and Stump to dinner.

20

Great fun. Agnes looked a perfect *poem* in her blue dress designed by Crane. After lunch she, Mr. A, and I went to the Arts and Crafts Exhibition in the New Gallery—it *was* a treat! Such tapestries, caskets, embroideries, bookbindings, silver and copper work, vessels and goblets, chests, beds and chairs, drawings and designs, pottery, jewels, gesso work, enamels and ivory work, etc: etc: of marvellous grace and beauty. (JJ, 22 Oct. 1896)

Back home, writing in her private journal, in German, and in old-fashioned *Handschrift* for extra secrecy, she admitted with horror: "If he finds something beautiful, then I too at once think it is beautiful. It is ghastly, and I am fighting hard against it, but so far without success. Can he really have a hypnotic power over me? That would really be appalling! I must tear myself free, for it cannot be that I . . . " (JJ, 15 Oct. 1896).

As a child, Janet had gone to art classes in Sevenoaks, with a Miss Halhed, who "wore strange homespun loose sacklike clothes . . . girded herself with embroidered and studded belts and clasps and chains from Bulgaria, donned little Finnish fur hats, and beads from the Andaman Isles" (RA, 34). When she came back from Paris, Janet rejoined the class at once. It was one way of filling up her intermediate existence at Godden Green. But then, not long after the Arts and Crafts exhibition, Miss Halhed decided to rent a studio in London for her Saturday-morning class, and the studio she chose was a converted skittle alley in the garden of the Magpie and Stump. Janet joined the class at once and, inevitably, would go in to lunch with the Ashbees afterward. When the spring series of classes was over, Janet wrote in her journal: "I am sorry also that the Magpie and Stump lunches are over. They have been very pleasant and gay, and Mrs Ashbee always kindness itself towards me" (JJ, Mar. 1897). CRA continued his gentle indoctrination of her, sending a copy of *Sesame and Lilies* and a mild taunt about her life being "all holiday, all plums and no dough, an indigestible diet" (EL, 28 Apr. 1897).

In the spring of 1897, Janet revisited Germany for a glorious few weeks of music and the renewal of friendships. At a music festival in Bonn, her impudent autograph hunting brought her face-to-face with the well-known pianist Leonard Borwick.[4] "I can hardly believe that my wish of years has been realised at last, and that I have got to know Borwick personally! The idea is so delightful that I continually go back and gloat over it. . . . We had some interesting conversations about Mr Ashbee and his jewels—Knole, our mutual friends in Berlin, pictures" (JJ, 26–27 May 1897).

In August, Borwick who, as it happens, was gay, came to stay at Godden Green for a few days. He came on his bicycle, and Janet made two journal entries. In one, taped together for greater privacy, she quotes from the Brahms song *Die Sonne scheint nicht mehr,* and in the other:

> His eyes are wells of blue honesty, clean and fearless; wide and solemn when in earnest, dancing stars when in fun. (All this sounds like the raving of an idiot, but it is sober truth. I am too old and serious for Backfisch-Schwärmerei.) . . . All Sunday afternoon we sat in the garden, I nominally reading, really watching—looking at Goodwin's water-colours, and CRA's jewels, over which latter we thoroughly agreed. . . . On Saturday he goes to Chartres . . . in November he intends going to Petersburg—alas, alas! Five or six months at least. I daren't hope ever to see him here again. (JJ, 3 Aug. 1897)

For all her protestations about maturity, it almost seemed she was in love.

Yet, barely three weeks later, after only a fairly short journal entry about the death of her much loved "Grannie" Forbes, comes the long description, on 23 August, of the horseback ride with CRA, during which, almost without preamble, he proposed marriage, and she, virtually speaking, accepted.

---

4. Leonard Borwick (1865–1925) was a well-known international concert pianist who became a friend of Janet and CRA.

CHAPTER 3
COMRADE WIFE
1897–1898

IT required considerable courage even to contemplate such a radical change in his way of life. Marriage as such was not what he really wanted, but it was emerging as the only way of distancing himself from the complications of life with his too much loved, and too loving, mother, and his two increasingly unhappy, unmarried sisters. And it was easy enough to describe the kind of young woman he would look to marry. She must, of course, be intelligent; receptive, especially in the field of the arts; and above all young, so that she could be trained to help him in his lifework. Most important of all, she must be sensitive enough to appreciate that this marriage would not be conventional, for she would from the start have to understand and accept her role as "comrade-wife." The more he saw of Janet Forbes, the more he hoped that she might fill most of these requirements. And perhaps the undefined, almost tomboyish quality she had about her would boost his courage to the point of proposing.

When Janet got in from that momentous ride, she got out her treasured journal and made an eleven-page entry. It was, she wrote, "truly a strange wooing" (JJ, 26 Aug. 1897). It had begun with a huge discussion of sympathy:

> whether antipathy at first sight changes, (yes), or whether sympathy once felt can die (no) . . . whether entire and perfect sympathy was ever possible between two beings, which last we agreed in denying. Another long pause, while we rode gently through the green lanes. "Are we two sympathetic to each other?" he asked. "Not wholly." I again rejoined, trembling for what might come. Another long pause . . . "In what respects am I not sympathetic?" was the next question. I was

staring at Shamus's mane, and answered haltingly: "Oh, in various ways—it is so difficult to specify." What a coward I felt! . . . [W]hat an opportunity for clearing up an unsympathy, and clean thrown away. . . . Did I fancy it, or was there really a slight hesitation, as he said quietly, "Do we sympathise enough to be man and wife?"—I dared not look at him, but answered, "I don't know. It is such a big question. I must wait and tell you later." "Think it over quietly and I will ask you again." (ibid.)

He went back to London the next day, and Janet was left to try to make up her mind.

She spent two days in a purgatory of doubt. Sometimes she felt "the sunshine of being almost sure he is the right man for me . . . that he would really be my *will's master,* without which marriage would be a living death for me." At other times, she had the thought "that we do not love *each other* at all, but merely are in love with each other's qualities: I with his *marvellous* intellect, his unique artistic temperament, his wide knowledge, his kindly nature—he perhaps with my veneration for him, and my companionship rather than love as a wife" (ibid.). Finally, her course seemed fairly clear:

> Neither of us will, I firmly believe, ever be "violently in love," as the phrase goes, neither has an emotional or demonstrative nature, and I expect we shall make the soberest, staidest, most gravely comic pair of lovers the sun ever looked on!
>
> I had a very grave talk with Father this evening—he is quite of my opinion . . . But he would like to see more ardent affection on both sides, so we are to have a 6 months probation, and not consider it an engagement till the end of that time. (ibid.)

He was hardly the life partner her mother and father would have chosen for her. But Janet had always shown a considerable will of her own, and her judgment had been trusted. What could her father do now except get her to agree, at least, to a year's engagement?

CRA, meanwhile, had written to her again, developing his ideas:

> Comradeship to me so far—an intensely close and all-absorbing personal attachment, "love" if you prefer the word, ... for my men and boy friends, has been the one guiding principle in life. ... Some women would take this, and perhaps rightly, as a sign of coldness to their sex, and they would shrink from a man who revealed himself thus. ... *That* depends upon the woman. I have no fear that you will misunderstand ... you are the first and only woman to whom I have felt I could offer the same loyal reverence of affection that I have heretofore given to my men friends. Will not the inference be obvious to you? There are many comrade friends, there can only be one comrade wife. (EL, 2 Sept. 1897)

She answered: "I think you need have no fear of my misunderstanding you, or deeming the point in your character of which you speak 'coldness to the sex.' On the contrary, I hope very much to be able to enter, tho' at first in a small, yet in an ever-increasing measure into the circle of your comrades, myself being one of them" (EL, 4 Sept. 1897).

CRA then broke the news to his mother. "Thus you see," he wrote, "I beat an honourable retreat from the Magpie and Stump, I could not have lived with the sisters any longer" (EL, Aug. 1897).

In October, Janet flew the first kite about the chance of their being able to live in a CRA-built house. He quickly replied that it had occurred to him too. He had some building land on Cheyne Walk, and would put a proposal to her father. "There is just room on it for a little house that would suit you and me. I have not at present the capital that would enable me to build for my self, but possibly he might care to become our landlord, and I pay him the interest on the money laid out in the form of rent" (EL, 7 Oct. 1897).

He had also been thinking of their life together in another part of London. The workshops of the Guild of Handicraft were now at Essex House in Bow, a handsome eighteenth-century house looking down on the Mile End Road. There he had built up a working community of men and boys, some forty or fifty strong.

> You could help me greatly, and the influence you might exercise would be considerable. I have often longed for one of my sisters to take an intelligent or helpful interest in my work there, but neither of them has ever had any real care for it. . . . Think it over. I know you don't want to be merely an ornamental wife! My ménage there is of course *very* simple, but it is not uncomfortable, though naturally very bachelor-ish. . . . You would in any case I think like to come down with me on my regular evenings, preside at my boys suppers, direct their music, and help in many ways a woman can. . . . The old place is very dear to me, it would be the brighter for having you in it, and we might watch the building of our permanent home at Chelsea from it. (ibid.)

But any hint of actually living in the East End, with its poverty and criminal associations, was quickly nipped in the bud by the Forbes parents.

Their refusal may even have helped speed up work on the Chelsea house, for the plans were ready and went to Godden Green for comment before the end of October. Janet tackled them immediately, writing,

> I rejoice at numerous cupboards and other household additions. The kitchen is ever so jolly, and the second floor has resolved itself capitally. I like the cut-off corners of your room too, but you know, I think there ought to be a fireplace in the drawing-room, for the music room will be mighty full of wind and bogies at times. . . . And DO GIVE the maids a cupboard in their bedroom! This is I feel is most important for their comfort. (EL, 3 Nov. 1897)

These were the first of Janet's many commonsense suggestions for the improvement of CRA's sometimes less-than-practical house plans.

Because their engagement was not official, it proved very

difficult for them to meet and discuss anything informally; besides, CRA was always frantically busy. His workmen were making furniture for the palace of the grand duke of Hesse at Darmstadt, and in September he was showered with impatient telegrams from Germany because the czar was visiting Darmstadt in early October. "And he has to sit in my chairs," CRA told Janet, "eat off my tables, switch on my lamps, turn my door handles, and generally admire Essex House productions—the men are in a high state of excitement" (EL, 15 Sept. 1897). At the same time, he was working on a belfry screen in the church at Seal, near Godden Green, paid for by Janet's father, and translating Benvenuto Cellini's *Treatises on Goldsmithing and Sculpture,* which was to be the first publication of his Essex House Press. "You shall transcribe it, *if you can*" he wrote to Janet, "but I fear you won't be able to read it as it is so abominably written being mostly 'train and omnibus work!'" (EL, 8 Nov. 1897).

They might have hoped to be together at Godden Green for Christmas, but then there was a change of plan, and Janet, Nevill, and their mother set off for St. Petersburg to spend Christmas and New Year with their Russian cousins. Janet sent CRA graphic descriptions of her relations, the Carricks, and of their way of life. "We have great fun, and seem to have lived here for ages; the *Wohnung* is very comic and old-fashioned, all *hung* with Russian and Persian carpets." She wrote of the sublime singing in St. Isaac's cathedral; of her cousin Valery, a keen radical and Socialist who turned out, to her delight, to be tremendously keen on Edward Carpenter; and of a long but enjoyable evening dancing the mazurka (EL, 25 Dec. 1897).

But, in spite of all these excitements, and all the new impressions, what both CRA and Janet called "the Demon Doubt" beset them during this month, when they were more than usually cut off from each other. On Christmas Day itself, Janet had written, "As for the Demon, I've had several fights again, and don't feel sure of myself by any means, physically or

27

mentally; oh, I *do* hope it will all vanish—what *shall* I do if it begins again on my return? Do help me to fight myself free from these ghastly doubts" (ibid.). But there was no real way that CRA could respond to this plea. He was far from accepting the prospect of marriage without panic, and his letters to Janet were by no stretch of the imagination love letters. What he wanted, without actually putting it into words, was an intellectual partner who would be an addition and an adornment both to his work and to his life, who would lavish on him all the feminine care that he got from his mother—without the maternal fussing—and who would make no physical or emotional demands on him, such as might be expected from a "normal" twenty-year-old wife! Not being able to spend Christmas at Godden Green, he had spent it in Paris with Leonard Borwick and Philip Dalmas, also a musician and also probably a homosexual.[1] They spent much of the time in Dalmas's fifth-floor flat, living like bohemians, trying to invent a new form of musical drama.

After this week, which was obviously as disturbing to him as Janet's Russian visit had been to her, he wrote her one of his most revealing letters. There are six quarto pages of it, written on both sides, and in it he describes meeting the Demon Doubt in person, as he walks home in the fog to Chelsea from an evening with Lionel Curtis and his closest friend, Goldy Lowes Dickinson.[2] The Demon follows him home and, set-

---

1. Philip Dalmas was an American pianist and composer, apparently of some promise, and a friend of Carpenter and Borwick, as well as of CRA and Janet. They visited him and his family in the United States in 1900.

2. Lionel Curtis (1872–1955) was a public and civil servant. CRA repaired J. M. W. Turner's old house on Cheyne Walk for Curtis and his friend the artist Max Balfour to live in. Both served in the South African war, and Curtis stayed on to work there under Milner. Goldsworthy Lowes Dickinson (1862–1932) was CRA's closest and lifelong friend. A much loved Cambridge don, scholar, pacifist, and homosexual, he was the gentlest and kindest of men. Janet was very fond of him.

tling down on the end of his bed, uses every argument against bringing a woman into his life. "Wives encroach and make increasing demands on the heart," he says. "She'll want more and more and more, you'll see if she doesn't, more than you have accommodation for." CRA replies, "I've taken precautions on that score, she knows perfectly well what my views are on such subjects, she knows that the position I offer her is one of complete equality with all my other comrades, and beyond the fact of her being my only woman comrade, I can offer her nothing better in the world!" The Demon responds:

> "Doesn't it occur to you that all these pretty devices, and theories . . . may all drop to pieces after marriage . . . ? Soon after marriage a woman claims a sort of proprietary right over her husband's heart—she lays a kind of embargo on it—she brooks no intrusion of others . . . even if her sense tells her that it were both in her own and her husband's interest to leave him more rope. . . . Then one of two things will happen, either you'll make her miserable, or you'll give in. In the latter case . . . " (and he glowed red depths of condolent misery) "your friends will drop off one by one, you'll loose your influence over others, the work at Essex House will become more and more admirably organised for she'll help you with that pluckily, but the soul will go out of it, the boys will shrink from you, as from an old mentor who no longer understands them, for you will be their young friend no longer, in short, you'll loose your magic, the most sacred thing you possess—your power over men—and why? When the wife comes in at the door, the comrade flies out of the window." There was a long pause, broken at last by his hollow, dusky voice. "It's all a mistake, a great mistake, a mistake from beginning to end. A man with your temperament and principles in life ought never to marry—and you'll see that I'm right one day." (EL, 11 Jan. 1898)

This letter missed Janet in St. Petersburg, and followed her back to Kent, throwing her into fresh agonies of uncertainty. But what could she do with her life, if she let her own Demon

Doubt put things into reverse? The empty prospect steadied her resolve.

In early March 1898, news of their engagement got out, as a result of Agnes Ashbee gossiping. CRA was furious, and wrote to Janet: "I do not now see any further object in withholding the announcement . . . so sit down and write your letters. As for me, I shall write to my conventional relatives, and to a dozen of my friends,—the rest must find out the way the wind goes, there are too many to write to. I can't be bothered to do it, with all my other work" (EL, 8 Mar. 1898).

He did indeed continue to be punishingly busy. The guild was in the process of being turned into a limited company, and they had just bought the equipment from William Morris's former Kelmscott Press to start their own at Essex House. He wrote, "Great jubilation . . . next Monday there will be vans of presses and gages and chairs and tables and paper and machinery—lock, stock and barrel—moving East from Hammersmith. We are thinking of a musical procession!" (EL, Mar. 1898). Janet could not so easily banish her doubts with work.

But once the wedding date was fixed, and the Demon Doubt banished, officially at least, the remaining two and one-half months were packed with activity. There was the last detailed planning for their house on Cheyne Walk, number 74, and the last proof corrections for the Cellini *Treatises.* Janet was in charge of the wedding invitations, which presented enormous complications, partly because CRA had issued a general invitation to the whole of the Guild of Handicraft. Mrs. Forbes used all her guile to extract from Janet the secret of where the couple were going for their honeymoon, but CRA wrote from the island of Sark, where he was recovering from bronchitis in the company of his mother, "the less you talk about it the better . . . and remember too, that the maternal jurisdiction over your movements ceases on the afternoon of September 8th" (EL, Aug. 1898).

At last, on one of the hottest days of the year, the wedding took place in Seal church, its modest fourteenth-century interior now resplendent with the small gold suns on CRA's belfry screen. The "Little Mother," as from now on Janet too alluded to Mrs. Ashbee, was supported by all three daughters, with Frances, the only married one, providing her two little boys—Cecil, aged six, and Guy, four—as pages, bewitching in white satin. The only important personage not present was CRA's father. He maintained a dignified silence about twenty miles away in his country house at Hawkhurst, if he knew of the event at all.

Janet wrote of it in "Rachel" as "a day of unreal excitement, half terror, half delight. In the morning she put on new and fascinating clothes, everyone regarded her with veneration, almost spoke in whispers to her, and touched her as they might a holy thing. It was wonderful. She was now quite certain it was 'all right'; she felt exalted, supremely happy. Her old nurse wept as she dressed her. . . . CRA looked unfamiliar and more than usually alarming in a frock-coat" (RA, 53).

One small thing did, for a second, give her pause, to surface again in her consciousness only long afterward. As they took their seat in the carriage to drive back home from the church, she looked up at him—and saw tears pouring down his face. Was it only the beauty of the ritual in the beloved King James's Version, or could it also have been the realization of the ending of an infinitely precious part of his youth? She wondered about it only later.

Her doubt was soon swept away by the excitement of the reception and the lighter-hearted ritual of the cutting of the cake. Then she went up to change into her going-away clothes. The wedding had in many ways been unconventional, but had the biggest secret of all leaked out, it would have been vetoed by Janet's parents and CRA's mother as just too outrageous. The secret was that the couple, after entraining for London, planned to spend their wedding night at Essex House, going on the next day to a cottage in Alfriston, Sussex, for a more traditional continuation of their honeymoon.

Soon the growler jolted them along the endless length of the Whitechapel Road, the noise was distracting in the summer evening, the smells in that heat, horrible.

To Janet it was all symbolic. It was she who had suggested and planned that their first night was to be spent in East London, in the heart of CRA's work, and she welcomed the uproar and the dirt as a sort of baptism.

It was darkening as they drove up to the stately old house. ... The housekeeper, a comical staunch old servant of the family, opened to them and led the way with a flickering candle upstairs. They passed along an echoing corridor to a little bedroom. Besides a rickety chair, a table, a washstand with a square of household soap, and the shabby cast iron little beds under their checked coverlets, the room was quite bare. It had a faint smell of hearthflannel, smuts, and from without, that Whitechapel smell of fried fish which permeates everything.

"Alf and Sid ain't gone yet, Sir, shall they bring up the box?" piped the old lady in her rough treble; and bustled away to see to supper.

In a bewildered way Janet took off her hat, and laid it on the bed. Two lads, laughing and scrapping in the passage, knocked and at once came tumbling in with her big trunk of entirely unwanted new clothes. Whistling a tune, they pounded each other off into the darkness again.

Janet followed CRA into the next room, and ate with indifferent success, a little East End supper. It was stiflingly hot. The open window into the garden let in smuts and puffs of hot night air laden with more smells. Janet felt sick, and strange, and desperately frightened. All her wild invented theories by which she had in vain tried to explain to herself what "The Marriage Night" meant, came into her head. From the Bible to Wagner, she went through all the mysterious passages, but she still had not found the key.

In the hot darkness she undressed, slipped into her lacy nightgown, and hid like a hare under the bedclothes.

CRA was unpacking in the little meagre bathroom, and

with every sound that came through the partition her terror increased. Her mouth was dry like a chip, and she huddled among the pillows, her eyes wide and aching.

When he came in with the candle, she saw an unknown man in unknown flannel garments, who smiled at her reassuringly, tucked himself up in a matter of fact way, and blew out the light. (RA, 55–56)

8. Essex House, 401 Mile End Road, London, ca. 1900

33

CHAPTER 4
THE HOUSE WITH THE
COPPER DOOR, 1898–1900

FROM Essex House they went to stay in the Clergy House at Alfriston in Sussex, a medieval house just acquired by the National Trust and, apparently, let to their two friends Lionel Curtis and Max Balfour. This stay was the beginning of Janet's liberation. The weather was perfect, especially for swimming, and she cast off her stays before her first bathe with CRA in a symbolic gesture. She never wore stays again until middle age. But at the same time, there were old loves to be propitiated. On the first day of their honeymoon, CRA wrote to his mother, "I shall always love you more than anyone else in the whole world" (EL, 9 Sept. 1898). And Janet, who had written to her father, had a letter from him ending: "Oh my darling, you are in my thoughts night and day, all day long. Be happy, very happy; and give a thought of love occasionally to one who ever worships you" (EL, 10 Sept. 1898).

Surprisingly, CRA did not get restive for a full fortnight, during which they cycled, walked, swam, and read aloud to each other. Then they moved on to Millthorpe in Yorkshire for Janet to meet Edward Carpenter. Her account, in what was from then on their joint journal, reads:

> At last I have met Edward Carpenter, and Philip Dalmas, two personalities of the greatest human interest and vitality, and they have both far exceeded my expectations. The wonderful face of the former, with the great magnetic brown eyes, the strange tender lines about the mouth . . . The feeling of home and of peace and satisfaction that you feel at once in the atmosphere of his cottage, the absence of "Things," and of their attendant fuss and care, make an evening spent with him a scarlet letter in the calendar. (AJ, 1 Oct. 1898)

Though at the beginning Janet's journal entries showed signs of trying rather too hard, they soon introduced a refreshingly personal flavor, for she wrote with dash, and had no eye on publication or posterity.

The Little Mother joined them at Millthorpe, and they went on to Birmingham to visit artist friends there, and then to stay with old Colonel Shaw-Hellier, one of CRA's gay patrons, in his old country house near Wolverhampton, to which CRA had recently added a chapel. Janet reported on

> [t]he dear Colonel, so simple in his aristocratic surroundings, and yet so much in keeping with them. The "frank and free" look in his blue eyes, and the naiveté about the mouth, are but indices to his delightful personality. . . . There is something pathetic in the fact of the old soldier and aristocrat living all by himself in this grand place, labouring to improve it, pottering about the farm and garden, reading daily in the new Chapel . . . and maintaining the old fashioned pomp and ceremony around him. (AJ, 16 Oct. 1898)

9. 74 *(right)* and 75 Cheyne Walk, London

From the Midlands they came home to 74 Cheyne Walk, the house that CRA had designed for them. It had a strange front door, sheathed in copper and decorated with two large carnations of the type known as pinks, which were the emblem of the guild. The ménage à deux had really begun.

Janet had to run the house and cope with two servants; entertain an assortment of artists as well as public figures; associate with aristocratic and industrial clients, who might be wooed into giving financial support to CRA's projects; and, last but by no means least, get along with the simple craftsmen and boys of the guild, and their wives and families. If she managed, it was partly that she was under a kind of anesthesia. It was all, as she would often say, "so interesting."

> Should she run a mill-girls' club over the river, district visit for the vicar in the hideous Chelsea slums at her door, learn to do it more scientifically by working at a C.O.S. office?[1] There were also thrilling lectures at the polytechnic, a rapturous swimming bath and drill hall to keep up her exercise, and she felt she must know how to cook. . . . CRA's attitude towards his wife was a strange one; he left her to find her own experiences, to get to know people in her own way, and to taste, touch and handle things just as they came, even if she hurt herself.
>
> For the first time she came into contact with poor people, really poor, not the comfortable cottagers she had known at Godden Green. Her gift of naturalness was of great value to her, and . . . she found it easy and delightful to stray into all kinds of homes, and hear every sort of tragedy and comedy from her neighbours. Many of the big facts of life she thus learnt for the first time, her ignorance being colossal, but she was neither shocked nor depressed. (RA, 57–58)

After the terror of her wedding night, what was missing on the emotional and sexual side (she was as yet completely un-

---

1. The Charity Organisation Society was founded in 1869 to bring system into a mass of small private charities.

awakened) was made up for by the sheer excitement of all the other new experiences. She was "at liberty to go and come, and invent occupations for her solitary day. She was the owner of a latch-key, a house of her own with a view on the river, and a good husband who had entire confidence in her wisdom and power. It was all too good to be true" (RA, 59).

One by one she was introduced to all his friends, and was thus initiated into the idea of comradeship. With Goldy Lowes Dickinson she established an immediate contact that lasted for life, and he was much impressed by the originality and clarity of her thinking. George Ives, a prison reformer, a writer, and founder of the Order of Chaeronea, a secret gay society, became a true friend, and so did Laurence Housman, the artist and writer, and brother of A. E. Housman; his sparkling letters to her, always triggered by one of hers, span many years.[2] And then there were Lionel Curtis and his artist partner Max Balfour, who lived nearby in Chelsea. They were all gay. But it was not only Janet's unsexed quality that made them so quickly open their hearts and minds to her, but also her complete frankness and ability to accept them as they were. Here she is writing about an evening with Ives, while CRA was out at a dinner in the city:

> We had a real good talk of about an hour and a half, and perhaps got to the bottom of things. . . . "What tragedies I've been through. How can I be thankful enough that it's over, and that I shall never have my boyhood back! And never love again. I'm quite dead you know, I've killed my soul. Oh yes, it's LOWER I admit . . . but such a relief to have no more pain, and life LOOKS so beautiful from a distance!" "When did you join the Cause?" I ventured. "As far back as I can remember, when I was a small boy, and I COULD not understand why

---

2. Laurence Housman (1865–1959) was the brother of A. E. and Clemence Housman. A writer, playwright, illustrator, and, though a confirmed homosexual, ardent supporter of the cause of suffrage, he was one of Janet's real friends, and a most prolific and faithful correspondent.

such a wonderful thing should not be sanctioned. And ever since I've felt it and hoped and striven, and now I've put all the love I have into that . . . and although we of the Cause KNOW nothing, we hope a great deal. Personally I've no fear of Death, only I hope it will be quick.

"Let's see the ring," I said. "You promised to tell me about it." "Well, it's all symbolism, you know," he added diffidently, handing me the heavy silver ring with the name of the battle of the Greek lovers, and the little device like a double fork. "Do you understand it? You see it's 3 links of a chain, and the end links are open—d'you see? I can't possibly tell you more than that."

I only half saw the meaning, but I felt the spirit, so it was all right. "The thing I CAN'T understand," I suggested, "is Jealousy!" He leapt up in his chair. "Yes, Yes," he cried, "I'm so glad you feel that. It's inconceivable to me how anyone who really loves, can be jealous. They DON'T love, those people. Jealousy must be a disease. . . .

"I haven't been in love now," he said meditatively, "for 3 or 4 years, and I never shall be again." "But isn't it rather a pity," I said, "to kill yourself off quite so soon? For after all, it's very beautiful." "Ah, you're too young," he replied. "You don't know the tragedies I've gone through, and all the people I've been in love with." I could not repress a broad smile while I said I supposed I'd been more fortunate than he.
(AJ, Nov. 1899)

Just then she heard the sound of the copper door, and her husband appeared, very tired, "in a demoralised-looking dress suit" (ibid.).

Of the two whose Alfriston cottage they had honeymooned in, she wrote soon after their return to London: "After a very dull dinner party came the contrast of a delightful hour at the Turner House, with those two, favoured of the Gods, Balfour and Curtis, and Canon Rawnsley. The possibilities of an American lecture tour with Charley were discussed . . . It was grand fun sitting on the big sofa before the fire, Curtis throwing out exciting suggestions, . . . Balfour sitting and smiling in

10. Janet Ashbee, photographed by Frederick Hollyer, ca. 1900

his royal way, and looking exceedingly beautiful" (AJ, Dec. 1898).

Janet was learning fast! Casting away her stays on that first swim was not an isolated gesture signaling liberation, either. She soon started smoking as well and wearing sandals. "[I]n pursuit of a theory, her clothing became severely practical. She

39

never got to the last ditch of sexlessness, the puttycoloured Jaeger underwear; but all lace, frills and ribbons with which her trousseau had been adorned, were now excised. Her every day dress was a braced skirt and jacket of green Ruskin serge, with a cap to match. The neck of the blouse was cut low, and she wore a string of amber or lapis round the throat" (RA, 58). She joined the Healthy and Artistic Dress Union, wrote some articles for its journal, and was later on its committee with Walter Crane and Mary Watts.[3]

One of the friends she made through the union was a young and attractive woman called Gwendolen Bishop who, though married, soon started taking part in the Guild of Handicraft's plays and river expeditions, where she became a great favorite with the boys. Janet found her fascinating and enigmatic.

On her, even Jaeger seemed right, she had a slender and shapely body, she walked like a willow-tree in motion, and yet she had something Eastern, almost feline in her grace. . . . Before the scornful glances of her strange eyes, green like jade with full sleepy lids, Janet dropped the last shreds of her feminine weakness and followed her heroine into battle against the conventions. . . . They did not talk of anything deeper than clothes, but it was done in a symbolic way, and all the importance of raiment as an index of character, was insisted on. (RA, 63)

With time, Janet discovered that this radiant creature had a husband, though he was rarely mentioned, and that they lived in a flat. And then she and CRA were invited to dinner.

The chief features of the evening that stuck in Janet's memory were that they sat at an immensely long narrow black

3. The articles mentioned are "The Dress and the House, No. 2," *Dress Review* 1, no. 4 (Apr. 1903): 43–47; and "Clothing Made Easy," *Dress Review* 4, no. 13 (July 1905): 217–18. Walter Crane (1845–1915) was an artist, craftsman, designer, and prolific book illustrator. Mary Seton Watts (1849–1938) was an artist and designer. In 1886 she married the painter George Frederick Watts, and in 1895 she designed the remarkable Watts Chapel at Compton in Surrey.

table, that the room was stencilled with blue lotuses, and that a tall jonquil grew out of a brown Cornish crock. That cats kept getting up onto the backs of their chairs, and that remote, at the end of the table sat Mr Bishop, a legal-looking man in gold spectacles who had been coerced into wearing a brown velvet coat. The only things that seemed to belong to Gwendolen, were the jonquil and the cats, and possibly the coat.

Janet thought her wonderful, and CRA too felt her power, and liked her clean boyishness. . . . Her husband hardly spoke, and seemed a little worried by the cats; the whole evening he sat, looking rather tired, and watched his wife with worship in his eyes.

Janet dismissed him as a nonentity. (RA, 64)

In the spring of 1899, Janet was recruited for a nonspeaking part in *Beauty's Awakening: A Masque of Winter and of Spring*, organized by the Art Workers' Guild. Nearly all the important artists, architects, and designers of the Arts and Crafts movement who lived in London were members of the guild, and on this occasion they came together in uneasy and sometimes chaotic collaboration for a performance at the Guildhall in London. CRA contributed some of the designs, and wrote some very contentious doggerel for the libretto.

From a secluded sofa corner in the music room at 74 Cheyne Walk, Janet recorded her impressions of one of the rehearsals:

[T]he gentle Walter Crane, vaguely passing from group to group, the worst chairman of a meeting imaginable . . . and Wilson who looks like a seedy bank clerk and who is perhaps the greatest artist of them all. . . . The funniest . . . was the little wizened ballet-master Espinoza, who has drilled most of the Opera of Europe. . . . He was in raptures over Whall's demon drawings.[4] "Ah! *mais*" he exclaimed, "*cela sera très drôle, très original.*" Then he lifted his little coat-tails, and tripped

---

4. Henry Wilson (1864–1934) was an architect and designer. Janet's high opinion of him is now widely shared. Christopher Whall (1849–1924) was the leading stained-glass artist of the Arts and Crafts movement.

about in the style he had already assigned to "Jerrybuiltus,"
sending even the sober Crane into fits of laughter.
(AJ, 9 May 1899)

Janet was playing Venice, one of a procession of "Fair Cities"
(plate 2) culminating in London, which was the hopeful theme
of the masque. It was against her better judgment, for she was
a shy performer, but she was supported by CRA's sister Agnes
as Florence and by Gwendolen Bishop as Rome. And it was
not too serious. Athens "discarded anything below her little
crêpe-de-chine dress on the plea that 'the more Art, you know,
the more Nood!'" and London, "an effete looking Baroness,"
became "greatly agitated about her crown, a colossal copper
one we made at Essex House—it had to be buttoned on under
her chin, and even then the poor thing had to balance the
weighty trophy like a muffin man his tray" (AJ, July 1899).

When it was all over, Janet wrote a piece for the journal
summing it up, and the list of artists taking part sounds like a
roll call of that moment in the Arts and Crafts movement:

The Great Masque has come and gone, like the gorgeous
flower of a hothouse plant, and like a flower too, transitory,
and now quite dead. . . . With all its work, its thought, its
beauty, its fun, and its failures too, it has quite gone; but
Fairmond is still with us in the genius of the many artists
who gave themselves to create her.
    The fun of the whole thing strikes me before even the
beauty—such a queer lot of men and women were brought
together . . . the mild and benevolent Dragon (Lionel Crane)
who so considerately offered his tail for Trueheart (Paul
Woodroffe) to prod every time he stepped round the stage
(for all the world like a chicken stepping out of its shell). . . .
[T]here was the flippant Constantine (Gerald Moira) forever
playing the fool, and winking, with his crown awry, and pok-
ing the solemn ones with his sceptre; and there was May
Morris, the Majestic, the Mournful, the Morose St. Helena,
with Wilson's lovely cross. . . . Then Wilson's Lamps that
looked so beautiful on paper, and turned out such dull shape-

less masses of silk, their subtle symbolism quite lost in the half light—and Davis's children, no failure about *them*, they were quite wonderful, as the four gray winds blew them all about the stage, their little leafy ragged reds and browns, and ambers and emeralds turning and twisting in the dance. . . .[5]

Hundreds of humourous little touches rise up in the memory; the little pink Cherub (Louis Whall) who was fed on cold pork pie at midnight to keep him awake; the insufferable Titian (Hugh Stannus) who set everybody right, and then got in everybody's way, and had to be squashed systematically; and the Greek youths (from the Guild of Handicraft) who were so ashamed of their bare knees, and always thought people were looking at them.[6] . . . And the Jury boxes where we dressed, where the March lambs were forced into their hot woolly coats, and cherubs coaxed into tights with much cake and ginger beer; where the butterfly skipped over barriers to avoid the scoldings and the active comb of her mother, who snapped every five minutes: . . . "You *are* a little worry tonight! You'll ruin the whole masque!" (AJ, July 1899)

During the first two years of their marriage, CRA continued to be inhumanly busy, designing for all the fields of guild work. In 1898 and 1899, the Essex House Press alone produced five items, all of which Janet edited and proofread; the strict training of both her old governess, Miss Stoy, and of her Paris tutor stood her in good stead. Her spelling and punctuation were impeccable. She got full credit for having collated and edited

---

5. Lionel Crane (1876–?), the son of Walter Crane, was an architect and artist. Paul Woodroffe (1875–1945) was an illustrator and stained-glass artist. He later lived in Chipping Campden. He was a colleague of Laurence Housman, but Janet found him gloomy and feeble. She and Laurence referred to Woodroffe as the *bête grise*. Gerald Moira (1867–1959) was a decorative artist, working in gesso, stained glass, mosaic, and other media. May Morris (1862–1938), the daughter of William Morris, was a designer and embroiderer. Louis Davis (1861–1941) was a stained-glass artist, a pupil and associate of Christopher Whall.

6. Hugh Stannus (1840–1908) was an architect and author of works on decorative art, metal casting, and the like.

the various versions of Bunyan's *Pilgrim's Progress,* and her in-stinctive reactions about works to be produced must have been very useful, in particular for the little vellum series of "Great Poems," the first of which appeared in 1900. Among the artist-illustrators who were cajoled into doing frontispieces for these poems were Walter Crane, William Strang, Reginald Savage, and Laurence Housman.[7]

Janet wrote after her first meeting with Laurence:

> You'd never think on reading the sad little legends he has written, that he had such a modern personality. . . . He came gaily down into the big room, his thick black hair cocked up and the sunniest smile in his eyes, seemingly bent on having a good time. WE certainly did, for he is full of delightful stories, which he lets slip daintily enough with a demure smile. And we gave him scope for plenty of them, for we talked shop as hard as we were able, and each luckless brother artist came in for his share. (AJ, Apr. 1900)

Laurence remembered this occasion twenty years later, when writing to Janet at length about their friendship. "You did give me an early shock by standing to receive your guests in your own house, like an Italian Renaissance altar-piece, with two boy acolytes supporting candles on either side of you! But that I put down to the decorative CRA and not to you. Your wifely duty was merely to carry it off—which you did!"

A constant factor in CRA and Janet's marriage continued to be their independence from one another. Her acquisition of new friends and new activities of her own shows it. "Charley and I have kept our old friendships," she wrote, "and made new ones, both, of either sex in perfect liberty and happiness" (JJ, Jan. 1905). All things considered, the marriage had started pretty well.

---

7. William Strang (1859–1921) was a painter, wood engraver, etcher, and hard-drinking Scot. He and his wife, Aggie, became two of CRA and Janet's best-loved friends. Reginald Savage (ca. 1886–1933) was an illustrator and wood engraver. Later he illustrated CRA's privately printed book, *Peckover.*

CHAPTER 5
THE LADY OF THE GUILD
1898–1900

WHEN she became the Mistress of the House with the Copper Door, Janet also became the Lady of the Guild. She had known the men and boys for some time, of course, but now she was eager to enter more fully into their world. On Wednesdays, she and CRA would cycle down to Essex House "separately, CRA holding it dangerous to cycle *à deux* in London, and Janet gloried in threading the traffic of Fleet Street and Whitechapel Road. Besides having a little band of workmen's sisters and daughters to a sewing party and to tea, she spent hours in the workshops watching the men, learning [about] processes and people. At seven the younger men and boys were free to join her and CRA round the supper table" (RA, 59).

Her unconscious role was the Youthful Hostess, the "aide-de-camp" of her husband, and almost playmate of the boys.

11. The metalworkers of the Guild of Handicraft, ca. 1900

The old housekeeper looked after everything, so for thirty-six hours Janet was free of care, and rollicked in her dignified but dirty surroundings like a schoolgirl.

> The suppers were lively and very popular, and to be young enough to be invited was considered a privilege. Mrs Kirtland's pies and excellent shoulders of mutton and raisin puddings were a vast attraction to the hungry and growing, but there was something besides. The personal atmosphere was warm and honest. Humanly, as apart from intellectually speaking, they were all, during that hour really equals. CRA had unquestionably the power of seeing and knowing the human boy, through his class, of loving him, and begetting love in return. . . . It was not that he was a King among Cobblers; it was rather that his truest, most beautiful because most natural self shone out when he touched his fellows through their mutual humanity. . . . At the Whitechapel suppers Janet was no hindrance to this intercourse . . . He treated her as an extra, and a more charming boy. At the same time she gave that touch of house-mother to the gatherings, which was the only kind of femininity that really appealed to her husband.
>
> After supper they all gathered round the hearth in winter, and sat on the mangled lawn in Summer, cigarettes and pipes were lit, and they sang old songs with choruses, and rounds and catches; CRA had a very sweet tenor voice and a real feeling for good music. . . . They also read plays, sitting round the lamplit table, Shakespeare, Dekker, Ben Jonson, and Beaumont and Fletcher. (RA, 60–61)

On Thursdays, Janet would visit the wives of the guildsmen, who plied her with cakes and celery, watercress and new bread. In this way she spent "many hours in the fastnesses of Custom House, West Ham, Stepney, Clerkenwell, East India Docks. She got to know her East London pretty thoroughly; and being entirely fearless and unselfconscious, she never once encountered anything but courtesy" (RA, 61).

Weekends were mostly spent at the primitive cottage called Poynetts, at South Benfleet, in Essex. Before, CRA had simply put up a tent in the garden, when he and his boys cycled out from the workshops on Saturday afternoons. Now, Janet was brought down to "this Robinson Crusoe–like establishment":

> She had command of the one bedroom, while CRA kept nocturnal order among his boys in the tent, and took them out for an early dip in the Thames estuary, by Canvey.
>
> Janet delighted in the freedom, even in the squalor of these days. Dressed in her shortest and most disreputable skirt, she cycled down often through half a foot of Essex Mud, or in scorching summer suns. And it was romantic to climb up the hill and then, plunging down thro' the woods, dragging the cycles across rabbit-haunted fields at dusk, and over stiles, to click open the little gate and stand now among flowering tulips and lilies of the valley, and now breast high in purple and crimson poppies. To right and to left closed down folds of the low Essex hills, and beyond, a pearl-grey streak, the open Thames. (RA, 62)

12. Janet on the guild river expedition, 1899

47

She went on her first guild "river expedition" in August 1899, a week of rowing down the river Wye with the boys. It was an unheard-of activity for a young woman of her background, even though, as a concession to propriety, she had a female companion. She rowed with the boys, cooked for them, walked hand in hand in the dark with them, hearing their confidences with a natural simplicity, and let them, when anyone who wanted to, lie with a head in her lap as she read aloud. Around the nightly campfires, she led the singing with gusto and a trained musician's skill. It is hard to single out any one of her accounts as giving the whole flavor of that "sunshiny sparkling week":

> To my great relief the introduction of my sex does not seem
> to have interfered with the unconstrained jollity of the Boys.
> ... Varley was a delightful companion; he captained my boat
> and proved a skilful navigator and such a willing helper when
> the boat struck rocks or shallows, and we all had to tuck up
> and jump out and shove her off before she drifted round or
> capsized. We had only one big talk—one evening outside
> Monmouth, when he and Cyril and I lay round the camp fire
> ... and watched the swirls of mist coming up the valley.[1]
> Then we launched out and talked very large indeed, on into
> the night, and even lifted just one little bit of our soul cur-
> tains, yes, even Cyril. ... It is now no rare thing to win a
> smile from him, and occasionally, I even find his long cold
> fingers twisted into mine, and (by the camp fire be it under-
> stood) feel the roughness of his tangly hair against my face.
> (AJ, 13 Aug. 1899)

Janet was, of course, unaware that he was falling in love with her, though her disarming obliviousness of her own sex helped prevent the relationship from getting out of hand.

---

1. Fleetwood C. Varley (1873–1959) was an enameler who had only just joined the guild. He was a great-grandson of John Varley, the watercolorist. Cyril Kelsey (ca. 1881–?) was an apprentice silversmith, and one of CRA and Janet's biggest "counseling" problems.

Lewis Hughes, a young, big-eyed Welsh blacksmith who looked like an organ-grinder's monkey and was therefore known as "Jacko," was the most obliging of the boys.[2]

> He has the most perfect temper of them all, which naturally got taken advantage of; it was "Jacko, you go for the milk," "Jacko, lend a hand with the porridge," "Jacko, bale out the boat there's a good chap," and so forth to all of which occupations he brought his broad smile. And how he enjoyed the recitations at night! "Are there any moorre?" he would say with the soft Welsh accent, after each poem. . . . He was one of the younger lot who stripped for the rowing and looked like young gods and turned a lovely warm colour, but got dreadfully burnt and sore. "My skin seems too tight," said Sam, and "Oh, my jacket is so much too heavy for me" wailed little George.[3] These two babies were a valuable addition, and typified the coming generation. The small printer's devil Simeon Samuels (called Sambo or Fred by request!), is a quick little Jew, very careful and very good-humoured—he kept all my accounts on a piece of newspaper. (ibid.)

Charlie Downer, another of the young blacksmiths, was the jester of the party.[4] He kept everyone laughing

> with his wonderful witty mimicry, and comic little gestures and remarks, not to mention his songs, and the "flare-up" he

---

2. After Lewis Hughes (ca. 1883–?) left the guild in 1902, he worked as a coal miner and a milkman, and was heard to be in trouble with the police, to CRA's great distress.

3. Simeon "Sammy" Samuels (1885–1973) worked in the Essex House Press and then with the guild jewelers, but was too young and too Jewish to leave London when the guild moved to Gloucestershire in 1902. He kept in touch with CRA and Janet for the rest of their lives. "Little George" is probably George Colverd (ca. 1885–?). A silversmith and keen soccer player, he came to Chipping Campden with the guild in 1902, but went back to London soon afterward, hoping for a place on the Millwall Reserves.

4. Charlie Downer (ca. 1877–?) was a blacksmith and dependable comic in guild plays. He went to Chipping Campden with the guild, and continued working there after the liquidation of the Guild of Handicraft Ltd. in 1908, with his fellow blacksmith Bill Thornton.

49

13. The guild river expedition, encamped before Tintern Abbey, 1899

gave us on the last night at Tintern when we revelled until
past midnight. . . . He it was who cheered us when it rained,
. . . and when we had all to bundle out of the train at
Gloucester in the midst of a ragged supper, and each seizing
rugs, opened sandwich packets, knitting, loose cards, blazers,
frying pans, and the kettle, run madly for the train. (ibid.)

Whether in the guise of another sort of boy, or of a rather
special girl, Janet was accepted as one of them. And though she
was always "Mrs. Ashbee," never "Janet," her absolute honesty,
warmth, and irrepressible humor made the label unimportant.
They probably hardly considered her sex as such, any more
than she did. Or she, theirs.

In December 1899, the guild produced one of its Jacobean
plays, Beaumont and Fletcher's *Knight of the Burning Pestle*,
and took the show to Charterhouse School. This guild play
was Janet's first, and she wrote:

It has lost none of its freshness in its 300 years' sleep, and the
merry humour comes home to us in much the same way it

50

did to James I's subjects. . . . CRA presented a somewhat wild appearance in his open red shirt and shaggy white beard. . . . Taken altogether Cyril was really the best—he spoke well and clearly and looked charming as Master Sutton's scholar, and more so as the fantastic, gorgeous "Pompiona"; his great blue eyes shone with excitement, and his girlish face under the green veil and black tresses, was the prettiest thing in the play. (AJ, Dec. 1899)

These were the heady days of the guild, when it looked as though it could only expand and grow—the dream made flesh. CRA was reflecting even then, however, on how formidable an establishment it had become, how intense its growing pains.

When she went down with an attack of the measles in the spring of 1900, Janet used her convalescence to compose an alphabet of the guildsmen, which shows how well she knew them all. These doggerel verses—there are forty of them—give to an extraordinary degree the atmosphere of the guild, and of the characters who made it up at the time. She pulled no punches:

> *I am THE WOMAN who made all these rhymes*
> *And I've read them aloud now a great many times,*
> *For I've fired them off without pity at each*
> *Unfortunate friend who has come within reach.*

The verses show the sureness of her character analysis, as well as her ability to aim the barbed darts gently enough for none to be taken amiss.

> *B—stands for Binning, our old Kelmscott comp,*
> *Who tells you of Morris with awe and with pomp;*
> *Suggest anything NEW, and it's 20 to 1*
> *He will answer you gravely: "It cannot be done!"*

> *And J—stands for Jelliph, the Labour Director,*
> *The Workmen's Rights, Mealtimes, and Wages Protector;*
> *He sings country songs with a sad solemn face,*
> *As he sharpens his plane the long shavings to chase.*

51

R—stands for old Ricketts, so quiet and prim,
Like a neat little tabby cat fixing the rim
Of each small silver pepper pot studded with coral,
So perfectly proper and faultlessly moral!

C—stands for Cyril, lithe, bony and odd,
With the nose of a demon, the mouth of a god,
The eyes of a seraph, the throat of a snake,
And the fingers and touch of a wizard, that wake
Old dim recollections of far-away lives
When we know we were mothers, and think we were wives.

One wonders what CRA made of that last stanza. His instinct was not to probe! Essex House itself is the core of it all:

E's Essex House, with the Workshops built round,
And Oh what a mess they have made of the ground!
For with football and hockey and jumping and running
And various mixed games devised with much cunning,
They've trampled and tumbled and rubbed up the grass
Till a brown patch of mud's all you see as you pass.

And W is for those memorable Wednesday evenings:

For after the supper is finished and done
And the newspaper battles re-fought and re-won,
We get out our playbooks and study fresh plays
And think out costumes and rehearsal days

Or sit round the fire in clustering rings
And talk of Utopias and other fine things.

Or out in the garden when summer comes round,
On the make-believe lawn we recline on the ground,
When the night wind keeps blowing and twisting the leaves,
And the low roar of traffic slips under the eaves,

And the little white pinks send up a faint smell,
And the rings of tobacco smoke float up as well,

And the stately old mansion looks on at it all,
Traditions and mem'ries in each bit of wall;

And our Catches go up to the Whitechapel moon,
And many a Chorus and many a tune
Remind the old place of the Earl and his train,
And the Workshop turns into a Palace again.
(AJ, Mar. 1900)

There were shadows in the spring of 1900, for the Boer War was now more than six months old, and CRA and Janet were shaken when both Lionel Curtis and Max Balfour enlisted. But their minds were on another part of the world, as they planned a lecture tour in the United States for CRA, on behalf of the National Trust. It was planned to begin in October, and in September, while CRA hurried to finish some drawings, Janet wrote to his dictation: "The great American Journey appears to be at last coming off. . . . Rolfe is preparing the way for it.[5] . . . We propose taking the little mother with us, and as we have only given her a week to decide, she will probably come. Any long maturing plans would be dangerous" (AJ, Sept. 1900).

---

5. Henry Winchester Rolfe (1858–1945) was an American academic and intellectual. He and CRA probably met at the Oxford University Extension Summer School in 1892. He helped organize CRA's U.S. trips, and they remained lifelong friends.

CHAPTER 6
AMERICAN BLOSSOMING
1900–1901

T HEY sailed to Quebec and took the train down to
New England.

> We were dumped down at Concord Junction at 6 in the
> morning, and I saw my first American sunrise, yellow over
> the yellowing trees. After a night in the sleeping car the
> crispness of the atmosphere filled us with fresh vigour, and
> we walked through those golden avenues singing praises to
> Autumn. . . . After breakfast at an Inn we looked up Professor
> Rolfe and his people. He has been working hard for us and
> the National Trust, and he is keen and hopeful about the
> results. (AJ, Oct. 1900)

After the lecture, they went to stay with Ralph Waldo
Emerson's son at his house in the country, a mile outside of
Concord. Janet sang old English songs, of which the most
popular was one of the guild's own river songs, "Down the
Golden Stream." "The supper was a merry Carpenterian meal,
corn cakes and maple syrup, baked apples and macaroni, and
fine American coffee" (ibid.). CRA lectured at Harvard, and in
Boston:

> We dined at the Nortons at Chestnut Hill.[1] He is the dearest
> old man in the world, and up to an intellectual battle of any
> kind. He flung down the gauntlet by declaring that he dis-
> liked all Morris's typographical work, type, paper, drawing,
> style, all *ugly*. This was great fun! It is excellent diet occasion-
> ally to eat wholesome prunes that we dislike. . . . In between
> our discussion on the advance of Negroes, the blessings of

---

1. Charles Eliot Norton (1827–1908) was a Harvard professor, distinguished
man of letters, and enthusiast for the Arts and Crafts movement.

camp life, the rapid civilisation of Western America, and the attractions of South Africa, I glanced at the Little Mother opposite. She was arguing excitedly with an old Professor, discussing Maeterlinck and Suderman with zeal and ignoring the fact that she was courting death by eating hot bread and ice-cream turn about! (AJ, Nov. 1900)

These encounters were exciting, but Janet soon became painfully aware of the tension generated by the Little Mother, CRA, and herself being so much together. Matters were not helped by the fact that the Little Mother, then nearing sixty, had just had a major operation and was probably still anxious about her health, and easily tired. In "Rachel," years later, Janet reflected on the notion of taking her along. Theoretically, the idea was excellent, but only a visionary could have planned such a mad combination of natures and hoped it might succeed. "Old Mrs Ashbee tried to be tactful . . . but she had of course to be the chief personage, the situation had all the horrors of polygamy, so to speak, and Janet knew for the first time the maddening tooth of jealousy. She cursed herself, she wept in secrecy, she despised her pettiness, she apologised to Mrs Ashbee for attacks of brusqueness, even of rudeness; it was all no good" (RA, 65). Laurence Housman had once tossed off a limerick about the Little Mother:

> There was an old bundle of tin-tacks
> Who talked in the very best syntax;
> Her wisdom was law,
> And she rasped like a saw,
>
> And cut off your head with a flintaxe.
> (Janet's "Baby Book")

Janet had never shown it to CRA, and now it could hardly make her smile. Her efforts to be all that was expected of a daughter-in-law were Trojan, but the relationship between her and the Little Mother was never easy.

From the East Coast, CRA traveled alone to Chicago, where he was to spend about two weeks, and Janet and the Little Mother joined him after a week or so. They stayed at Hull House, the settlement founded by Jane Addams in 1889 on Beacon Street, among the city's immigrants, inspired in part by Toynbee Hall.[2] Janet responded to Chicago with shock:

> When a man has finished with Hell, says a proverb, he is sent to Chicago; and when you first arrive you endorse the statement. Smoke, darkness, noise; the clashing of car-bells, engine-bells, steamer-bells; the grating of endless trolleys as they dash along the streets; the shriek of the American voice trying to make itself heard above the uproar. The rattle and thunder of the elevated railway, the unearthly buzzing of electric cabs . . . and the thudding of power houses that shakes a whole street. . . . To the East stretches the gray sea of Michigan, with its tides and storms and breakwaters. And along its edge, the dreary Park, flat, and grey too, in its winter dress—with dreary houses of the wealthy, horrid little pretentious castles of money, along the side. . . . "Our only merit" said Mr George Mead to me, "is that we still seethe."[3] And they *do* seethe. Out in the South at Hull House the pot is nearly boiling; and a curious mixture it is inside. Every race, every grade of human creature, seems to pour into the great caldron of Chicago—and what will be the blend at the last who shall say?
>
> Hull House itself stirs and mixes the brew, its clubs and meetings bring the motley crowd together—Russians and Greeks are taught English—the children get singing lessons, and what is even more valuable, the capacity for enjoyment—the boys have workshops—the young people dancing rooms—the older ones lectures. The great block with its fore-

---

2. Jane Addams (1860–1935) was a pioneer U.S. social worker. With Ellen Gates Starr, she founded Hull House in Chicago, after a visit to Toynbee Hall in 1887–1888. In her later career, she was a leading worker for international peace, and was awarded the Nobel Peace Prize in 1931.

3. George Mead (1863–1931) was a professor at the University of Chicago, philosopher, and keen supporter of Hull House work.

14. Mrs. H. S. Ashbee and Janet Ashbee, probably photographed in Chicago by Frank Lloyd Wright, December 1900

court of tiles attracts all sorts and conditions; it is a Beacon in that loveless street, 26 miles long; its fame has gone out through all the earth, and its words to the end of the world. (AJ, 30 Nov. 1900)

It was probably at Hull House that CRA met the architect Frank Lloyd Wright, with whom he later argued and theorized excitedly in Wright's home and studio in Oak Park. Wright must have used the occasion of this visit to take the magnificently dramatic photograph of CRA and the no less psychologically perceptive one of the two Mrs. Ashbees, sitting somewhat warily together. In fact, the whole Chicago episode seems to have proved overwhelming for the elder Mrs. Ashbee, for she actually made her will there, witnessed by one of the Hull House staff! Fortunately, the lecture tour provided op-portunities for Janet to escape from the difficult, triangular relationship and strike out on her own. From Chicago, at the beginning of December, she went on to Washington in advance of her husband and mother-in-law. She found herself in the fascinating new role of impresario, selling her husband to the lecture circuit. And she turned out to be very good at it:

> Mrs Hobson, whose heart I won right away, coached me up in the conventions of Washington Society. She is one of the dearest and cleverest and most charming old ladies I ever wish to meet; she said yesterday at lunch: "My Dear, you mind you eat plenty; can't go doing all these things with nothing inside you, although you look as though you've done them all your life. Strikes me," she added, "I'm doing the best work of all for the Cause, in feeding Mrs Ashbee!"
>
> A Mrs Hopkins here is also "running" me in more senses than one! Yesterday afternoon, after lunch with Mrs Hobson, she gave nearly two hours to running around with me and hunting for a lodging, we went to 11 places, all full! Finally found a delightful English landlady . . . who nearly fell on my neck when she heard English spoken. . . . [S]he is from 'enley-on-Thames, and gives me bacon and eggs for breakfast and a latch-key. . . . Mrs Hopkins was much exercised about me. She said, "I don't like your knocking about alone in a great city—you're too young and pretty!!! (this to you only N.B.)."
>
> Last night *"grand diner"* at Mrs Hobson's, *décolleté*, peacock and all!!! [see plate 3] . . . No women of any importance. . . . The daughter of the Russian Ambassador took me home in her carriage!!! I'm having a rare time! . . . Washington is crammed! If the worst came to the worst we could stow the Mother with me . . . and you go to Hopkins' Club. But I'll try and find other quarters. Never say die! Oh my God! I did sleep last night! I hope your talk on the 11th will be a huge success. "300 Bright Women"!!! I'm thankful to be free and alone! Always, yours in truth, Janet. (AJ, Dec. 1900)

Then another letter:

> Three Cheers for your wife! The Ballroom at the British Embassy is at your disposal! Lord Pauncefote says he will

invite anyone to hear you if you will make a list.[4] . . . I have
just had a confidential talk with his lordship, and he was quite
charming, and his daughters, (nice, plain, comfortable girls)
. . . would help me write out the invitations. . . . You would
have laughed to see me sitting in the great, gaudy room,
damask-curtained, chatting jauntily with the old thing! The
Clarks say all the parvenus in that set will pour in now, and
that our National Trust fortunes are made! . . . "He must have
fallen in love with you my dear," Mrs Hobson explained. "I've
never known him give the Embassy Room but twice, it's a
miracle!" (ibid.)

Following on this description, with a psychology unusual for
a barely twenty-three year old on a first visit to America, she
told him how he should approach his Washington audience,
warning him off his favorite, quasi-imperial theme of a "greater
England": "N.B. Your line at the Embassy must be emphatic
statements re centres already formed here, affiliations, names,
facts; some GROUND under their feet. . . . You must be as disarming and winning as you can. No 'greater England.' . . .
Remember, you are speaking to what is known as 'aristocracy.'
Be cautious with your JESTS . . . be careful of political allusions"
(ibid.).

It was a journey of contrasts. From the glamour of the
British embassy in Washington, they went on to New York,
where they found themselves in Chrystie Street House, a shelter for homeless men and boys, just off the Bowery on the
Lower East Side. It was nearly Christmas, and CRA takes up
the story:

Janet picked up with David Willard at Hull House. He told
us if we liked to rough it, we might come, so here we are. The
letters announcing our arrival miscarried, so when we arrived
there was no Willard. It was the oddest entrée you could
imagine into this piggie little house in Christie Street, and we

---

4. Sir Julian Pauncefote, first baron Pauncefote (1828–1902), was a lawyer and
diplomat. He was the British ambassador to the United States from 1893 to 1902.

59

were SO hungry. One after another the lads dropped in and stood around in a circle, and let us talk to them. The strangest growths of Bowerydom! . . . Of the lads that received us and made us welcome this strange Sunday, 4 were thieves, one was mixed up in a murder case, another had been a burglar (he looked harmless enough), another was an unfortunate little Neapolitan—Antonio the Dago, who was to be shipped back to Italy and two others had run away from their respective homes, and were given up as impossibles. We soon made friends, and life soon opened up as it usually does when you take off your gloves. We had had a sandwich at 1 o'clock and were rather looking for a hot supper after our long cold journey, instead of which, a gaunt, empty table.

When it came to 9 o'clock, no host, no victuals, and the "Little Mother" beginning to droop, I mooted the matter of food in a general way, as a dry biscuit forsooth! One of the lads slipped out and in a few minutes returned with some unground coffee, and a huge, flat, Dutch sugar-capped cake! My word how we enjoyed it. I found out afterwards that he had financed the treat out of his own pocket, but it was as courteously done as you could imagine. (ibid.)

Not surprisingly, the squalor of the Bowery proved too much for the Little Mother, and the next day CRA wrote that she had collapsed.

She thinks it is picturesque, but otherwise a wee bit too rough for her, so we found her a little apartment to herself in a more distinguished part of the city, and Janet and I stay on. Carpenterianism, the simplification of life, is sorely tried by the absence of a bathroom. We fetch water in a pail from a most evil-looking yard at the back of the house, upon which look five other houses, and our rooms measure 7 feet across. Item: there are 40 or 50 people in every house, item: 50% of them are continental cosmopolitans. Item: that means Jews. Item: there's an epidemic of smallpox. (ibid.)

Sheer discomfort beat CRA and Janet too in the end, and Wilfred Buckley, soon to become the American agent for the Essex House Press, persuaded them to move into his flat on East Fifty-sixth Street.

After an almost too sumptuous Christmas dinner with Buckley's in-laws, Janet escaped again, this time to visit a friend from her Paris days, Mabel Terwilliger, who was now married and living in Syracuse, New York. They decided to visit the Roycroft Workshops at East Aurora, from which Elbert Hubbard published his magazine, the *Philistine,* and preached a noisy gospel of the Arts and Crafts.[5]

> Everyone has heard of Elbert Hubbard, the crank, the Socialist, the Book Maker, the Heretic, the "Anarkist" with a K, and most people have seen the queer stuff they turn out at the Roycroft shops, all colours and types, and papers and bindings, with now and again a successful fluke. We just took the train, Mabel and I, yesterday afternoon from Syracuse, and got to East Aurora at nightfall, as the snow was settling down thick along the roads. It WAS a funny situation. We stood on the track, our night gear in a little grip, and wondering what the next move was to be; we didn't know a soul in the place. Mabel turned and said: "Now look here, we'll just walk around to Mr Hubbard's place and ask him what we're to do. It can't be far!"
>
> So we picked up our skirts and tramped along the country road . . . (like a couple of damsels-errant seeking our fortunes) out into the night till we came to a sort of chapel with a light burning in a window. A passing Roycrofter saw us hesitating on the side-walk. "You go right in," he said. "You'll find Mr Hubbard there." So we walked in. There was a home-like Carpenterian breath about the place, a fire blazing between two great sea-horses, a bare table piled with books and papers, trophies of Roycrofters hung along a string with a score of little dried sea-horses (the emblem of the shops), pulls of new pamphlets, pages of books, and a queer, red-headed fellow poring over a newspaper. He looked up and took us two girls as a matter of course.
>
> "You sit right down," he said, "guess Mr Hubbard'll be in right away, you want to see him I spose?"

---

5. Elbert Green Hubbard (1856–1915) was a salesman, at first of soap for the Larkin Company of Buffalo and then, at Roycroft, of Arts and Crafts sentiment and objects. He died in 1915, on board the *Lusitania.*

15. The first Roycroft Print Shop, East Aurora, New York, ca. 1898. Photo by Frances Benjamin Johnson. Courtesy of the Roycroft Arts Museum and Boice Lydell.

So we set the grip on the floor and waited. Presently the door opened and Hubbard came in. It was like having a Holbein picture uncovered before you. A tall, well-made fellow, clean-razed with a firm chin, and that electric sort of look that "people with souls" (as Ives persists in calling them) always know how to kindle. He took off a vast black felt hat and shook hands. Mabel explained the situation. At my name he turned to me.

"Are you any relation of C. R. Ashbee?" he asked, smiling. "I know him quite well. I didn't like to ask if you were married," he added with a twinkle. "You didn't look like it somehow. Have you had supper?"

We explained that the grip contained sandwiches, and that we only wanted his advice as to a hotel, and we would come back in the morning. He laid a hand on my shoulder, and his brown eyes snapped at the fun of the thing.

"Now," he said, "you just come right along and I'll put you up at my house, and tomorrow we'll go through the shops."

Well, we followed Fra Elbertus, as he calls himself, out into the snow, feeling a pleasurable excitement as to the style and extent of his household. He opened the door and called in:

"Here, Bertha, I've brought you two good Philistines, they want some supper, and I'm going to put them up in the front room." A dear little lady with the same luminous expression, a small girl clinging to her gown, came out and greeted us, and we were shown into a room with two snowy beds, apparently made ready for any tramps who might chance to come by. Downstairs a large round table was laid it seemed with endless places, and plates heaped with crackers and cookies and cranberry jelly, apples and a vessel containing that terrible thing known here as tea.

16. The Hubbard family in 1898. *Left to right:* Sanford, Bert II, Katherine, Elbert, Bertha, Ralph. Courtesy of the Elbert Hubbard-Roycroft Museum.

After supper they said they were all going to a concert, "And these two girls," Fra Elbertus pointed to us, "are coming along with us. Now put on your rubbers, I guess we'd better start." Quite a lot of Roycrofters set out for the concert, which was creditable enough for a village affair. . . . When we got back, we all went up to the big Workroom and I gave them a talk about the Trust and the Guild. They were an ideal audience, they caught all the points, and joined in the laughter, men, women, and boys, it was lots of fun! . . . This morning, breakfast at 7.30, buckwheat cakes and syrup, shredded wheat and fried apples, Millthorpe again! Their three great boys were out camping up in the wood, we saw their pictures, splendid young chaps, just the sort you'd expect from such a manner of life.

The Workshops were great rooms, well lit and aired and warmed. The buildings are of stone, "hardheads" they call them, which the farmers brought in carts off their fields, and Fra Elbertus bought for a dollar a load. Great beautiful bits of purple and brown and grey, put crudely together by the Roycrofters who keep their builders living near as the mediaeval folks did, and in the intervals of book-making lend a hand to spread mortar or adjust a cornerstone. The rooms are fine; just plastered with huge adzed beams, holding up the roof, and wainscottings of grey oak which Hubbard and his boys felled last autumn out in his woods.

From a single copy of *The Philistine* published a year ago as a joke, this community of printers and others has grown up, till now close on 200 folk are employed.[6] The cash comes in from 100,000 subscribers to the monthly *Philistine*, at a dollar a year each, which amply pays wages, prints books, makes gardens, produces excellent carpenter work, and a little good smithing, and enables a delightful crank to run what appears to be an ideal community. . . . If he also makes good profits who's to blame him? . . . The nicest part is that Hubbard has a fine sense of humour, and sees the joke of the thing as much as anyone. . . . In the library are specimens of the Roycroft binding, poor stuff most of it, but wonderful considering the

---

6. The *Philistine* was actually first published in 1895.

5 years only of growth. He has 8 or 10 presses worked by a gas engine, and one little forlorn hand press that he uses for pulling special proofs. What the place lacks is someone with a strong instinct of beauty, who will refuse to pass those inorganic designs, and the colours that fight. At present they go on the "do it as well as you can" principle, which is very human; but they turn out a lot of poor work.

In the little forge which smelt of home, they were making some hideous gas-brackets, great unconstructional things, just for the want of knowing the first principles of design. . . . He promised to come and see our little workshops in Bow.

"You know the townsfolk and the Church people won't have anything to do with me; I'm such a heretic you see. I have girls around in my shops that respectable folks wouldn't look at. You wouldn't mind *The Philistine* though; I guess you're a bit of a heretic yourself!" (ibid.)

Reflecting on Hubbard's enthusiasm, Janet decided that it had been "the funniest of Birthday treats" (ibid.). She was twenty-three that day.

From New York, the three of them went on to Boston and the last of their lavish dinner parties. "It's really a good thing we're to sail so soon," Janet wrote,

for many more dinners after the pattern of last night would make a wreck of even my digestion. Beginning with grape-fruit and curacao, and ending with that particular variety of ice-cream known as "Individuals" (an architectural arrangement with a base of golden candy and a pinnacle of strawberries with cream in between), it was a proof of how lucrative a business running street-cars may be. Old Mr Whitney, having made his fortune in a straightforward way, untroubled by ethical qualms, felt it his duty to tell me how unpractical any Guild-and-Country-Scheme would be.[7] That it would have to be capitalised by a philanthropist, and that any movement thus artificially bolstered up . . . WOULD NOT LIVE. We had a

---

7. Henry Melville Whitney (1839–1923) was the organizer of the Dominion Iron and Steel Company in Cape Breton, Nova Scotia.

noble fight for it, and as I skipped every other course, I kept the whip hand and preserved my optimism. We finally made an agreement, that I would return in 20 years time, visit his steel workshops in Nova Scotia, where at present he is building halls and libraries for his 3000 work people, and tell him how our little Utopia in England was getting along.
(AJ, Jan. 1901)

They left for Britain soon after, to be greeted off Fastnet by the news of the death of Queen Victoria. They were thus in time to stand in the bitter January cold with the huge crowds lining the streets for the funeral, and to sense with them the passing of an era.

CHAPTER 7
THE LAST OF LONDON
1901–1902

WHEN they came back to 74 Cheyne Walk at the
end of their journey,

it was a miserable raw January twilight day. The electric lights
were burning, and the fog crept in. They walked all over the
house, round the big hollow Studio, into the little panelled
dining-room, and at last to the tiny green library.

"It is good to get home," said CRA, and he took Janet in
his arms. It was the first real kiss, a kiss that did not mean
goodnight or good morning, but just feeling. Janet thrilled to
her very spine—and in that hour her love for CRA the man
was born. (RA, 66)

In "Rachel," Janet referred to this moment as "the crown after
the martyrdom" (ibid.). Perhaps she was trying, in retrospect,
to pinpoint the first stirrings in herself of sexual feelings, in
part stimulated by the jealousy she had—to her shame—felt
during the American trip whenever she, CRA, and his mother
had been together.

The record of Janet's life, during the next fifteen months or
so, is a series of holiday episodes; there is little of her daily life
in the house on Cheyne Walk, but much of weekends in the
guild cottage of the moment, visits to friends, and guild river
expeditions. Life is spent outdoors, plunging into rivers as she
plunged into life, feeling the warmth of the sun against her
skin.

At Whitsun 1901 she was at the Court House, Long
Crendon in Buckinghamshire, which was then being repaired
by the National Trust and had been temporarily loaned to the
guild.

17. Holidaymakers at the Court House, Long Crendon, Buckinghamshire, Whitsun 1901. *Left to right:* Charley Downer, Reginald Beddome (a friend of the Ashbees), Janet Ashbee, Sid Cotton, Cyril Kelsey, Beatrice Creighton (another friend, lying down), Lewis Hughes, and C. R. Ashbee. Courtesy of King's College Library, Cambridge.

What a perfect holiday we are having, and what a lovely land this England of ours is! Here we are in the heart of the agricultural country, green fat pastures along the valleys, rich brown ploughland on the hills, and dotted down wherever a fine site offered itself, these wonderful villages. How these mediaeval fellows knew where to plant their towns, priories and churches! Crendon starts low down and climbs up, one straggling street of yellow cottages, tiles and thatch, alternating with, every now and again, an Elizabethan Inn, till you reach the church on the highest point, and close by it, our Court House.

How cosy the low length of its roof makes you feel, with the great Gothic chimney rising at the end, the chimney up which so many witches have flown, and plenty of room for them too, you say, through that stupendous flue from the

Ingle nook! The dear holiday sun has been with us all the while, and though he dried up the garden a bit more than we liked we did not grumble. All the flowers were alive, and our little new-made lawn a foot high, with tufted grass, just created for lazing on. We rested our heads on the rim of turf, and dreamed of how lovely our garden would be next year while one of us read the immortal "Huck Finn," his joys and his escapes. (AJ, Whitsun 1901)

She spent the morning with her friend Beatrice Creighton, "in the fields lying flat with our faces to the sky, and feeling the rich, generous sunlight stream through to our very marrow" (ibid.).

Charley and the boys took it out in bathing, and it was like a chapter from Sir Philip Sidney to hear the little company come singing up the fields from the river, all the cockneydom blown away with the wind.

Turn Amaryllis to thy swain,
Thy Damon calls thee back again,
I know a pretty, pretty, pretty arbour nigh
Where Apollo, where Apollo dare not spy.
There you shall sit, and whilst I play
Sing to my pipe a roundelay.

Then we would hear Lewis, very sober, with his rich Welsh accent:

As I was going to Strawberry Fair
(Singing, singing, buttercups and daisies)
I met a maiden taking her ware (Fold-de-dee!)
Her eyes were blue and golden her hair,
As she walked on to Strawberry Fair
(Ri-fol, Ri-fol, Tol-de-riddle-li-do,
Ri-fol, Ri-fol, Tol-de-riddle-dee!) . . . and so on.

It all seemed perfectly natural and proper, and belonged as much to the place as the actual buttercups and daisies beneath our feet, or the bunch of lilacs that our poulterer sent round with the eggs this morning.

69

In the evening we cleared the builders' rubbish from the end room, and the boys fetched down old scraps and chunks of timber from the upper chamber, and then, my word, did we make a blaze! We gathered in a circle round the ingle-nook, brick-bats, wheelbarrows, hods and pails of lime didn't matter a bit, we were determined to have our Sing-Song in THAT ROOM at any price, and poured just a scrap of paraffin onto the mountain of wood. When it caught, we were wild with joy. Charley Downer let loose his River Expedition War-Cry, and we cheered at the flames as they roared and crackled up the chimney. It was a regular Jolly-Art-14th-Century-Elizabethan-Fire . . . and we had a fine Sing-Song round it. . . . [1]

When we had gone through our usual songs and catches, we sang the superb Hymn of Agincourt, and the Gregorian verses rolled and rang under the beams. . . . And then Charley Downer sang us the following, which CRA had specially written for him, and for our house-warming:

Came Kate the Queen long ages ago
Up at the Courthouse high on the hill,
Her knights, her squires, her ladies gay,
Under the chestnut bough:—
Tapestried walls a wonder to weave,
Rustle of silk in wimple and sleeve,
Past as a dream on a Midsummer Eve,
And we by the Ingle now.

Have ye seen the flood aswirl on the Thames
Up at the Courthouse high on the hill,
Or the witches leap in the lightening flame,
Under the chestnut bough?
Have ye seen the rift where the willow tree stood,
And the thorned bullock's heart dripping with blood,
As the White Man of Notley rides in the wood—
And we by the Ingle now.

(ibid.)

---

1. *Jolly Art* was a phrase used by the guildsmen to describe Arts and Crafts tastes and objects—"a Jolly-Art fishknife," for example.

The guild's tenure at the Court House came to an end in the summer, after disagreements with Octavia Hill of the National Trust, "the lady in the mushroom hat," as CRA always called her.[2]

They found another cottage, Waterside at Drayton St. Leonard's in Oxfordshire, and CRA, who left the organization of the move entirely to Janet, wrote to greet her arrival: "I imagined you locking the doors of OUR Courthouse, and picking the last few flowers, and shaking the dust off your sandals, and thundering down the mainstreet in your violet sunbonnet, sitting on the top of the Elizabethan chest of drawers, holding a Glyon dish and muttering imprecations on the venerable head and mushroom hat of Octavia Hill" (AJ, Aug. 1901).

They had some wonderful times at Waterside, perhaps because of the charm of its small scale, and Long Crendon was soon forgotten. Janet went down there with Sid Cotton (plate 6), a boisterous, crazy, forgivable cabinetmaker, known in the guild as "the Mad Hatter," and wrote to CRA:

> Behold us sitting entirely idle, "under the chestnut bough."
> Sid is irrepressible, and so painfully affectionate that I have to
> be very firm. . . . [W]e thought a swim would have its
> charms. As I had no bathing suit Sidney regretfully re-
> nounced the idea of a diving lesson, and we wandered knee-
> deep among the hay, the sun blazing on us, and all the fields
> full of hot summer scents. I picked a lovely bathing place and
> sent Sid off to the next field. You can't think how luscious the
> water was, and how I lay and roasted on the bank after a
> swim. . . . Sidney is getting so "obstreporious" I must go for a
> cycle ride to keep his spirits down; Drayton always gets into
> one's blood. We both wish you were here, and send you our
> love. (ibid.)

The guild river expedition that summer was down the river Severn:

---

2. Octavia Hill (1838–1912) was a philanthropist, a pioneer of improved urban housing, and cofounder of the National Trust.

We feel the sun burning through the tent-side onto our faces—we get up plunge naked into the amber water—we lie on the bank and get tanned all over, and even when we feel the thistles underfoot as we race up and down the meadow drying, we sing with pleasure. When I say we I mean Gwendolen Bishop and I, the other 12 are round the bend of the river doing just the same thing. . . . Gwendolen is a splendid comrade—her dreamy enjoyment and passivity brought to her by her Hindu blood are an excellent brake on my impetuosity, and I enjoy every moment of her society.[3] . . . I always think of her more as a beautiful boy than a woman, in spite of her womanliness and grace. She looks as if she had just stepped out of a Morris tapestry, as she swings, sandalled, along the field in a blue gown with a little red breast-harness, and the lovely hair about her shoulders. (ibid.)

In September, the guild went to Hallingbury Place in Essex, where they had decorated a new billiard room, designed by CRA, for the Archer-Houblons.[4] The work was finished, and now there was to be a cricket match, Essex House versus Hallingbury village. It brought together all that CRA cared about: the best of aristocratic tradition, history, and "the Boys." The weather was perfect, and everything was "right"—except they lost the match, as CRA wrote:

So far from thrashing the yokels, Essex House has been royally beaten. Never was there such a licking! . . . But life all round was so lovely, as it always is at Hallingbury, that even a thrashing more or less, seemed to matter little after all. When the match was done, the brake was brought down to the Pavilion on the beautiful green sward, the tea-things unpacked, and we had an enormous meal in the evening sunlight. . . .

3. There is no further explanation of Gwendolen Bishop's Hindu blood. She was the youngest daughter of William and Jane Bernhard-Smith.
4. George Bramston Archer-Houblon (1843–1913) and his wife, Lady Alice, whom CRA adored, were aristocratic clients who took a great interest, financial and benevolent, in the fortunes of the guild.

In the centre of it all was Lady Alice, loveable, queenly, observant, missing nothing. . . . She told me the boys should wander where they liked, see what they liked and assemble in the Hall afterwards, for they would be sure to want to know how the new room looked, in which so many of them had had a hand. So we went to the island and bathed, and then round to the farm, to the cows and pigs, and then along the Haha and by the gardens, and last to the formal pond, round the shadows of which walks the ghost of the wicked Lady Morley; Jacko was particularly anxious to know about her, so I told him what I knew, and a little more. We finally wandered back to the house through the avenue of cedar.

Lady Alice who has followed the life and fortunes of Essex House step by step with intimate interest, was delighted when I told her of what Charley Downer had whispered to me as he looked at his iron grilles: "I say, doesn't our billiard room look fine!" And if we Cockneys have been humbled by our licking, our pride came back to us, as it always does, in satisfaction at our own craftsmanship. We spelled out the coats of arms of all the Houblon intermarriages we had painted, and compared the white pinks on our blazers with the modelled monogram of the Guild on the Hallingbury ceiling, and we concluded that it was emphatically our room.

Miss Houblon won the hearts of the boys by plucking them roses which they stuck in their buttonholes; and when the whole party crowded at the door to see us off, and the carriages were filled at our departing, our captain, it was prettily done, rose up with the whole XI, waved his cap, and gave three cheers for Lady Alice. (AJ, Sept. 1901)

There are glimpses of life at 74 Cheyne Walk: of the guild's birthday feast for which the Little Mother baked the cake, appearing at the end of the meal from behind a curtain "like Salome with the bread knife, silvery, in her grey silk and grey hair" (AJ, June 1901), and of "a good evening with friends . . . music and real conversation and no wrong notes in either. . . . Arthur Wauchope, the attentive listener, and Sylvia, beautiful in blue and old lace. We put the lights out and sat round the

18. The music
room or studio at
74 Cheyne Walk.
From *Moderne
Bauformen* 2
[1903], pl. 75.

fire while Leonard Borwick played to us, Bach and Schubert,
Schumann and Brahms, in his own naïf and elemental way"
(AJ, 23 Feb. 1902).[5] The piano on which he played would have
been the strange, rectangular grand, made by Broadwoods, that
CRA designed as a wedding present for Janet (plate 5). Its in-
terior was painted with designs in a Burne-Jones–William
Morris manner symbolizing music, with a poem woven
through them, also of his making:

5. Arthur Wauchope (1874–1947) was a soldier and administrator, chief of the
British section of the Berlin Control Commission from 1924 to 1927, and high
commissioner to Palestine and Trans-Jordan from 1931 to 1938. Janet met him
earlier in 1901 at Porthgwidden, the Spottiswoodes' house in Cornwall, and he
remained her dear friend for the rest of his life. Sylvia Spottiswoode (née
Tomlin) was the wife of publisher Hugh Spottiswoode. They were probably
friends of Janet from Godden Green days.

I dreamed that in a garden once I lay
Where three strange women garlanded with vine,
Rose and woodbine, and trelliced from the sun
On pipe and lute and viol played to me.

At the bottom was a sleeping figure, symbolizing Beethoven, whose music had a very special meaning for CRA because of the Little Mother's playing of it.

Janet's musical skills, at this time, went into collecting and editing the folk songs, ballads, and modern tunes that were the repertoire of guild sing-alongs and that she and CRA were now bringing together to be printed at their own press as the *Essex House Song Book* (plate 7).

In November, she went to Cambridge and met the musicologist Arthur Somervell.[6]

> He said he had come across our new piano at Broadwoods, played on it and liked it. . . . I told him of our Songbook, and for the fun of hearing the jealous musician snap, quoted Fuller-Maitland's excellent little book of County songs.[7] "Ah yes," he said, "What a pity he didn't make more of those melodies—such meager accompaniments—he might have done so much better." I smiled, and remarked that one generally had to substitute one's own for any composer's setting to folk tunes. (AJ, Nov. 1901)

The weekend cottages, the guild river expeditions, the *Essex House Song Book* more subtly, and perhaps also the journey to America had turned CRA and Janet to thinking of the possibility of finding a home for the guild in the country. The lease on Essex House was due to expire in September 1902.

---

6. Arthur Somervell (1863–1937) was a composer and the inspector of music for the Board of Education.

7. J. A. Fuller Maitland (1856–1936) was a music critic and connoisseur. Janet was probably referring to Lucy Broadwood and J. A. Fuller Maitland's *English Country Songs* (1893), on which she drew heavily in the editing of the *Essex House Song Book*.

19. The High Street, Chipping Campden, Gloucestershire, ca. 1900. Courtesy of Alan Crawford.

On their way back from the guild river trip down the Severn, in August 1901, they had gone to see Chipping Campden in Gloucestershire. The town had been a center of the wool trade in the Middle Ages, and then of the silk industry, and what attracted CRA, apart from the incredible beauty of the place, was a large, unused silk mill, as well as a number of empty cottages that could be reconditioned and rented for the guildsmen and their families. In November, he went down there with the foremen of the guild:

> A sort of foremen's beanfeast at Campden today to spy out the land—and it was certainly not one of nakedness. . . . We went over the silk mill again, measured it up, peered through the green and bottle glass panes, studied the girth of the

plumtree growing round the stone-work, tipped the old mad woman with the ringlets, climbed up and down the empty 17th cent. houses, explored the town hall and the reading room, asked endless questions & finally in the words of the exceedingly stolid Bill Thornton, the foreman of the smithy, professed ourselves as "very agreeably surprised." There now, the country has charms after all, and it seems as if the Great Move were at last coming off. (AJ, 14 Nov. 1901)

There were doubters among the guild's supporters; one of them was Gwendolen Bishop's husband, Gerald, who was interested in current ideas about garden cities, and thought the project was too small. "He says we ought to combine with other heads of business, and do the thing cheaply" (AJ, 23 Feb. 1902).

But in December the guild met in committee, and the men decided by a majority that the move to the country should be made. CRA and Janet were at Waterside for Christmas, and Lewis Hughes caught the train and walked eight miles through the snow to bring the news. Not long after he got there, they heard carolers outside the window. Janet went to the larder humming,

Down in the cellar
See what you can find
If you like our singing
We know that you'll be kind.

She produced a huge Godden Green cake for the children. Then she and Lewis Hughes sang slowly "As I Sat on a Sunny Bank" three times, to teach it to the children. "I thought of the little Russian Jews in the Bowery, and how I had taught them that song a year ago; and these small folk were just as quick, for they sang it after us, true and clear without a fault. Then the cake was cut, and they held their breaths while a slab was dealt out to each. . . . We felt the successes of 1902 coming towards us" (AJ, 28 Dec. 1901).

One day in March, she was walking home along Cheyne Walk and saw the door of number 74 open, and the housemaid talking to a stranger.

> I arrived in time to usher into the hall an old gentleman dressed in a cocoa-coloured ulster and a craped silk hat of that exactly cylindrical form affected by Parisians. I knew from recollections of a Nicholson drawing, that it must be Whistler, whom the Waltons had sent round to look at the house.[8] He has since decided to take it. For Alas! our dear little 74 is soon to pass from us for two whole years, but one cannot expect to live in a Gothic house at Campden without a proportionate London sacrifice! It took me back almost within touch of Ruskin and Hammerton, and the other people in the "10 o'clock" to have the little, horrid, cantankerous curled perfumed creature on the floor before me. I hope I did not show the antipathy he raised in me, a purely physical one I believe. He gave me the impression of an old, old man trying to be young and sprightly, and aping the oddities of youth, or rather of an old monkey copying the affectations of man. . . .
>
> No doubt it is interesting that such a celebrity should occupy your house, but to think of him using the intimacies of the home that even 3½ years have made very dear to you, is dreadful.
>
> Let us hope he will refrain from painting on the walls sarcastic comments on the builder of the house, as he has been known to do before. (AJ, 6 Mar. 1902)

Soon, such considerations were pushed into the background, for in April the extraordinary transplantation of the Guild of Handicraft had begun. The Cockneys were moving to Arcadia!

8. E. A. Walton (1860–1922) was a painter and an associate of Whistler. Ashbee designed 73 Cheyne Walk for him in 1896–1897.

CHAPTER 8
WHITECHAPEL TO CAMELOT
1902–1903

THE first years in Campden were joyous and exciting. The guild became a showpiece in its new home, and there were almost too many visitors, from Europe and America as well as nearer at hand. John Masefield, a new friend, wrote a poem, at Janet's request, to celebrate the town.

> *Campden town*
> *Is quiet after London riot;*
> *Campden street*
> *Is kindly to the feet;*
> *Campden wold,*
> *So bonny to behold,*
> *Is merry with the blowing wind and glad with*
> *   growing wheat.*
>
> *Campden fields*
> *Are covered up with buttercup,*
> *And bluebells slight*
> *That tremble with delight;*
> *Cuckoos come*
> *When blossom's on the plum*
> *And blossom's on the apple trees in petals red and white.*[1]

In the Great Move, they had managed to combine "Arts and Crafts" with "Back to the Land," and the situation seemed to be full of hope.

It is hard in today's world to imagine just how gigantic a step the move must have been. Many of the guildsmen had little

---

1. Janet Ashbee, ed., *The Essex House Song Book* (Chipping Campden: Essex House Press, 1903–1905), sec. 5, p. 1.

79

20. The silk mill, Sheep Street, Chipping Campden, ca. 1906. Courtesy of the Guild of Handicraft Trust, Chipping Campden.

experience outside their London streets, the sights and smells of Whitechapel and Bow. How would they manage without the city lights, the trams, the fish-and-chip shops, and the music halls? How would their wives manage without being able to run in to Nan's or whatever relatives lived near? And how would the country community receive them? The Campden population at the time was only about 1,600. As it turned out, the settling of this whole group of people—about 160 men, women, and children—into the quiet of this small town in its unspoiled countryside, although an extraordinary event, seems to have gone quickly and smoothly. The workshops came separately, the Essex House Press and the enamelers being the last to arrive. The old silk mill became the guild workshops, and Braithwaite House in the High Street a hostel for the younger men combined with a guest house. Janet and

CRA moved into a partly fourteenth-century house also in the High Street, which they renamed Woolstaplers' Hall.

CRA kept his architectural office at 37 Cheyne Walk, and actually still spent much of his time in London, leaving Janet in charge of the practicalities:

> I have just prowled round our domain, guttering candle in hand, to make sure no visitor, human or otherwise, is present, (a dog belonging to one of my local aides de camp, entered before supper, and made off with my Godden Green pheasant, so caution is necessary!) and I need hardly say it is ghostly and uncanny. . . . About half the things have come, confusion reigns, and of course all the unnecessaries like sofas and cushions, and the cello arrive by dozens while mere details such as towels and knives and cups wait till tomorrow.
>
> As I stood in the Hall at about 4 o'clock, watching the staggering of two giants with the cabinets, a soft, cat-eyed dame approached, veiled in black, and regarding my straw-covered and besmudged person with gracious kindness said: "I am Mrs Carrington, can I do anything for you?" as who should say: "I am that I am. What wilt thou?" I willed nothing . . . and waited for her to go, which she soon did, extending a black-cottoned hand—Ugh! (AJ, Apr. 1902)

It was the vicar's wife.

Janet was enjoying herself:

> My Dear Husband
> How vastly dull you can be! Well, it's so delightful here that I'll heap more coals on your head. The door is open showing the garden which I found time to tidy and sow with many seeds yesterday. Starlings are giving their long whistle among the apple-blossom, and the sun blazing away. The house is chilly though and a fire pleasant. . . . Sid by the by has been Whitechapeling frightfully with the local damsels. (AJ, 3 May 1902)

A few days later she had the boy in for

> not exactly a carpet talk—but an admonishment. We went for a long ramble . . . struck over the fields to the Millstream,

21. The garden at Woolstaplers' Hall, Chipping Campden, ca. 1905. Courtesy of Alan Crawford.

where Lord Gainsborough is going to build us a swimming bath, and through a cowslip meadow up a little hill, where we sat on a hurdle and looked at the grey town tucked under its cover of evening smoke, the church tower keeping guard at one end, and all about, the cloudy orchards, gray, white and green. Sid's blue eyes looked angelic; he might have been meditating on his possible entrance to paradise. (AJ, 5 May 1902)

Janet was soon summing up the local personalities likely to impinge on the lives of the guild and its members. Louis Dease was the agent for the lord of the manor, Lord Gainsborough, and

all the town knows him. . . . "Speaking from the Estate point of view" is one of his favourite preambles, or, "In his Lordship's interest I really feel I cannot . . ." etc. . . . The Gainsboroughs are as yet an unknown quantity. The Earl seems a harmless, gentle creature who seeks peace and ensues it, the Countess a clear-headed able woman, a manager, but

kind and motherly. . . . I cannot imagine that we shall be able
to break the immense barrier of conventionality which divides
us. . . . Their poverty might make it possible; or our frank refusal to be classed anywhere in Campden Society, which
seems greatly to puzzle the inhabitants. (AJ, 3 June 1902)

The vicar, Thomas Carrington, was an important figure in
the town, but to Janet's mind, he was

one of those who retard the coming of the Kingdom on Earth
by their aggressive stupidity. His wife is a bigot, slippery and
truculent, but of the stuff that would burn you with green
fagots if you denied one of the 39 articles. She and her daughter patrol the town, which they have divided up into districts,
clothed in self-righteousness, and armed with pale pink
parish magazines. . . . Oh! this Church of Englandism makes
you sick when it runs in grooves like these! . . . The other
Sunday evening we all returned from a cycle ride to Warwick;
I daresay we did look as if we were enjoying it, there not appearing any valid reason for concealing the fact, as the whole
battalion sailed down the hill, just as the Vicaresses, senior
and junior, were taking their post-devotional walk before
bed-time. The sight of 12 young people rejoicing in their
youth, was however too much for them, and they considered
it a just punishment to cut us for a week! (AJ, June 1902)

By August, CRA was compelled to write Mrs. Carrington a
stiff note, having got wind of her trying to discover the "theo-
logical opinions" of the guildsmen.

Janet was soon involved in the local schools:

I find something wanting in my day, if I have not either been
with the children in class time, or had them in our garden to
learn songs or help with the vegetables. . . . They have
brought me plants and seeds, made the marrow bed, staked
the tomatoes, planted sweet williams and pansies, and over-
powered me with nosegays. I have constantly to refuse gifts of
rabbits and kittens.

Sometimes we go for rambles to Northwick Park, or
Broadway Tower, to the amazement of "the gentry," who

83

regard me and my little train as incomprehensible altogether. But the schools are bad and inadequate . . . and it is no good lifting your eyes to the Church for help for she is dead. Will the new Education Bill do anything for us? (ibid.)

The move to Campden had meant the loss of some old faces as well as the advent of new ones. Cyril Kelsey, one of the deeply loved "problem children," had gone off to fight in the South African war, but now there was Fred Partridge, a silver-smith from Barnstaple, of whom Janet wrote:

He is excellent fun . . . has beautiful grey eyes that are set deep and look very straight, but cannot keep serious for long together; a rugged face with a good brow and jaw, shaggy hair . . . and a mouth rather too curved and unstable to be quite safe. He affects what the boys call the Jolly Art style of dress,

22. *Alec Miller,* William Strang, 1903. Pencil drawing; 13¼ x 9¾. Courtesy of Jane Wilgress.

84

complete from flannel shirt to sandals. . . . The last comer is Alec Miller, a Glasgow wood-carver, who promises well. He is refreshingly simple and direct, and has his lowland accent yet strong upon him. His great brown eyes and pleasant irregularity of feature call out instant confidence. . . . He is 23 and has been carving for 10 years. (ibid.)

Alec later recalled his first guild sing-along, and how they

all trouped into CRA's library, perhaps a dozen or 15 of us, and found the Ashbees and two friends; a quick-eyed observant woman, and a quiet, dark man with a pointed beard. Presently, the boys being all seated on the floor, CRA pointed a minatory finger at the lady, and in a singularly sweet tenor voice began the song: "Mrs Webb, Mrs Webb lend me thy grey mare" and so for the first time I heard that splendid song "Widdecombe Fair" with the refrain sung as: "Old Uncle Ashbee and all."[2]

The visitors were Sidney and Beatrice Webb, who were staying nearby, and Alec already knew of their *History of Trade Unionism*. This get-together was an example of the easy way in which the Ashbees introduced distinguished friends and colleagues to the company of the guild; Jack London, William De Morgan, and Walter Crane were later visitors.[3]

The first Christmas at Campden was lively with caroling throughout the town. "14 little neighbours' children in red riding hoods and coloured lanterns," CRA wrote, "and some ½ dozen grown-ups habited in black gowns or white hoods to

---

2. Alec Miller, "C. R. Ashbee and the Guild of Handicraft" (typescript, National Art Library, ca. 1950), 16.

3. From 1892, Sidney (1859–1947) and Beatrice (1858–1943) Webb made a formidable partnership as social reformers, historians, and writers. They wrote and lectured extensively on many aspects of economics and the social order. Jack London (1876–1916) was an American novelist. His *People of the Abyss* (1903) was based on his experiences in the slums of East London. William De Morgan (1839–1917) was a potter of great originality in the Arts and Crafts movement, and later a best-selling novelist.

keep the little band together" (AJ, 25 Dec. 1902). He and Janet spurned such modern songs as "While Shepherds Watched" or "We Three Kings," and the singers were coached in an older, richer mixture of faith and wassailing. There was a Christmas house party at Woolstaplers' Hall, including Gwendolen and Gerald Bishop, and much rehearsing for the first guild play in Campden, a repeat of the previous year's production of Ben Jonson's *New Inn*. Proceeds were to go to fund the building of a swimming lake outside the town, and all sorts of friends rallied to support this first Arcadian dramatic enterprise. Goldy Lowes Dickinson, whose sister May was acting in it, came, and so did the Strang family in force, and John Masefield, a new friend whom Janet described as one of those "stimulating people who excite you like champagne or keen air" (AJ, 17 July 1902). CRA played the lead role, and wrote that the guests were "quartered out and over the way and round about. . . . The village clamoured for an extra night, which we duly gave, also there was a matinée for the County, likewise a success, though little Lord Gainsborough slept peacefully through 3 Acts" (AJ, Jan. 1903). It made all the difference, he noted, having Lowes Dickinson, Strang, and Masefield to play to.

Quiet intervals were rare during those first couple of years in Campden, for Janet was confided in and appealed to from all sides. She seems to have gone almost daily into the old silk mill during morning or afternoon breaks, the times at which the boys especially moved around clutching mugs of tea, to see what was happening in the other workshops. These moments were of the greatest value, when problems about lodgings, or plans about lectures, sport, or drama, could be brought up informally.

In May 1903, she went to London for a brief visit, and part of it was spent being confided in by Cyril Kelsey, who had come back from South Africa, and by Gerald Bishop. It was probably in the friendly informality of Christmas at Campden that Janet had had a first chance to pry open the shell of reserve

23. Gerald Bishop,
ca. 1900

that was Gerald's defense against the problems of his and Gwendolen's marriage; a few weeks later, Gwendolen left for Italy on a journey of self-discovery. Gerald was asked down to Campden again on his own. That visit was the fateful February evening when, as Janet wrote in "Rachel," "he had prayed for her help, and she had leaned to him over the abyss" (RA, 70).

He had written to her to seal this first "recognition," saying that, with the "masculine habit of codifying which is strong in me I have got you down in my mind-tablets as a New Fact in my life. I hope you don't mind being tabulated in this unceremonious fashion—there is a special pigeon-hole into which you fit quite beautifully, and will I hope, come to feel quite at home there" (GMB, 21 Feb. 1903).

Now she spent a whole evening with him,

in his lonely rooms in Queen Square. He has been preparing
with a sort of forlorn hope against Gwendolen's second
home-coming—when? SHE is gaining (we hope) experience
and appreciation in Florence; "seeing LIFE" is I believe the
right term, and he waits in this queer little 18th century
abode, and now and again hangs a curtain or makes a book-
case. He has a homey restful way with him; brown eyes,
brown-coated, soft-footed, the pleasantest host after a long
day. He was delighted to show it all to someone fresh; and
prepared supper in his solitary little kitchen with the zest of a
child in its picnic meals. He is one of those who have gone
through the flames and the smell of the fire is not on them.
All the experiences of this awful year have not robbed him of
his sweet serenity and sane, level philosophy. . . . He drew
Gwen's last letter from his pocket and read it to me as we sat
over the fire, the first human home-letter since she left in
January, it had been like meat and drink and physic to him.
All the absurd little questions and bits of news . . . after the
morbid ravings of former letters, were subjects for our joy, almost for our tears. "Love is not made of cast iron" he had said
to me at Easter in his bitterness. . . . "No, but it is wrought" I
replied. And here it was, at the touch of Gwen's finger, as
strong as ever, perhaps too strong for her good . . . and by the
kindling of his eyes, and shaking hand, I can tell that Gwen's
power over him is mightier than any reasoning.
(AJ, May 1903)

With their growing understanding, Janet began to reappraise
her heroine of four years earlier.

In that summer of 1903, she and CRA went on a journey to
South Africa, with her parents and her brother, Nevill. In
preparation for it, and perhaps also as a reaction against rural
conservatism, Janet decided she must learn to ride astride.
Laurence Housman, in whom she confided, was not sure of the
wisdom of it: "I would like to see you riding in your own way
in any other part of England, but in Campden you want to
scheme your life to be as useful and as acceptable as possible in

24. Janet riding astride, 1904. Courtesy of King's College Library, Cambridge.

directions which a revolt in the saddle might help to make difficult" (AJ, Apr. 1903).

But she was not deterred, recruiting the help of George Hart, one of the guildsmen who had served in the army, and wrote to CRA:

> George met me at 6.30 at Broad Campden, and we changed my saddle, and retired to a solitary flat meadow, where G. proceeded to give me a military riding lesson with personal illustrations. He made me mount and dismount, trot, gallop,

with and without stirrups—he was perfectly serious, and I learned a lot. He says it looks fine, and quite natural and sane. He is the only one "in the know," and I think quite to be trusted. After supper we had a splendid metaphysical discussion. (AJ, 20 Apr. 1903)

The South African trip seems to have been taken mainly for the sake of Nevill Forbes, who had developed tuberculosis three years earlier, but CRA, whose natural hopefulness was always magnified by journeys, was exploring the possibility of establishing a branch of the Guild of Handicraft in the Transvaal. He wrote a great many journal entries on the trip; Janet did not write so many, but hers are among the most graphic. At one point, they abandoned her parents and brother, looking for more adventures, and found themselves in Kimberley:

> [W]e had had enough of the beaten track, so we cut the painter yesterday, leaving the family despondent, but sustained by the conviction of their wisdom in preferring trains and hotels, (i.e. security) to carts and farms (i.e. risk)! It must be terrible to arrive at an age when you dislike risk!! . . . Staying, in this gaunt hotel we observed, and I must confess avoided, a little furtive man with no chin and a 4 inch wound, barely healed, along the temples; also a cavernous cough.
>
> But last night, on coming from the diamond mines into that enormous empty drawing room, furnished entirely with linoleum, there was the little chinless man at the piano, an old and rattle-throated Collard, ringing up Bach Fugues to the flies on the ceiling. The shock was so great that we were galvanized into immediate acquaintance, and, music tearing down brick walls of reserve in that marvellous way it has, I found myself, half an hour after, playing Beethoven Symphonies with him à *Quatre Mains*, and introducing him to Brahms *Balladen*. We had no time to learn anything of his history, save that he works in a lawyer's office, and thirsts for music in this hard, flinty town, consoling himself, when he has driven out his uncongenial fellow lodgers, with Romances and Rhapsodies all alone among the linoleum. (AJ, July 1903)

The party was home again by the end of July. Nothing came of the idea of a branch in the Transvaal, but CRA brought back to the guild some orders for furniture.

When Gwendolen turned up again in September, Janet made a long entry in the journal.

> She has come back after 8 months holiday more lovely and winning than ever to look upon, and I am trying to get to her point of view. . . . One thing strikes me, she is harder; hard, with a streak of bitterness, the obverse of which is a crystal laugh with the ghost of sneer in it, that makes you shiver a little. One does not go off alone for 8 months and leave one's husband in a Bloomsbury flat unless one has a problem of some sort. But the queer part of it is that Gwen seems to have shaken off her part of the burden in the South, and come back to Gerald empty-handed so to speak, free of all qualms, conscienceless, almost soulless, a very Undine! . . . Poor Gerald! I asked her today as we were basking by a hedge on Dover's Hill . . . "Tell me, why are you fond of me?" "Because you are beautiful" she said earnestly. I gasped and was silent (AJ, Sept. 1903).

CHAPTER 9
THE FIRST SHADOWS
1903-1905

THE Webbs came to Gloucestershire again that summer, and Janet was in Woolstaplers' Hall, just getting ready to visit them at Aston Magna, when she saw two wonderful ladies, evidently not indigenous, rustle up to our threshold; one of them gave an appreciative poke with her sunshade to the 1840 bay window, and said in a stage voice, "Look, darling! Isn't this too exquisite? *Quite* the most beautiful thing I have ever seen!" And with that Minnie opened the door, and shewed in Lady Elcho AND Mrs Patrick Campbell![1] They both wore that air of coming to see a curiosity which always annoys me; but I was swept into my own drawing room with their skirts, and simulated an easy cordiality. I was just warming up to my subject and trying to choke off their fulsome admiration, when Mrs Pat crackled her black "glacé" train into a chair, and leaning forward with the tragedy of a Melisande, said hoarsely: "Tell me what it feels like to be as strong as that!!" This nearly did for my gravity, but replying that it felt like a cow who feels nothing at all, I resumed the showman, and soon got them into the High Street, the Guild being their real objective. . . . "I suppose you've had a lot of monks and that here, haven't you?" asked Mrs Pat, pointing to the Market Hall, which in some dim way I suppose suggested cloisters—when with a sudden scream, she hurled herself, Paris opera cloak and all, in front of the historic Station bus. Her aim was to rescue from death

---

1. Mary Charteris, Lady Elcho (1861–1937), was a leading lady among "the Souls" and a friend and patron of the guild. The Elchos' country house at Stanway was near Chipping Campden. Mrs. Patrick Campbell (1865–1940) was a famous, almost legendary actress, closely connected with George Bernard Shaw.

92

a horrible little dog, called I believe a gryphon, into the details of whose breeding it is not good to enquire too closely. She clutched the little beast up out of the dust, and hid it in her neck with a kiss.

"Isn't he too adorable?" she said. "He has Mary Elcho's eyes he has, and Arthur Balfour's nose, and Wemyss's whiskers!" The likeness was indisputable, but one loathed the way it was said.

We hurried through the works pleading our engagement. "Oh that's all right," said Mrs Pat, "we're going there too!"— and she caught up a great green enamel chain which matched her glass ornaments to perfection, and flung it over her head with a finished gesture.

At the Webbs's,

the little room was strewn almost spontaneously with Blue Books; for the tea tray a scanty space was cleared amongst the shelves of MS and Statistics, and the Webbs received us with their delightful air of conscious seriousness, an unbending from habitual toil as it were, a concession to the frivolous neighbourliness of friends. Withal a dubious glance was reserved for Mrs Pat, who with her clothes and her gryphon took up a third of the available space. Clearly she wasn't expected in the train of the aristocrat. But even Kings have their jesters, and as Lady Gainsborough says, "Mary Elcho always likes to have these *outré* people about her you know!" However, she had to be put up with. Sidney Webb sat on the edge of his chair, and tried to let himself down to her conversational level. His wife chose the simpler way of ignoring her altogether. But Mrs Pat was not going to be ignored. She was being snubbed, so she would play to the Gallery! The fiscal policy did not interest her, nor the educational status of Campden, nor the beauties of Batsford gardens—what SHE wanted was to talk about herSELF!

And gradually, as by a magnetism, we found we were the Gallery to which she was playing, and that, do as we would, she swayed us to her mood, and we laughed at her extravagant clownery. She rocked herself on the window seat having secured her audience. "Yes," she drawled, "It's really delightful to be a complete lunatic—you see nobody expects anything of you, you have no standard to live up to," and with a meaning glance at Mrs Webb, "and you can have a real good time!"

Mrs Webb drew herself up and flushed pink. This was too close to home to be passed without challenge. She glanced at her notes about the room, and remarked in her most Webby manner: "Well, of course, if you're writing the history of Local Government, you can't exactly be a lunatic." Mrs Pat laughed, having the best of the situation. "Can't you?" she jeered, "Why, I should have thought that was just what you would be under those circumstances!" (AJ, Sept. 1903)

Now that they were in Campden, Janet relied more on correspondence to keep in touch with friends, and particularly to joust with Laurence Housman. Her letters to him do not survive, but his to her give a sense of the witty, teasing debate they carried on.

I do believe you LIKE to be misunderstood, because whenever you get onto a postcard, or into an envelope, there is always some attempt at a misunderstanding trying to bite the end of your pen! Now there are some people I find it quite impossible seriously to misunderstand, but they are the very people it is nicest to entangle in an argument, because no harm or hurt can come of it. And you happen to be one of these. . . . Heavens! I hope this letter does not sound sentimental or patronising. How can I be patronising when I don't know whether it is spelt with an "s" or a "z"? (AJ, Feb. 1904)

At the end of November 1903:

IF I arrived very dirty, with nothing but a toothbrush in my pocket, in pursuit of the beautiful and true, on December 4th, would you take me in for the night? And not sit on me too controversially? I hope to be walking back to London then; I should come to you via Stratford-on-Avon, so you could flaunt a bicycle in my face if you wanted to be nasty. I post clean shirts ahead of me, so if you say "Yes" you will understand a brown paper driblet when it arrives. (AJ, Nov. 1903)

And after meeting CRA in London: "My memory of his

conversation is vague as I was chiefly concerned with the way he buttons his cuffs—how, I can't tell you, there was a sort of *'il n'y a pas de quoi'* air about them, like a 'Swiss roll' coming undone. He also wore a napkin ring instead of a scarf-pin, so he managed altogether to look as if he had come for luncheon bringing his sheaves with him" (AJ, Aug. 1903).

Throughout the year, there was a steady stream of people coming to check up on the Cockneys in Arcadia. "The visitors come and go here so thick now," CRA wrote,

> that one has to hold oneself in fairly tight if one is not to let one's work be interfered with. We find it best to have them in the country house manner, in batches at weekends, so that they entertain each other. . . . Last week it was a voluble and quickly intelligent violently freethinking little German jew and his wife, Mr and Mrs Eckhart from Manchester, immensely interesting both of them, rich, sympathetic, but as hard as nails. A fortnight before, a charming young American professor . . . from Kansas was it? or Oklahoma, I forget—he also "wanted to know you know," and so came to our Arcadia. This week we have the oddest crew. Laurence Housman, in pursuit of that Will o' the Wisp, the Simple Life, walking on foot from Hereford to London, protesting against railways, and sending his pack on to us by train, as avant courier of his coming. Staying in the house with him are Granville-Barker the actor, . . . and a curious and interesting Jesuit, one Thorpe.[2] He turned up at my office last week . . . "wanting to know, you know" and so also drifted as a flake of snow, in at our door. (AJ, Nov. 1903)

Housman and Granville Barker, allegedly collaborating on a play, stayed three weeks, sharing the simple meals prepared for the young men of the guild at Braithwaite House.

---

2. Harley Granville Barker (1877–1946) was an actor, actor-manager, and dramatist, as well as an influential producer and critic. Janet and CRA always claimed that he was "ruined" by his wealthy American second wife. Joseph Thorp (1873–1962) left the Jesuits not long after this visit, and worked as a writer and designer in the printing industry.

The guild play that Christmas was *The School for Scandal*, with CRA as Sir Peter Teazle; afterward, Janet went to stay with her parents, spending a day or two in London on the way. On the train down to Godden Green, she wrote to CRA:

> You will marvel that life is still present when you hear what yesterday was like, . . . but Lud, Sir Peter, now I am wound up, bless you, and with £200 in my pocket egad! what's fatigue? I can make it up to Godden Green, where by the way, you are expected on Saturday. Well, my life! I thought of you improving your mind at the lecture, while Gerald and I were dining, theatring, and afterwards (oh, what of the censorious world!) supping in the Strand at midnight. . . . Oh it was fun! Its glorious to have a crowded week of frivolity! Well, yesterday was the cap—and a field day for "The Professor." We met at the International, where we disagreed over nearly every picture, but the superb jewels sealed up the breach, and we sat and revelled in the most wonderful Whistler seascape I have ever seen. By this time we were thoroughly in the mood to enjoy each other's society, so we had an amicable lunch, and then came the triumph, when we walked into the New Gaiety dress circle like lords, and allowed ourselves to be diverted. As a matter of fact the piece, "The Orchid," . . . was very funny and almost free from vulgarity. . . . When we had sat for three hours, we thought it was enough, so we left before the end and went to the tea place. We were joined by Alf, George, Sammy and Lewis and had great fun.[3] . . . All merry except Lewis, who is out of work again and was very silent and down. . . . [H]e made my heart ache he looked so wistful. (AJ, Jan. 1904)

The jaunt was organized by Cyril Kelsey. They all went on to Drury Lane where it was Standing Room Only, and spent four hours in the crowded pit, being fed chocolate by Sammy

---

3. "The Professor" was the guild nickname for Cyril Kelsey. Alf Pilkington was a cabinetmaker, known in the guild as "the Wild Man of Poplar." He left the guild in 1900 to enlist for South Africa. The others at this young men's reunion with the Lady of the Guild were George Colverd, Sammy Samuels, and Lewis Hughes.

25. The bathing lake at Campden, ca. 1905. Courtesy of King's College Library, Cambridge.

Samuels while all around "dined copiously on Bass and sandwiches and oranges" (ibid.). Afterward, Cyril called a hansom cab, and he and Janet went back to Chelsea "more dead than alive. . . . It's no use, I can never get up any righteous indignation for 'The Professor'—a person with a voice like that, who thanks you so prettily, . . . well, I suppose one wouldn't be a woman if one remained consistently harsh" (ibid.).

The great event of the summer of 1904 was the Grand Opening of the Bathing Lake. This event was the culmination of many months of effort, both in raising the money and in organizing the actual digging. It might have been thought that the entire community would rejoice at having such an amenity, but with their long-held ideas about a freer and healthier lifestyle, CRA and Janet seem to have underestimated how shocking it may have seemed to the locals that boys and girls might actually swim together, even in the almost total coverage of the bathing suits of the time. And perhaps the real outrage was the idea that swimming instruction would be during school hours! Janet found herself up against Lady Gainsborough, who wrote to say she felt that things were being rushed with the school managers:

> Please forgive my plain speaking, but as I am double your age, and began to be interested in these matters before you were born(!), I have had time to learn that one has to have untold patience in order to carry through the smallest reforms or improvements. . . . *"Tout vient à qui sait attendre"* has been my motto, and I have lived long enough to prove it, which may be of some consolation to you, who are young, impetuous, and almost too kind-hearted. (AJ, 22 June 1904)

Janet was incensed by the note, but thought to show her proposed reply to Rob Martin Holland, a friend and a director of the Guild of Handicraft Ltd., who wrote: "She writes of course *"en grande dame,"* but this is natural to her, and especially natural when she wishes to give you friendly advice from the pulpit of age and experience! . . . Such a letter as you have written would declare War to the Knife, and is therefore impolitic. . . . Oil the engine, and don't get grit in the bearings, and your reforms will come through, for they are driven by the greatest of all forces—energy!" (AJ, 25 June 1904).[4] Janet wrote a milder version, regretting "that such an important part of every child's education should not have the managers' encouragement. One has only to look at the anaemic and sickly women (I could cite a score) and girls here, to grasp how their physical development has been neglected" (AJ, 27 June 1904).

Once the excitements and the tensions of the opening of the bathing lake were behind them, both CRA and Janet took separate holidays, CRA with three of the young men of the guild, sketching in northern France, and Janet to Oxford where she

---

4. Rob Martin Holland, later Holland-Martin (1872–1944), was a director of Martin's Bank and other concerns. He and his dynamic wife, Nell, were good friends and advisers of CRA and Janet, though Janet always felt CRA compared her unfavorably with Nell, who had produced six sons.

had been lent a house, complete with a maid, for three weeks. She had a variety of friends who visited, including Gerald Bishop (Gwendolen had gone off again), her father, and CRA too, when he came back from France. She enjoyed "that queer atmosphere of Lotus-eating that always floats around Oxford, a dream of beauty and joy in the senses while it lasts" (AJ, Aug. 1904). But she also had business to do, trying to organize a grant for the Campden town band. On CRA's suggestion, she went to see the head of the Appointments Board at Trinity, a Mr. Raper.[5]

> It is always fun to beard these Fellows and important persons in their lairs, and instructed by the Scout, I walked into a very dusty and interesting room. It was full of writing tables, papers, books, bronze and jades, porcelain and ivories—all in complete confusion; and when the little old, grey-bearded man stepped into it, he finished the picture. He telephoned me into communication with the proper people for the job; and then began the adventure!
>
> "Don't go!" he said, as he walked backwards and forwards colliding with bits of furniture. "You know, I really know you quite well—I tried to buy your portrait last year—of course I didn't know it was you—but I recognised you the moment you came in." I was thunderstruck, and not very sure how to take the old man's agitation. "Yes, it was in an exhibition here; "A Lady in Red" [see plate 4] was the name—and I felt I wanted to live with it—but the price was too high—Not for its value, Oh no! But for my means. And now I see YOU! It is all like a dream!—Don't go! I want to talk to you."
>
> I remembered the portrait well. I had stood to my old friend Miss Halhed years ago in Chelsea, it was not a very good picture, and I could hardly fancy it hanging beside the Reynolds and the Holbein. As I meditated, the old man was staring into my eyes. "I shall not leave for my holiday today," he said, "I must see more of you. Can you dine with me alone

---

5. Robert W. Raper (1842–1915) was a classical scholar, conservationist, and fellow at Trinity College, Oxford.

tonight?" (Curiouser and curiouser, said Alice.) "I shall be charmed" I replied gravely, "shall I come here?" "No, I'll show you the way." He seized a hat from the pile on the table and took me upstairs and downstairs and out across a quad, and finally pointed to a dark portico. "There," he said, "go in through that door at 7.0 tonight and I shall be waiting for you inside."

It was too diverting to resist! We met at 7.0, in what proved to be the Common Room of the College. My host in spotless evening dress approached me with a piteous air! "Imagine!" he said, "my dear old friend Vernon Lushington has turned up and I HAD to ask him to dinner—my disappointment is acute—any other night but this—we shall not be alone as I had hoped, but he may go early! . . . [6]

When the other old gentleman appeared, Mr Raper unselfishly . . . made a grey and nebulous foil for his friend's conversation. We were the oddest trio in that sombre heavy room, and the butler must have wondered why and where the white muslin and green zephyr guest had been picked up.

At last he left . . . and my little host sighed with relief and conducted me into further depths of dusty apartments. We reached a remote cubby hole chiefly filled with books and containing one small sofa. Here we sat down and talked very personally. This was the old man's desired hour. I was loth to close it down, but it was growing late and I saw no end to the atmosphere of "Realised Ideal" in which he was wrapping himself. After much protest he seized a coat and hat and a huge bunch of keys, and sighing heavily, turned out the lights. We stumbled downstairs and out through the big iron gates. The night was quiet and black. "Are you aware," said Raper, "that we are entirely alone in this garden? This evening is like a dream—a dream." At last on my doorstep, he bade me a hurried good night. (ibid.)

As a postscript Janet added, "I wonder whether, now that he has known the original, he will buy the portrait?" (ibid.). He did. And after he died in 1915, it was left to Janet.

---

6. Vernon Lushington (1832–1912) was a writer, judge, and conservationist.

In September, Janet and CRA went over to Hamburg for the lavish wedding of his cousin Elizabeth, who had reached the summit of grandeur by marrying into the Nord Deutscher Lloyd shipping family, an image to be lived up to. To CRA, the materialism was very disturbing. "The Old Hamburg was beautiful, if a bit prim, the new Hamburg of Bismarck's *Zollverein* was vulgar" (AJ, Sept. 1904). Janet wrote:

> I of course was taken over for inspection. Six years a wife, and not yet introduced, and all the aunts and uncles and cousins eager and waiting to call me "Du" and clasp me to their ample breasts. But as a matter of fact I have far more affinity to them than Charley. He has still enough of the diluted German in him to be terribly insistent on being English, and I watched him stiffen into a super English *hauteur* as the expensive cousins chirped and chattered. On the whole I think I passed muster. Of course I was not really a wife; I was not known to give dinner-parties to 35 habitually, could not make more than one kind of soup. . . . I did not dance, above all, I had no nursery. Charley however HAD succeeded in selling things, (a forlorn Guild salt-cellar smiled at us from among silver-gauze sashes and nipped geranium heads on the dinner table). (ibid.)

In November, Janet spent some time in Birmingham with old friends, the Arthur Dixons, and went to a meeting of the Socratic Society to hear Gilbert Murray read his new translation of the *Troades*.[7] Birmingham, Janet wrote,

> is a wonderful place, a curious mixture of Bourgeoisie and Romance, dullness and intellectual activity, materialism and spirituality. . . . Mrs Dixon had planned one of her delightful dinner parties for me last night, and as Friday was the only night the Lodges could come, Arthur Dixon had to forego all the excellent meats provided; in fact it was against his ritualis-

---

7. Arthur Dixon (1856–1929) was an architect and designer of the Arts and Crafts movement, High Churchman, and leading figure in the Birmingham Guild of Handicraft.

tic conscience to have even the social conviviality that day, but
he stretched a point for me! Our end of the table was dis-
tinctly gayer. . . . I had asked to sit opposite Lodge, so as to
catch that splendid look—and the quartet rippled from
Euripides thro' Marlowe to Shaw and back again—we felt
like fresh whetted knives.[8] The other end, a quieter background, showed Lady Lodge, a large and pleasant person
with no special outline, who sits very loosely to her 12 children, and to her responsibilities in general as wife of the principal of Birmingham University. Her husband thinks her the
most beautiful woman in the world; this gives her an unfair
advantage, but must be agreeable!

On the other side of poor Arthur Dixon, whose green eyes
twinkled sadly at me from behind a mountain of conscientious salad, sat Mrs Catterson-Smith. Her principles and her
temperament alike are against the wearing of evening dress;
and an enveloping garment of black, without form, and
void,—a rudimentary opening at the throat, and large
bunches of grapes fashioned in seed pearls, and hung about
the shoulders, represented to her the limits of decorum. She
has the terrible effect of a suction pump;—approach her, and
every idea will leave you, you forget the English language,
and the power of laughter. The whole company felt it, and
struggled. Mrs Pinsent's crimson velvet, and my crimson
damask on either side of the table acted, however, as non-
conductors, and preserved the life of the remainder.

Catterson-Smith himself, who is so beautiful, one forgives
him much, even his wife, talked quietly of Old Time
Socialism, of methods of teaching drawing, (he is now Head
of the Birmingham School of Art), and of Fabianism. After
dinner Mrs Pinsent and I settled down in the back drawing-
room, and talked Workhouses, Special Schools, Lunacy,
Physical deterioration, etc.[9] She is an eminent novelist, and I
understand her "No Place for Repentance" made quite a stir

8. Sir Oliver Lodge (1851–1940) was a scientist, a student of psychic phe-
nomena, and the first principal of the University of Birmingham.

9. Robert Catterson-Smith (1853–1938) was an artist and designer associated
with William Morris in the work of the Kelmscott Press, and had been recently

some years ago. She has brought up three children in a thoroughly rationalistic and material manner—no place for Religion—and is now on the Royal Commission for enquiry into the provision for the feeble-minded and crippled. Her negation of the Spiritual is almost amusing in the light of such splendid work as she does, constantly, voluntarily, and amongst the most hopeless and despairing section of the community. (AJ, Nov. 1904)

The guild play that winter was *As You Like It,* tailor-made for Campden with its rural world. CRA, of course, played Jaques, but around Christmas he was suffering from lumbago and had to go to Droitwich for a spa cure. Charley Downer, who was a natural as Touchstone in the play, wrote CRA that the rehearsals were going well, but that they all hoped soon to have the "Actor-manager back, and enough brine in his body to turn our Bathing Lake into a Sea Bath." Work, he added gloomily, "is still very quiet here with us" (AJ, Dec. 1904).

Janet had found herself on the defensive about the guild as early as the spring of 1903, and had written to CRA then of her forebodings: "Have we been deluding ourselves all these years thinking that we were doing any sort of good work? . . . Will 2 or 3 years see us out? Is it all going to bust? . . . Here is Liberty putting £10,000 into the Cymric Silver Co. and we struggling to get our hundreds, and having to pot-boil with vile brooches etc. to make ends meet" (AJ, Mar. 1903).

The brooches were not all vile by any means, but the problem of keeping workers on through slack periods, and letting them make things for "stock," was a very real one. The move, idyllic though it had been in many ways, had created its own difficulties. In London, if there was a fall in orders, workers could get casual jobs in their trades with other firms, and come back again when things picked up. In Campden, it was

---

appointed headmaster of Birmingham Municipal School of Art. Ellen Pinsent (1866–1949) was a novelist, a rationalist, and Birmingham's first female city councillor.

impossible. Also, the guild had a showroom in the West End of London, a necessity now that they were in the country, but also a drain on their resources. Every time there was a success, anxieties receded. But by the summer of 1905, the third anniversary of the Great Move, the signs were becoming difficult to deny.

And for Janet, there was the growing ache of her childlessness.

CHAPTER 10

THE BULGING RED BOOK

1901–1908

FROM the moment of her marriage, Janet's lively contributions had gone into CRA's journal, though she did not totally abandon her own, which she had begun on her return from Paris in 1895. What she called her "little bulging red book" was the last of these nine volumes, and it had been started the week before CRA proposed to her. It was not filled until 1907, and the entries were very intermittent. In fact, they are less a record of events than outcries. She wrote nothing in it for three and one-half years, from the autumn of 1897, after their engagement, until June 1901, six months after they came back from America.

In this first entry after her marriage, she wrote,

[H]ow queer it is to see all the doubt and hesitation and childishness of that momentous summer 97!! . . . and somehow I feel I must just write up the Romance as far as it goes. And it has become so much more romantic as time went on—that year of engagement seems chill and bare compared to the growing richness of these latter years. And oh! how right he was! Every day I bless his wise control of words and feelings during that barren year. His rare visits, and the coldness that saddened me then, and gave birth to those awful doubts were all the prudent suppression of an emotion that we had not yet grown into. . . . When I try to bring back how I felt even during our honeymoon—the experiment it all was, the tentative way I approached him, my fear of appearing foolish in his eyes, with our frank comradeship of these days, I can sing for joy that such a husband has been given to me. . . . *Doubt?* Why, I should as soon doubt my own existence as the fact of our love now. (JJ, 11 June 1901)

The next entry comes after another two years, in September

1903, six months after she and Gerald had become "facts" in each other's lives, and the guild had already been eighteen months in Campden.

5 years since that lovely hot brilliant momentous wedding day when we both rushed into the unknown; much is now known, and each scrap and wisp of knowledge leads to better happiness and wider love.

One of the known things that has come by little and little, seems to be that we are to stay just us two. I have fought against this, and at first it made me very miserable, and now every while and again, I just take and nurse the Pity of it. . . .

Charley is one of the people who have "a genius" which is as much as saying that they are not dominated by sex—and what sex desires he has are all homogenic.[1] Dimly I have always known this, appreciated it, and naturally, (who would not?) left plenty rope—always reserving the hope and conviction that STILL somehow the sublime other thing would happen, and I should not be ashamed among women. I am certain now that it will not happen. With all his affection for me, and the lively and delicious understanding between us, he has I know not the slightest physical desire for me ever. It is like asking a horse to be a stag—it is an impossibility to expect it . . . though there are times when I clench my teeth to padlock Nature, it is seldom, and becomes more seldom with disuse. . . . I see many complete and beautiful married lives round me with no children, men and women who have work to do in the world not as fine and obvious and direct perhaps as child-bearing, but still decent work that takes the energy of both to the hilt.

Some price has to be paid for marrying an abnormal man. And it is worth oh how much! to have the quick comprehension, the tender gentleness. . . . In face of his powerlessness to feel with the body, I will curb the hot love that struggles to get past my padlocks. . . . In perhaps two years the padlocks will be welded together, and the keys thrown into the sea. . . .

---

1. *Homogenic* was CRA's preferred term for *homosexual,* learned from Edward Carpenter.

106

The sacrifice of the animal to the spiritual, in me, *by myself*
alone, in silence, must be better and saner than the open
sacrifice, for nothing, of the whole being, grovellingly begging
for an impossible boon to be thrown to the animal part. And
when the keys are *lost,* perhaps it will no longer be felt as any
sacrifice; but may be forgotten, atrophied, and merged into
the larger work of bearing other, less selfish, if less glorious
burdens.

But while I still have the keys? (JJ, 5 Sept. 1903)

This entry was written at about the same time as one of
Gwendolen's reappearances, and if Janet had defined Gwen's
state as "a kind of sexual anaesthesia," she herself was only just
beginning to emerge from something very similar. Gerald's
need of help and understanding would not, on its own, have
begun this awakening. She was, after all, frequently called on
by lame ducks of all sorts, often older than herself, who came
to her for what they felt to be her strength. It was, above all, the
warmth that she felt in Gerald's presence that began the awakening process. This warmth, and a very caring way of taking
charge of her, of relieving her of responsibility, contrasted with
the complete, sometimes almost chilling, independence that
she had experienced from the beginning with CRA.

In some of her "red book" entries of this time, there is an as-
sumption of a certain ferocity in making love:

Well, there's a good bit of physical basis before you get to
the sexual act, and a hungry person will live a long time on a
little. I feel often and often, why not shut the door on it once
and for all? . . . Why not live with just the happy morning
and evening kiss, the touch of the hand, and the look that can
mean everything? . . . Oh how many years would I not give to
know it in even its brutal completeness.
(JJ, Mar. 1904)

Between the moonlit silences of sleep
I felt a hand that touched me in the night,
Cool on my naked shoulder, and delight

Pulled at my veins, and sent the surging deep
From head to foot. And as I knew my Dear,
And trembled at the contact of his hand,
I felt that he could never understand
The normal woman made of love and fear.
So once again, loving and fearing much,
I prayed for pain, for mastery, for fire,
For passionate conquest, even for brute desire,
Anything but this temperate, gentle touch.
And as I glowed and prayed, the hand grew light,
I kissed it—and it slipped into the night.

(GMB)

The red book also describes Janet's difficult feelings about her mother-in-law.

> The jealousy I am wracked with stands on a singular plane. Between Charley and his mother there lie only 21 short years, hardly longer than the space between his age and mine. A bond of unusual strength ties them together. . . .
> [M]arriage connotes however a devotion more complete, even to the merging of body in body. This is what the average man and woman demands, and naturally demands, of marriage. To a nature like his the cry for this complete union is a foreign cry; and the relationship with his mother is to him a perfect relationship. . . . *He is safe,* safe from the eternal cravings of sex, which, as they do not touch him, he can have no conception of nor pity for. The dread for him lies in the possibility of "a scene"—the picture of the unsatisfied woman.
> (JJ, Jan. 1905)

She despised herself for this jealousy, and avoided situations where they might be *à trois*, where "the dearest of comrades" turned into "a dour, morose, resentful man, ready to contradict and on the perpetual defensive" (ibid.).

In the summer of 1905, CRA and Rob Martin Holland were in conference about the business prospects of the guild, and CRA was left very depressed, writing to Janet, "The world is not going as well as it might. Not at all. . . . Rob was here on Saturday and Sunday, and he was very down about things. Finance, mainly—we are not marking time, we are losing money. . . . If people won't buy things, the logical outcome is that one must cease making them" (AJ, June 1905). But then he got a commission to design a house in Hungary—his work was well known on the Continent, where he had exhibited often. Furniture for it, of course, would all be made by the guild. He left for Budapest in late June, returning in early July.

While he was away, Janet wrote a song on the theme that had been exercising her much over the past eighteen months. It was to Gerald.

Friendship and love have no barrier between
And when I look in your eyes gray-green
All the Love and Friendship since Adam was made
Come knocking at my temples and make me afraid.

Your tender voice and your serious smile
Call me to think of you all the long while.
And when I see you and suffer your touch
I know I am a woman and I love overmuch.

Now that we're young we think we don't care
When old age lays his white hands on our hair;
While I feel the blood in your fingers running red,
Time is timeless and Death is dead.

We are alive and we'll love as we may
For we are growing older every day;
But I know when I look in your eyes gray-green
That friendship and love have no barrier between.
                    (JJ, midsummer night, 1905)

And then, almost as though she felt unable to handle the way things might be developing—or as a kind of warning signal—she sent the poem to CRA in Budapest, writing,

I have made a find in a ballad book, an old Welsh song which seems to me to have some points. . . . [T]he book merely puts "Old Welsh Air, words traditional." . . . What date do you put it at? The words and tune go so well together they seem to be contemporary, early 18th century? . . . Come back soon and hear it sung! For the rest, between workmen, swimming, neighbours, the garden, Shelley's Plato, tea-parties, births and weddings, I am kept busy, but rather want someone to tell it all to. . . . I hope you are taking huge orders as my wages from you are two months overdue. (AJ, June 1905)

She used the same ruse about finding the song with Masefield, but he was not deceived. "It is a most lovely thing, I think it the only really living love poem of the last three centuries. I showed it to W. B. Yeats who thought it most charming; and to Frank Sidgwick, who was stricken breathless by it. And now will you please be very kind and tell me where you found it, and whether you wrote it yourself" (AJ, ca. June 1905). And Gerald, to whom she also sent it, wrote, "Do you know, as I read I said, 'No, she has not found this, she has written it herself,' and even after I had read your criticisms and comments, the thought lingered" (JJ, midsummer 1905). From then on, Janet often sang it at informal evenings and gatherings, yet somehow the song kept its secret.

In August, Janet and Gerald went cycling in Norfolk.

Each church along their road was to them a sanctuary. As the heavy door of each was pushed open, and they two alone, warm and sentient human beings, stood in the chill dusk, her hand slipped into his, as a child's hand slips at twilight into the elder brother's. . . . "Churches are for week-days," Janet said. "On Sundays they go dead."

They sat on a wall bounding a forlorn little graveyard from a green lane. It grew dark, faint gleams were still in the sky, the silence was complete. Gerald laid a reverent hand on her wrist.

"Dear little sister," he said, "what have we done to deserve this happiness?" . . . The hunger for the touch of affection

which had been crying out these long years, was being stilled.
. . . She stooped and kissed the hand that held hers. . . . She
heard him pray for her joy. (RA, 73–74)

It was only in 1908, when she wrote "Rachel," that Janet admitted to her arrogance in believing that she had some special
strength with which to handle "this strange unorthodox devotion, this friendship that was love," while denying it completion
(RA, 76). Her conviction had persuaded Gerald and herself
that such a relationship, which stopped even before a real embrace, let alone intercourse, need not destroy them both.

Supposing that, one quiet windless night
I left my bed and climbed the little stair,
And you should dimly feel me standing there
Among the darkness, warm and live and white.

And if I came and woke you with a touch
And roused the passion choking in its bands,
And you rose up and held me with your hands
By my two shoulders, trembling very much;

And if about your pulsing throat I wound
My fingers with instinctive warning tense—
THEY would not serve to bar the gates of Sense,
But our own souls, standing on holy ground.

For I know we could keep the balance true
If in your arms I lay, the whole night through.
                                        (GMB)

In today's world, the kind of self-control she and Gerald
were practicing is thought pointless, if not positively harmful.
If you are being "spiritually unfaithful," does the additional un-
faithfulness of the sex act really make so much difference? But
Janet was a child of her time and background, and in her
scheme of things it made an enormous difference. And Gerald
loved her enough to respect this reluctance, though perhaps he

III

realized better than she did what it was going to cost them both.

At the end of 1905, she made what was almost the last entry in her private journal. It was a plea to CRA that they abandon any further pretence at sexual intimacy. Against it is written in pencil, in a later hand: "Luckily, this was never sent or said." At almost the same time, she wrote another poem intended for CRA, called "Rosewood":

When I am dead, then take this little key
Open the rosewood door, pull out the trays,
And there a chronicle of rainbow days
In sheaves of ranged letters you shall see.

Dated through many years of happy strife,
What will they mean to you, these writings dim?
Nothing, and less than nothing; though to him
Who passionately wrote them, more than life.

Within his heart, hidden and guarded well,
There burned the flame you need to make you whole;
The love that blazed beneath that self-control
How strong and clean it was, these letters tell.

Build up the fire, now that you have read.
His love may light the world when I am dead.

(ibid.)

Gwendolen, meanwhile, came and went. Early in 1906, she wrote Janet that, however little chance they now had to exchange ideas, she wanted Janet to see and criticize two poems she had written "out of the heart of me." One sought Buddha somehow to "silence the anguish of my cries," and the other was called simply, "Blinded with Tears":

Love in the valley
With bowed head
Sings a dirge
Above her dead.

Ah blind of heart!
Can'st thou not see
How from the hill
He looks on THEE?
    (AJ, Feb. 1906)

Unless Gwendolen, now calling herself Daphne, was so self-absorbed as not to notice or care what was happening between Gerald and Janet, these verses could almost be telling Janet not to hold back any longer. There was perhaps not much left, by now, of her relationship with Gerald, for in the summer Janet alluded to his having been, for the past two years, "stamping out the smouldering fires" (GMB, "The Crystal Bowl").

Gerald was now not only a trusted friend, but also one of the guild's financial advisers, and during 1906 and 1907, he and Janet were increasingly together. When she was with him, she "suddenly felt safe" (RA, 78). He was the only one of her circle to see that she "was not the self-reliant woman, the tower of strength, that even her most devoted friends thought her. . . . [H]is name for her: "Little One," which nobody had ever thought of giving her, moved her almost to tears" (RA, 79–80). CRA interpreted their contact as a happy comradeship; he could not recognize the risks or the signs of strain of unfulfilled yearnings that he did not himself feel.

In the summer of 1906, the Essex House Press, a fairly self-contained department of the guild, was closed down. The associations with Morris made the closing especially bitter. And the future of the whole guild as a limited company, which it had been since 1898, was coming into question. By midsummer of 1907, CRA was in such a state of depression that Janet persuaded him to go for a holiday to Scotland with Alec Miller. Since Sid Cotton's and Jacko's departures, Alec had become the most loved young man of the guild, and, as one of its mainstays, he was completely in CRA's confidence. There was absolute equality between them, apart from age, though CRA was still always "the Master" to Alec. Alec regarded Janet, who was only a couple of years older than him, with a deep, almost brotherly affection. Janet could think of no better way of being useful than by entrusting CRA to Alec, hoping that the young Scotsman would be able to help him accept the inevitable.

At the end of 1907, the Guild of Handicraft Ltd. went into voluntary liquidation, though many of the workshops continued on an independent basis. One of the many friends who wrote to commiserate was Arthur Wauchope. Janet had written to him, probably with some bitterness, reminding him at the same time that she was just about to be thirty. "It's nonsense my dear to talk of failure; think how many have come under the influence of the 'Campden touch'" (AJ, Dec. 1907). But the sense of failure grew; it was not only the loss of the guild, or of "the Guild Idea" with which she had been so long involved, that left a sense of emptiness. There was for Janet personally the growing fear that she was losing her ability to maintain the complicated three-way relationship among herself, CRA, and Gerald.

By the spring of 1908, the strain was becoming too great. How long could she go on giving CRA the comradeship and the affection that he needed, while responding with the other part of herself to Gerald? In March, she fell ill with diphtheria, though it could also have been the first onset of her approaching breakdown. Her father took her away to convalesce in a quiet little hotel in Sussex, and she wrote to CRA, "There ought to be a great deal of God here, according to Yeats, for there is certainly 'Nothing'" (AJ, Mar. 1908).[2] She added that Gerald had turned up.

> We all whizzed to see Rye and Winchelsea—most wonderful little fairy-tale cities on hills with obsolete rivers and shipping, and strange men in chocolate serge, baggy trousers, and oh! the churches! Gerald had no luggage, but knowing Father

---

2. Janet was referring to the essay "Where There Is Nothing There Is God" in Yeats's *Secret Rose* (1897).

was to be golfing all next day, Sunday, I made him buy a
toothbrush and two handkerchiefs at the Post Office here,
and put up at the hotel. Father was delighted to meet him,
and we had two lovely walks on Sunday, and lots of French
poetry seated by a haystack. (ibid.)

All in a whistling rain
And wreathed about with mists,
Seafog in grey-white twists
Drifting about the plain

A little haystack brown
And lonely we espied;
To shelter in its side
My dear and I lay down

Upon that faery throne
A King and Queen were we,
And all that wide country
Belonged to us alone.

A book was on my knee
The leaves turned in the wind
At will; with heedless mind
We let them flutter free.

We were alive and young,
Glowing from feet to head;
The lovers were long dead
That those far poets sung.

We did not greatly care
What those dim singers meant;
So pale and lacking scent
Their ghostly roses were.

Your shoulder was my bed
I could not see your eyes—
But through your low replies
I felt your breath instead.

Outside our fragrant nest
No whisper could I hear,
You, only, I knew near,
Your two hands round my breast.
(GMB, "For G. M. Bishop")

But the concealment weighed on her increasingly, as did the fear that she might make some slip; deception was almost impossible to one of her spontaneity. She had kept all of Gerald's letters and poems to her from the first "real" letter, five years earlier. But now she panicked, and added a verse to "Rosewood" for CRA:

I made to LOVE a sacrifice of words
Five years of letters on a burning pyre;
And as their ashes trembled in the fire
Their souls flew back to me like little birds
I felt each exquisite and plumy wing
Brush past my cheek, and circle round my brow;
They nestled in my neck, and even now
As in a dream I hear them coo and sing.
Brilliant and dazzling, opalescent, red,
Sea-blue, and snowy-feathered, soft and warm
My eyes are blinded by the loving swarm,
Or was it tears for all the innocent dead?
And now, dear lad, there is no fastened gate—
The rosewood chest is bare and desolate.
(GMB)

This act gave her a certain relief, at least from the thought of discovery, and of a total misunderstanding of her and Gerald's relationship.

In May, and perhaps part of June, CRA was away in Sicily with Alec Miller. He and Janet had been there, at Taormina, the year before, when he had made the first plans for a house there for Colonel Shaw-Hellier, and Janet had no illusions about the old colonel's ménage, humming with beautiful

26. Plockton. As the waters of Loch Carron rise, this part of the village becomes an island.

Sicilian boys; now CRA was going to inspect the building work. He was back in early July, and Janet, still in need of recuperation, got ready to go to Scotland on her own. She had arranged to borrow a cottage at Plockton in the western Highlands, looking out over Loch Carron, and was there from at least the middle of July and for much of August. At some point, Gerald joined her.

In "Rachel," Janet wrote that an older friend had told her earlier that she was on the edge of a precipice. "Yes, the precipice is there," Janet had replied.

> "I know one carries one's life in one's hand, but you don't know how strong we are, and oh! it is so gloriously worth while!"

It was worthwhile. To feel the blood pulsing under Gerald's wrist, to see those grey-green eyes that the world thought so "quiet" ablaze, to hear his steady voice shaking, and yet to know him under perfect control . . . and to know herself, what it was to tremble with love—this was being alive. . . . [S]he was living up to the hilt, as she felt this strange completion of her life, lit by two stars. . . . She loved CRA, she loved her many friends, but this was different. For the first time she now loved passionately, and this love had shown her how she COULD feel, what she lacked, and now, what she doubly longed for. . . . Surely, surely it was good. (RA, 94–95)

The cottage was a haven, a charmed circle. "It really is Arcady," she wrote to CRA. "Yesterday we rowed a mile out to a little isle full of heron's nests, heather, deep moss, and fir trees—and anchored in a little emerald bay invisible for all the world. . . . Here we bathed, naked and unashamed, plunging in again and again, the white shining bodies standing out against the pine trees, and we ran ashore to dry" (AJ, July 1908).

But what seemed like a haven of total peace, timeless, to be savored absolutely, without thought of what must come, was only the putting off of the day of reckoning. Here were two warm, loving human beings, continuing, from the highest motives, to deny to themselves and each other the very thing that both lacked in their marriages. For both, the strain was becoming too great. It became clear to CRA that the level tone of her letters had been deceptive. They had lulled him into believing what he had wanted to believe, that on her return everything would revert to normal. But the storm center toward which Janet had been drifting now enveloped her, and she was in a state of breakdown.

CHAPTER II
AMPUTATION
1908–1910

THE final parting from Gerald was in the heat of the August crowds at Birmingham station. "She heard the click of the hansom doors, and felt Gerald's kiss on her fingers before she wheeled off. She saw him standing bare-headed, his lips tightened, amid the racket of the terminus. It was their last meeting" (RA, 96). They would not see each other again for a long, long time. Janet arrived in Campden in a state in which she was unable to make the simplest decision, and humbly submitted herself to the idea of going to her parents' home. Godden Green received her, but not even Nurse Parsons, who had looked after her as a child, "rising out of the floor like Erda" whenever she was needed, or her father's deep love, could help with the nights and days of insomnia and nausea (ibid.). Eventually, Janet had to be admitted to a London nursing home, under the care of the eminent neurologist Henry Head. Today her treatment might have been tranquilizers, or long months on the psychiatrist's couch. Henry Head's treatment was of another kind.

He found her, as a patient, refreshingly direct and truthful, even in her state of clinical depression and despair, and he used a mixture of reason and ultimatum. He quickly realized that her leaving CRA would be so total a betrayal that she would not be able to live with it, and that it would destroy—sooner rather than later—her and Gerald's love. So he pushed her toward the other course, an instant and total ending of the relationship with Gerald. Janet put herself unreservedly into Dr. Head's hands, and her immediate and complete trust in him, plus a steadfast determination to follow whatever course had been decided on, brought her back from the brink.

Almost unbelievably, she was only a fortnight in the nursing home. Then Nurse Parsons collected her and took her straight down to Southampton to board the liner on which she and CRA were due to set off on another American lecture tour. Her pen had not lost its sharpness, and she dismissed the other passengers as "a dull tribe of wiry, white-haired American ladies bent on 'a good time,' a few good-looking, vulgar young women, and two queer effeminate boys; but on the whole nobody that one 'wanted'" (AJ, Oct. 1908). She had probably started writing "Rachel" while still in the nursing home, and now she finished it on the boat. Writing it was part of her therapy. While CRA worked on his lectures, Janet sat on deck wrapped in a rug against the chill, or in a secluded corner of the saloon, filling sheet after sheet. Ultimately, it ran to more than one hundred typewritten foolscap pages, and she showed CRA the first draft before the end of the voyage. He read it at once, and the perceptiveness of much of her self-analysis, and her analysis of him, must have been a kind of shock treatment for him too.

She thought of Gerald "sitting, really alone now, in the little room in Soho," and she thought of all that she had lost in her philosophy of life, all her "theories of men's and women's intercourse, built up on insufficient premises, her creed, her religion; the basis of her philosophy, the starting point of her loves and friendships" (RA, 98–99). By Dr. Head's brutal injunction, no one from her old life was to write to her at all for six months, though a number of friends, even Gerald, asked CRA to transmit their love and thoughts. It was only her phenomenally sturdy constitution, and the meetings with old and new friends during this American journey, that slowly began to have an effect. She noticed too that CRA was beginning to look after her in a way he never had before. As a rule, he "was not good at 'looking after' people. He had not the subjective imaginativeness that quickly sees and feels the wants of others" (RA, 97).

They arrived in New York in the last week of October, and went to stay with Frank Taylor and his wife. Janet was charmed by them. "He is an extraordinary man, combining the most intense form of American acumen and 'money-sense,' judgement and energy, with a warm and simple loveableness, a schoolboy geniality and sense of humour. . . . His wife has that delicious Quaker sense of leisure and quiet . . . and a young zest in everything, politics, education, literature" (AJ, Oct. 1908).

She did not always follow CRA's tour, for there were any number of friends delighted to harbor her, and prevent her from doing too much. She had "three quiet days among the yellowing leaves" of New Jersey with Mabel Terwilliger,

> the same merry, childlike, affectionate creature she was fourteen years ago in Paris at the Padillas, and eight years ago when I visited her in Syracuse, and we went to Niagara and East Aurora together. We were at once immersed in reminiscences . . . our own adventures, past and future, and our husbands' careers, all rippled by as we sat sewing in that dingy, ugly old house, which none the less felt homey and happy by virtue of its very un-selfconsciousness. (AJ, 7 Nov. 1908)

A few days before Christmas, CRA and Janet renewed their acquaintance with Frank Lloyd Wright at Oak Park. Janet settled down in the playroom of the Wrights' house on the evening of 21 December and wrote:

> These have been quiet happy days in the circle of this beautiful family. Lloyd Wright is a strange, delightful soul—a radical original thinker working out his ideas consistently, as an artist, in his architecture—not bothering about the sociology of it, ("this destroys the art")—but putting up building after building in queer, square blocks. . . . Much of his building is to me, too bizarre and away from all tradition to be beautiful; and the decoration of squares and geometric lines I find fussy and restless. But he has big ideas, and is gloriously ruthless in sticking to what he believes. He has the head of a musician— a sad, thought-worn face, that smiles whimsically between almost fanatical earnestnesses. He is only 41 now, and his

121

beautiful wife 37, and they hardly seem like the parents of
their 6 splendid children, who range in age from 18 to 5.
There is something wonderfully tender and loveable about
Mrs Wright. With so many other of the best and finest
American women she has an abiding youngness—a supple-
ness of gait, gesture and smile—combined with that maternal
gathering-in elderliness which always brings tears to my eyes.
. . . Every tone of her voice rings with fearless honesty—
almost a defiant cry against sham—compromise and all dis-
loyalty—and cruelty. I feel in the background somewhere
difficult places gone through. . . . And I am certain, I hear too
beginnings of a different kind of sadness. . . . If her children
do not comfort her, she will be hard pressed. As yet, she is almost the girl still—slender and lovely—but strongly built—
and when she laughs, you forget the tragic lines about her
mouth.

But people do not kiss one in that way unless they are
lonely in the midst of plenty. (AJ, 21 Dec. 1908)

Janet was more perspicacious than she knew, and it must have
showed in her spontaneous thank-you letter, for Catherine answered that Janet may not have guessed how helpful her letter
had been, adding that one day, she might tell her more about
"that year" and why Janet's coming had meant so much to her.

They celebrated New Year in Helena, Montana, where
CRA was mobbed after a lecture by members of the Arts and
Crafts Society wanting advice on "achieving a standard of
beauty." "Holy shade of Plato," he wrote, "I don't quite know
what happened after that, but Janet tells me I hid under a palm
tree that was growing in a pot, and planted my back firmly
against a wall. My own recollection is only of intense heat, and
the thermometer about 90" (AJ, 31 Dec. 1908).

Then they went on to California and stayed with H. W.
Rolfe, now teaching at Stanford University, and his family.
"We took a delightful day off from the perfervid artificialities
of Los Angeles, and went out incognito with a packet of fruit
and bread, unbeknown to anyone, and before we could be in-

27. The Rolfe family, ca. 1909. Courtesy of King's College Library, Cambridge.

vited anywhere by telephone, and slipped off to the beach of Santa Monica, where we spent the day basking in the sun. We watched the waves, and a couple of Mexican boys catching clams in the surf" (AJ, Jan. 1909). Janet, of course, fell for the Rolfe children. "I have never had such an audience to English Folksongs as those two little girls. They sat entranced, their blue eyes getting bigger and bigger, taking me back after 'Love is Hot' and 'Friendship and Love' by demanding relentlessly 'What is it all about?' But best they liked the ship with the beryl stones, and 'My One my men, my Two my Men'" (AJ, 20 Jan. 1909).

Toward the end of February, they crossed back to the East via Colorado Springs. CRA summed up the tour for Alec Miller:

> 40 lectures at £10 each! which in this country with all the heavy railway journies—sometimes 4 nights a week in a train, is real hard work. But they have been a huge success. . . . At Leyland Stanford University, California, they gave me an audience of nearly 2000, the finest audience I've ever had; at Helena Montana, a little city, but a miners' camp 20 years ago, where the log cabins still line the streets, they turned out with the snow 12 inches deep, and gave me an audience of 500! (AJ, 28 Feb. 1909)

After a last stay in Concord, Massachusetts, Janet and CRA sailed for Sicily, where CRA threw himself into supervising the finishing touches on the colonel's villa at Taormina. By April, they were home in Campden again after an absence of six months.

Had the amputation worked? Had Janet really found new strength—not merely the pious hope of it—to start again in the same setting as before her breakdown, with nothing new to mitigate Gerald's absence? And how much had Campden

28. Janet Ashbee at the window of her bedroom, Woolstaplers' Hall, 1910

known? Apparently enough to fuel censorious gossip, such as the cruel suggestion that she had gone to America to "get rid of" Gerald's child.

There are few entries in the journal at this time; she obviously had little heart. Her own intimate book was filled by that year too, and she never kept another. But she expressed some of what she was feeling on their return in a few poignant pages added to the end of "Rachel," describing

the good-night minute, that golden time that Janet had learned to look forward to throughout the day. CRA, who had a queer atavistic notion that wives should go to bed before their husbands, came in to turn out her light, and unexpectedly sat down at her feet. He looked at her with his large brown eyes, shy of her still after ten years of marriage, and smiled his smile of the dreamer. . . .

He looked at her lovingly but it was a look so spiritual, so remote, that Janet sat up in bed and stretched longing arms out to him. She caught him by the two shoulders before his hands could protest, and bowing her head:

"Oh Charley, I do want it so dreadfully."

"I know, I know you do—."

His voice, the voice that had captured her sensitive and musical ear so many years ago, was tender and pitiful. But she felt even in its warm vibrations, that it was tender for her, pitiful for her; for itself it neither wanted nor was sorry.

"Perhaps it may happen still one day," he comforted her.

"No, it never will—and I am getting so old; and Oh Charley . . ."

"Yes?" His eyes were turned away in premonition. . . .

"Charley, I do . . . miss Gerald so. . . . It has been . . . horrible all these months. . . ." He looked down at her brown head, plaited up for the night; at her firm neck and ivory shoulders. He held her warm body in his arms, but she did not feel a fibre of him move to her. He was distressed, but he was afraid. (RA, 102)

Janet ended "Rachel" with this final paragraph, though she added a brief epilogue two years later:

What he did not know was, that through those five years he
had learned to love his wife. . . . What had been sympathy
and comradeship was now a stronger, more burning thing . . .
having won her without a struggle, almost without a word, he
now found himself beginning to court her in real earnest. He
did it very badly, he was still afraid. He dreaded her strong,
clinging arms and evaded her grey eyes when he saw them
clouded. But something had changed in his attitude towards
her; the ice had broken, and it was SPRING. (RA, 103)

Perhaps it was wishful thinking. But it began to work. At
Christmas 1909, she wrote a last poem called "Thanksgiving":

In the black night when twelve tolls,
It is quiet and primitive and warm;
God have mercy on all poor souls
Who have never lain in a lover's arm.

They do not know how the breath feels
Lifting the breast on which they lean;
They cannot learn how the mind reels
When the fingers touch unseen.

. . . .

In the grey dusk when three tolls
It is quiet and perfect and calm;
God have mercy on all poor souls
Who have never lain in a lover's arm.

As she wrote these lines, and perhaps not only then, the images
of her "two stars" may have blurred and merged in her subcon-
scious. Within a year after their return to Campden, she was
pregnant.

And then, when it was still little more than a wild and unreasoning hope, she miscarried.

Anyone with less courage and tenacity than Janet would
probably have had another breakdown. Instead, she got out the
first rough draft of "Rachel," cleaned it up, and typed it. In

126

April 1910, she sent it to John Masefield for comment. Because he cared both for her and for CRA, and because of the sensitivity of his previous criticism of her poems, and not least because of what she knew he guessed, she felt she could trust him to keep her confidence, and also give her an honest reaction. He replied at once:

> Thank you for your letter and the manuscript. I sat up late over it, then went to bed, lay awake nearly all night thinking of it, moved by it, then up at half past four, so distressed I wanted the agony at an end. . . . It is the only genuine thing I've read for years. . . . A splendid white thing. The beautiful parts of it took me by storm. . . . It is perfect as a piece of life and truth. As a novel: the gaps and jumps are too big. A good deal more is wanted. You leave out too much. . . . I feel the want of an explanation in a dozen places. . . . It would be a staggering book if you could finish it, write it all, fill in all the great glowing bones, which stick out so unfinishedly from the perfect head and heart. . . . It gave me a wicked night. I shan't sleep tonight either! . . . Hard on CRA? . . . One neither praises nor blames when one understands. So . . . God bless you both, and give us all understanding. (JJ, Apr. 1910)

Inspired by his enthusiasm, she answered immediately, and he wrote again: "I am thankful you are going to fill in your story. . . . Get the greatest amount of poignant life into all your characters. . . . You really are an extraordinary person. Go on, Go ON!" (ibid.). But it was not to be. Two months later, she was pregnant again. From then on, the prospect of real flesh-and-blood children filled her horizon.

CHAPTER 12
HOPE FULFILLED
1911–1914

O Mary Elizabeth A,
How early you came in the day!
With never a rag
To your back or a bag,
But we hope you're intending to stay.

And are you as dark as your Ma
Or a delicate blond like Papa?
Or will you instead
Be a Socialist Red,
Or remain a bald-headed Baba?

And will you continue to grow
Completely from topknot to toe
And placing reliance
On Art and not Science
Conceal all the things that you know?

For this is the secret my dear—
But I haven't got time for it here:
I'm off to a meeting
(Just time for a greeting)
Clock strikes, and I have to appear.
　　　　　　　(AJ, 26 Mar. 1911)

THUS Laurence Housman wrote on the arrival, in March 1911, of CRA and Janet's long-awaited first, at Woolstaplers' Hall. He knew well how much she had yearned for this fulfillment. The last two lines of the epilogue to "Rachel" were "Joy had come in the morning; she had only

128

29. The terrace of the Norman Chapel, Broad Campden, Gloucestershire, ca. 1908. Courtesy of the Guild of Handicraft Trust, Chipping Campden.

to be still in her Island of the Blest, and hug and hug and hug her wonder" (RA, 105).

In the hamlet of Broad Campden, about a mile from Chipping Campden itself, there was a ruined Norman chapel with a medieval priest's house attached to it (plate 8). About six years before Mary's birth, CRA had repaired this romantic building and adapted it to a house, for two particularly sympathetic clients, Ethel and Ananda Coomaraswamy.[1] Ethel was the sister of Fred Partridge, the former guild silversmith, and Ananda, a geologist, was increasingly interested in the tradi-

---

1. Ananda Kentish Coomaraswamy (1877–1947) was a geologist, art historian, and museum curator. He was first a popularizer of, and then an extensive writer on, Indian art, culture, and religions. His first wife, Ethel (1872–1952), later married Philip Mairet, who worked as a draftsman for CRA, and she became one of the leaders of the revival of hand weaving in England.

tional arts of India and Ceylon. Janet wrote that they had made the Norman Chapel, as it was called, into an enchanted place that "glows rose-colour with linen and Morris hangings and oriental crimsons" (AJ, 25 Jan. 1908).

But in September 1910, when she was not long pregnant, she had a long, sad letter from Ethel in India, saying that she was coming back, but Ananda would stay on there, and that the Norman Chapel would have to be given up. She was thinking of building herself a small cottage in Devon. Janet began to think that the Norman Chapel might be a better place than Woolstaplers' Hall for the bringing up of a family—it was larger, and away from the gossip of Campden High Street. CRA resisted at first, and then came around to her view. As it turned out, the house was not for sale, but CRA and Janet were able to rent it starting in July 1911; it would be their home for the next eight years.

30. Mary Ashbee on her mother's knee, 1911

Janet let every conceivable person know about Mary, and the baby was photographed from the first moment. Her father wrote at once: "I cannot wish you both any better wish than that your little girl should be all to you that you have been to us. TWO such as ours must be rare indeed" (AJ, Mar. 1911). Arthur Wauchope wrote warmly from India, but then, on being sent photographs, noted: "Captain Wauchope requests Madame Ashbee to send no more photographs of fat babies, either as picture postcards or in any other form, as such procedure awakens needless suspicions in the mind of his Commanding Officer, and undue merriment on the faces of his subalterns" (AJ, Apr. 1911).

In October, she sent a picture of six-month-old Mary sitting on CRA's knee outside the Norman Chapel to Laurence Housman. The suffrage campaigner wrote to Mary: "Tell your respected Papa also, that you look like a flower in his buttonhole, and improve his appearance greatly; just the finishing touch that he has always wanted, and I'm glad it's a little girl who has come to complete him, not a little BOY. You will help him to put woman in her proper place; . . . Bless you! You are doing a work in the world! . . . Tell your Janet of a Mama that I'm too busy for a letter to her yet" (AJ, Oct. 1911). There is also a happy photograph of Grandpapa Forbes with Mary on his knee. He died soon afterward, in December 1911, and, in a letter to Janet, Housman wrote: "What a patrimony! Thirty-four years of parental love, for which, on arriving at full years of discretion, you can find no blame. Fathers for such an epitaph might wish to die" (AJ, Dec. 1911).

But if life for Janet was in an exciting new phase, for CRA it was a different matter. He was nearing fifty, and for one still so full of restless energy—today he would be called a workaholic—the problem of finding a direction in life after the liquidation of the guild was acute. One of his schemes was to buy land for the guild near Broad Campden and divide it into smallholdings, so that the guildsmen who had stayed in

Campden would have more financial security. In this plan his chief ally was Gerald Bishop, who remained committed to the future of the guild. Gerald had married again and was living in Hampstead Garden Suburb. Janet could think of him more easily now that her hopes were fulfilled, and he was always a good friend.

In July 1912, CRA went to stay with the Tollemache family at Helmingham Hall in Suffolk, apparently to help with their remarkable library. He wrote Janet long letters describing how charming the whole family was, and how, when not deciphering vellum manuscripts, he was driven, in a "leisurely, feudal manner," around the five Tollemache villages. His hostess, he said, would welcome both her and baby Mary if Janet would be "content to rest and dream, and not want to be moving on to the next point" (AJ, 16 July 1912). Janet, now two months pregnant again, and not feeling at her best, found this condition unfair:

> Your letters are always interesting, but they generally make me angry, mostly I think because they show you at your very worst. You seem to slip out of my grasp and become again the self-conscious précieux you were when I found you . . . Mary to be "allowed" at Helmingham if, forsooth, *I* should be content to rest and dream etc. etc.
>
> The amusing thing is that in Broad Campden, at your door, you have exactly the same local conditions in petto— pure rusticity, 50 wonderful characters, memories, dreams, traditions, for the asking. But do you ever trouble to go and sit for an hour and talk to these people? No—it takes an honourable Tollemache to "take you on his personal calls" to note how they receive him!!!—as if Suffolk peasants were any more wonderful than Gloucestershire. (AJ, 22 July 1912)

CRA must have been surprised at what he had unleashed. "There. I have nothing else to tell you—and no commas to turn into full stops on reading over. I enjoyed your descriptions—so did others whom I read them to. And I suppose they will all go into the journal. Anyway not into my reliquary, that has the one only letter of yours that I should not care to read aloud—because it has one really personal sentence" (ibid.). As her outburst shows, Janet seems not to have appreciated that CRA, although he showed himself to be a surprisingly interested and effective father, was feeling excluded by her world of babies. For all her usual perspicacity, it did not occur to her that he could be suffering from simple jealousy, as well as the lack of her "comradely" involvement, her touch upon the tiller, that he had come so to depend on over the years.

In December 1912, he went to a King's College celebration dinner in London, a nostalgic and, as he recognized himself, unsettling event.

> Whether it was the exhilaration of the King's dinner or not, and the meeting of so many old friends, and all the youth and sap it made come up in one, I don't know, but turning out of the Hotel Cecil in the Strand, I had an adventure. The red Gods go in the Strand, you can see them if you look, and in the glitter of the electric light on strange and beautiful faces that pass and repass in the night. It is odd too how they search you out through the thousands. . . . Anyway, I was called. My first impulse was that of respectable and incipient middle-age, which bade me take no risks, but hop onto the nearest bus and fly, and then I thought that would be cowardly, so I looked round again. You must never do that, you must remember Lot's wife! It settled it for me, because the young Guardsman who had fired the train in me looked too. . . . Unless you snap the thing there and then, and stamp on it, it is good for you to carry it through, that is unless you are an ascetic or a puritan. But the Greek can't and I couldn't. This youth was very lovely, he came up to me and looked me full in the face. "Which way are you going?" I asked.
>
> "Oh, any way, my barracks are at Chelsea."
>
> . . . I've never had the courage to invite a Guardsman home to sup with me, but the beauty of his bearing, the grace of his speech which was pure Yorkshire, the reserve and naiveté with which he, so to speak, surrendered himself to me, like some delightful animal obeying its instincts, made him irre-

sistible. As I also was obeying mine, we marched back to
Cheyne Walk together, out of the glitter of the Strand and
down the Mall. It was going on for eleven o'clock as we
passed by Buckingham Palace, and the moon shone delicately
on Brock's white marble work in the Queen's fountain. For
once it looked really fine; when the red Gods are out, everything changes colour and comes out of itself. . . .

"I suppose you have lots of odd adventures out, o'nights?" I
said. "Lots!" he replied, and there was much meaning in the
word. . . . That he should go roving o'nights and pick up with
people like me seemed as natural as any other function of the
body or desire of the heart. When we kissed at parting, for he
had quite rightly to be back at his barracks by one, he said: "I
suppose we shall meet again some day?" "Of course," I said,
"and next time you come I'll have a better supper for you!"

The red Gods had done their work for both of us that
night, for my part I felt stimulated, and sappy, tingling in
every vein of me—knowing as the poet says, my naked soul,
and that I had taken what had been waiting for me.

White or yellow, black or copper, he is waiting as a lover

Smoke of funnel, dust of hooves, or heat of train—
Where the high grass hides the horseman, or the glaring flats
        discover—
Where the steamer hails the landing, or the surf-boat brings
        the rover—
Where the rails run out in sand-drift . . . Quick! ah heave
        the camp-kit over!
For the Red Gods make their medicine again!

It would be better perhaps if they made it not in the
crowded city, but as we have no prairies, sand-drifts or camp
fires on call every day, let us be thankful for the Strand.
(AJ, Dec. 1912)

Chris Robson, who was twenty-three, was the one person of
whom Janet, in later years, never really wanted to speak, probably because his was the one love among CRA's many homosexual attachments that had a very strong physical basis.

That first meeting was in December. In February, I was born and christened Jane Felicity, as Janet had planned. CRA had always wanted a boy, to be called David. Janet said, "It would not be good for your morals to have a boy!" He answered, "Please, PLEASE make it a boy. What's my morals got to do with it anyway! I like the name Jane Felicity, very nice,—but mere boy, John, Tom, Jock, Dick, or Jack—anything you like as long as you get the sex right—would sound much better. You forget my dear, that I am already the only male in a household of five women! It grows oppressive."

In March, he went up to Millthorpe to see Edward Carpenter. "Edward is wonderful as ever," he wrote in the journal, "—aging a bit, his hand a little shaky . . . but a curious aura is growing up about him" (AJ, Mar. 1913). His only regret was that Chris had not been able to join him there.

And then, in May, he threw any last convention to the winds, and went off with Chris for a Whitsun walking tour in Normandy. He wrote to Janet immediately from Dieppe, giving a detailed sketch of his traveling companion,

> so that when I introduce him to you, you will be able to say whether my judgement is sound, and you've been able to recognise him. . . . I feel extraordinarily soothed and made-over in his society, and after I have spent a night with him, refreshed, for he has given me some of his element. . . . For my part I need this other side of life still, I can't quite do without it—yet. Perhaps some day I may but it brings with it a gift of youth and it is regenerative.
>
> My dear, I do very much pity the heterosexual type of man wedded to a possessive wife. I suppose he isn't so sensitively organised as some of us, but it must be *very* difficult for him. . . . My love always, even though its wings, for the moment, are pointed from home. (AJ, May 1913)

Janet answered with her usual speed.

> Dear Lad.
>
> Yes,—of course I would rather know, than not know, and I would rather you told me what you feel you can. I should

hardly be human however, if I did not like to be "first"—and I confess I had a few tears this morning over the description of your lover. But I can never repay your understanding and generosity of 5 years ago, save "in kind," with counter-understanding when you want your romance. So bless you both. . . . The tulips in the square garden are like a dream of Arabia. The children send a kiss—they too are "young and regenerative!" (ibid.)

For CRA, this love went on until Chris's death on the western front in the summer of 1916.

Janet was pregnant again by the spring of 1914. She told Laurence Housman, who was deep in finishing a book, and he wrote: "Of all the ungrateful creatures, you are the snow-clad, ice-cold summit. Here have I been with child all the winter, and the moment proof of it arrives, I cut it in half and send you a portion to see how fine it is,—the other half being required by the printers for correction, and you give a sniff, and say, why have I ceased writing to you! I HAVE BEEN WRITING THIS BOOK TO YOU FOR MONTHS." But then he ended:

That thou may'st see the difference of our spirit,
I pardon thee thy babe before thou ask it.

And I hope it will be a fine one, and of the right sex, and will make a great public success of itself; and will say "uggum" to me on first meeting, which, being interpreted means: "Oh you beautiful poet, dramatist, novelist, take refuge in my ample bosom of affection from the stony-heartedness of my parent, my she-parent, for CRA is not as brutal as he looks.
(AJ, May 1914)

During that fateful summer of 1914, CRA had work in two international exhibitions, in Leipzig and in Paris. In June, while he was working on a planning competition in Dublin, Janet had another miscarriage. So when war actually broke out on 4 August, and all CRA's work more or less came to an end, both of them were in a state of depression. The immediate future looked dark and uncertain.

CHAPTER 13
FAMILY AND WAR
1914–1916

CRA described the mood of London that August: "There is a curious stillness and earnestness . . . an intense heat too, of weather too good even for the best of holidays—the sort of weather one looks back to as being part of river expeditions. All about the street are soldiers, patrols, armed wagons; and regiments in khaki march through the parks" (AJ, Aug. 1914). Laurence Housman, a confirmed pacifist, wrote more wryly, "London streets show human nature as ingratiatingly quaint as in a page of Dickens. They are full of self-conscious Territorials, all piping hot from school, doing their modest best not to look heroic, as they march along whistling through futurist moustaches, of girls they are leaving behind them" (ibid.).

CRA was to have spent the first Sunday in August on the river with Chris. "Now he is off with the expeditionary force— marching to Belgium—I presume whistling 'Tipperary.' We were to have had a bell tent and a boat, and to have exchanged yarns and lain among the flowers, and bathed and smoked, and we had planned a trip to Germany for the autumn" (AJ, mid-Aug. 1914). Janet, meanwhile, was recovering from her miscarriage.

In October, CRA described the Norman Chapel garden as a blaze of color: "Endless roses and butterflies and bees amongst the michaelmas daisies. The lavender stands in rich grey masses beside the dark hedges of yew, the Travellers' Joy is spreading its mantle of perfumed silver over plum and elder and thorn, while an orange and crimson shumax calls in the distance like a trumpet note. I have never seen a year so lovely, so tender and so full of colour. . . . Today I heard that one of our Guild boys was killed" (AJ, Oct. 1914).

The first Belgian refugees arrived in September, and CRA offered a house and some land on the guild's smallholding estate for a family of ten. The neighborhood turned out in force to help, and little Mary, riding on CRA's shoulders, added the finishing touches with a bunch of flowers and a basket of apples. Looking around him, CRA did not have many illusions about the patriotism of some of the people who had joined up from Campden. It was one of the ironies of the war that laborers' wives were better off on their allowances with husbands fighting than they were on the thirteen shillings a week earned working for British farmers at home.

It was a good question, though, what he should do. "I suppose," he wrote in November, "one had best give up and take to lecturing in America" (AJ, Nov. 1914). And he was, in fact, already working on a series of lectures for such a tour. But his active, almost youthful, and still romantic spirit fretted, longing to join in, and by December he was desperate "to find some Government billet during the war, all one's work being over for the time being" (AJ, Dec. 1914). But then, around Christmas, he was asked if he would maintain a liaison in the United States on behalf of the Bryce Group, an informal group of intellectuals and politicians initiated by Lowes Dickinson to work toward a possible international peacekeeping body after the war. It gave a sense of purpose to what CRA might have done anyway.

He set sail for New York at the end of March 1915, and then began a flow of letters between the Norman Chapel and America, sustained by faith—the Atlantic was already becoming dangerous—and patience at the slowness of their crossing. In the end, he spent much of the next two years in the United States, on three separate lecture tours. Janet wrote in April: "You will be amused to hear that the parting shot seems to have started a new baby; were it not that I am so keen on 'breeding'

I should be excessively provoked, just as I have dismissed a serving wench and settled down to a bachelor existence! . . . So now you can stay away as long as you like, so there!" (AJ, Apr. 1915).

A month later, she had had so little news that she wrote crossly: "[I'm] very disgusted to get a lot of rotten old newspaper cuttings from you. . . . [I]t is the last stage of ineptness. . . . [Y]our note doesn't tell me nowt, past present or future. I hope a railway journey will give you a chance. . . . I wonder if you are EARNING anything, or just rushing about?" (AJ, May 1915). Then a long letter arrived, and she was a mixture of jubilation and alarm at the recent sinking of the *Lusitania:* "It amuses me to hear of your operas, cars etc; but not one word yet as to whether you have given, or been paid for, ONE lecture, which I am naturally anxious to know! . . . I have awful visions of your livid head bobbing about among the wreckage and drowned babies; I conjure you—as Disraeli would say,—to come back on a true blue American line. Think of your unborn child if not of me" (ibid.). When he eventually wrote about the lectures, he explained that he was giving some ordinary professional ones and some on behalf of the Bryce Group; he enjoyed the second more, though the first paid better.

Letters were so slow that she often forgot what she had written, though she tried to remember the local gossip that would amuse him, and what books she was reading.

> I seem to have been alone so long that I can hardly visualise our cosy evenings with books and pipes; and I quite long for the mild irritation your unpunctuality induces in me, by way of a change. . . . What is the good of being married if you can't have a good grumble and be sure you are being understood? . . . Felicity is quite as old as Mary, and such a flow of language, and such MANNER. . . . Mary simply sits and stares at her in her Carinthia "haggard-beauty" naïve ingenuousness, and at the end of a great "speech" bursts out laughing, which of course F. loves. . . . I have the most awful nights, awake for hours, and frightfully restless. . . . I expect it will be twin girls, and their names are Helen-Caroline, and Susan-

31. Mary and Felicity
Ashbee, 1915

Margaret, and I have saved £45 in 5 months on my household
expenses, and think I deserve a pat on the back. (ibid.)

In one of the last letters to catch him before his return, she
quoted Mary as saying, "I suppose Daddy will have the same
sort of face he had when he went away?" (AJ, June 1915).

He was back by mid-July, and the whole family went down
to Saunton in Devon for a month by the sea. "We almost forget about the war," he wrote, "and think only of sand and stars,
countless and timeless things." But then came the news of the
death of one of CRA's best-loved guildsmen, Sid Cotton, by a
stray German shell. "Dear Sid," CRA wrote, "I recall him rowing naked on the Wye, with a wreath of yellow tanzies on his
head to keep off the sun. There was always laughter in his blue
eyes" (AJ, Sept. 1915). And he proposed this epitaph:

Here lies, near where the shell killed him, a young English soldier, Sidney Cotton, known and loved by all who knew him as the Mad Hatter. He was a cabinet maker by trade, of the Guild of Handicraft, and a light-hearted London Cockney. An Englishman of the new order that is to be after this infamous war is fought out; a democrat. He came back from Canada to answer the call of Democracy. He had nothing to loose, except what he willingly gave—his life; and nothing to give, except what was most worth giving—his love. "Where the City of the Faithfullest Friends stands, there stands the Great City." (ibid.)

In September, Chris Robson came back to London on leave, and they met again. CRA wrote to Laurence about the "singing of 1000 birds within" that Chris's visit had meant.

CRA left again for the United States at the end of September. Janet, who had stayed in Devon, left the children with their nannie and came back to the Norman Chapel by herself. The house was dead until the children reappeared: "[E]xcept when Mary was born, which can never be touched, I have never enjoyed more perfect happiness. They both look brown and rosy and sturdy and bursting with life and volubility, and hugs and questions. Too adorable. . . . It is quite extraordinary what, and how much THEY MEAN. The house and I feel absolutely changed in the twinkling of an eye" (AJ, Oct. 1915).

She was soon giving CRA the usual gossip. There had been battles with the local authority about the numbers in Alec Miller's adult-education classes; her own School for Mothers was flourishing—it was better, she was beginning to think, to be "a Tzar and do these things without Grants and Committees"; there had been great excitement about Lord Gainsborough closing a right of way, "because her Ladyship wants that bit . . . for her kitchen garden." "How are your lectures going?" she asked in mid-November. "I hope soon to see the colour of some money as I am getting very short" (AJ, Nov. 1915).

CRA got back to England just in time for the birth, on Christmas Eve, of the third disappointment, Helen Christabel. Laurence made matters worse by writing, "I hope David arrived ruddy and of good countenance. . . . Any news of Chris?" (AJ, Dec. 1915). Black in mood, CRA took stock "of this terrible year. . . . Work is no more. . . . As for the Guild, it is hanging by a thread. This week the blacksmiths shut up their shop and went their way one to London the other to Birmingham to make ammunition; a shop this in which there had not been a day's idleness in 21 years" (ibid.). Men from among the silversmiths, enamelers, and woodworkers had already gone one by one. "It is a strange ending to such a great endeavour. Is it an ending?" (ibid.). He still longed to believe that it was not.

He left in the middle of January for his third tour. Janet wrote to him about the new clergyman's "beautiful NON-clerical voice and speech, quite like ONE OF US! A charming smile, and a very nice, comfortable, un-martyred, rather city businessman's (fish-in-bag) kind of face. . . . You would laugh if you heard Felicity say 'conceived-by-the-holy-ghost-born-of-the-virgin-mary,' prestissimo! They are both learning the Creed, as I thought it best to get it in before the question stage" (AJ, Feb. 1916). This way continued to be Janet's somewhat down-to-earth recipe for the inculcation of faith.

"Felicity's midnight conversation," she wrote, "would charm the most savage breast . . . a sort of moonlight irrelevance and insouciance—a charming flippancy and good humour" (AJ, 19 Feb. 1916). She described my third birthday party and the saddening presence of her mother, whose powers were failing. "Mary remarked 'Poor Babushka, why DOES she worry so about the food? I dare say it's because of her husband having died, poor old lady!' . . . Mary is getting more like you than ever, especially in your most aggravating trait of putting off, conveniently forgetting, and gracefully sliding out of any boring duties!" CRA must have written hinting at yet another attempt at

"David" as soon as he should be back, to which Janet replied, "I don't want to think about anything but rearing this one, for this year. . . . So if you want your Second Establishment, now is the moment to start it!"

She seems to have been referring to CRA's account of his visit to Taliesin, Wisconsin, where Frank Lloyd Wright, long since separated from his wife, Catherine, was living with Mrs. Miriam Noel. CRA wrote:

> Well, they have a saying in the studios of the "Quarter Latin," "If you want to be an artist you must hang up your passions with your hat and coat before you enter the studio." Frank has done that. And so I should say, has the lady, a middle-aged woman, though I admit she dresses, shall we say, 10 years younger? . . . No, you wouldn't like her either, but then, what do we know, and why should we judge? . . . There's no fig leaf lingerie about the new morganatic relation. It is intellectual— of course with a physical basis. (AJ, Feb. 1916)

Janet's response was, in CRA's words, "unnervingly Saxon":

> I am amazed at what you tell me of Ll. Wright and his sec- ond whoring episode—I can't see why he can't make use of his wife's "physical basis" as you euphemistically call it! No, I should *not* have liked the arrangement, and I should not have gone there; not I think, out of disapproval, as it is not for me to throw stones at "irregularity" potential or actual—but be- cause I really do dislike the man, and his poses and all his talk and gas, and *parade* of it all. . . . The theatrical is always a bit disgusting—(you should hear Felicity say *Disgusting*). And you know whenever we want to be selfish or naughty (and all naughtiness is selfishness or fear) . . . according to your emer- ald theory, we should only have to say, "Well I suppose I am an emerald—*je suis comme ça*"—and plunge in ruthlessly. I suppose you will say Catherine wanted to "be the girdle round his waist" and *not* be hung up with his hat in the hall. You can't, however, have it both ways. When you and I were young, THE THING was for the wife to "enter into her hus- band's life"—(do you remember that preposterous letter you once wrote me in which you allowed me to "become one of

143

your circle of friends" Pooh). . . . The younger people now I
suppose hang their wife (if she is a "passion"?) up in the hall
and expect to find her ready for them at II P.M. But then they
must have another woman I suppose as an "Intellectual
companion."

Catherine evidently hashed it all up but I don't think as a
nature, apart from his *work,* that he is worth bothering about.
How silly of her not to divorce him. I can't stand such
pacifism—it's really a shade too Gospel on the Mounty.
Well—your letter doesn't really "require a reply," but it interested me profoundly.

I am afraid Mary will grow up wise. I would far rather
have her foolish, (virgin or not) like Felicity, FOR HER OWN
HAPPINESS SAKE. Felicity said yesterday that she had quite
made up her mind to "MAKE A MAGIC," but do you think she
would tell what? No, it is a "dainty secret" (delightful term). I
suggested she should make a magic and turn Helen into a
boy—She shook her sensible head. "Oh no no no NO!" she
said, "I couldn't do THAT. NO!" (AJ, Mar. 1916)

32. Janet Ashbee with Mary, Felicity, and Helen, ca. 1917

I was, apparently, the "most awful handful and the ringleader in all the enormities . . . a mixture of beefy vitality, lawlessness, vulgarity, fascination, coquetry, and the most appalling IMPU-DENCE in the fullest sense of the word. Coarse is a mild term to apply to the trend of her conversation" (ibid.).

The winter of 1915–1916 seemed interminable. "There has been the worst blizzard in these parts since 1878," Janet wrote at the end of March. "We were snowed in yesterday and today. Doors unopenable . . . a lot of yew trees not only bent flat but covered in lumps of snow, the TIPS FROZEN to the ground, so that I cannot release the poor things . . . drifts 12 to 14 feet deep on the road, and no vehicle could possibly pass for days" (AJ, ibid.).

As late as mid-April she was still writing, "I can hardly bear your descriptions of warmth and fruit; . . . we are perishing with cold; bitter black, blighting north winds . . . the children in thick extra jerseys UNDER their winter coats and beaver hats—Baby nearly blown out of her pram today" (AJ, Apr. 1916). But still she asked about his progress: "I . . . read with pleasure all your descriptions of . . . your favourite old ladies. . . . Your lectures to all those vague, altruistic Americans don't sound very lucrative, but I hope they were" (ibid.). He came back in June.

That spring, which had been so slow in coming, was the one that saw the start of the Irish rebellion, the long horror of Verdun, and the battles in Mesopotamia, where Arthur Wauchope, left for dead, had lain looking up at the vultures circling over him, waiting. Now probably only the sheer beauty of summer at the Norman Chapel helped mitigate the mood of near despair. The soft sunlight on the ancient stone of buttresses and walls, the rampaging color in the garden, was still lovely even in its partial wartime neglect. Chris was killed that July, though CRA did not know it till October. "They have killed Chris . . . " he wrote. "I knew it would happen of course,

Once put out thy light,
Thou cunning'st pattern of excelling nature,
I know not where is that Promethean heat
That can thy light relume."

(AJ, Oct. 1916)

But before the end of this cruel and accursed year, as CRA called it, an opportunity presented itself that was to give him five exciting and productive years' work, and new horizons for Janet and the family. An advertisement appeared in mid-December 1916, in the *Times Educational Supplement,* appealing for volunteers older than call-up age to teach English at a training college in Cairo, thus releasing younger British citizens on contract there for active service. CRA applied and was immediately accepted.

CHAPTER 14

CAMPDEN TO JERUSALEM—VIA CAIRO, 1917–1918

CRA used to say that if in doubt about some big decision, the thing to do was to consult Shakespeare. Take a pin and stick it between the closed pages of a complete volume. Then open the book carefully and see what phrase the point of the pin is pointing to. He claimed that when faced with the Cairo job in 1916, he had used this well-tried method. When he opened the book, the phrase the pin had pierced read: "Take her fair son, and let her make you happy!" So he did, and the whole world of Islam opened before him.

He sailed in February 1917, and wrote to Janet that it was turning out to be "a man's voyage. There are only four ladies, so the sum of necessary small talk is whittled to a minimum. My dear, if all women were like you, the world would really get on much quicker, for you can turn on the small talk to occasion, and yet not leave the other! God bless you!" (AJ, Mar. 1917). Janet's reply was: "I can imagine you in a blazing orgy of masculinity, being ever gracious to the feather-trimming or soupçon of ladies, who are like the mace in the fish pie. Your one compliment, or shall I say personal touch, was a great solace among the periods" (AJ, 9 Mar. 1917). She had started numbering her letters, to make sure that he knew he had got them, and in the right order. In the first of this series, she begged him not to be "too literary" (AJ, Feb. 1917).

She described my fourth birthday party in February: "[T]he guests all in clean white pinnies and Prout-ish hair bows assembled at 3.30. . . . No one was over five, and all behaved in a manner worthy of Buckingham Palace. The decorum was truly appalling" (AJ, 24 Feb. 1917). But by March she had heard nothing, and wrote, "I do wish I had something cheerful to tell

147

you, but the east wind is screaming round the house, and all three chicks are ill with a recurrence of influenza. . . . [T]hrough it all I have a sickening anxiety about them and you . . . and an aloneness I have never felt before. I can't think why I let you go" (AJ, Mar. 1917). Then she realized that she must be pregnant again—another parting shot! She told him in the too veiled idiom of a folk song, the meaning of which CRA missed completely.

At last a letter came from Cairo. CRA had arrived toward the end of March, and plunged straight into the job. "I never knew what the Middle Ages were like till I visited the El Azaar, the Arab University. . . . Thousands of men and boys, all sitting in circles round their teachers in immense open colonnades—exquisite architecture, reciting, memorising the Koran, reading, praying, eating their food" (AJ, 15 Mar. 1917). At the teacher-training college, on the other hand, he found his colleagues "cowed and disheartened by the ministerial system" and by the rigidity of the curriculum (AJ, Mar. 1917). But he soon met a few kindred spirits, in particular Will Stewart, head of the Technical School: "A charming fellow, and a great relief to all these timid officials and 'school-masters-*manqué*.'[1] . . . If they went about the slums of Cairo as Stewart and I do, and talked to the craftsmen—Arabs, Syrians, Copts, Greeks, discussed with them their actual workshop problems, they would get to learn how much of the 'Workshop or Guild structure' is still alive in the city" (ibid.).

Janet greeted these accounts of warmth and color with genuine pleasure, not unmixed with envy:

I am more than glad you have come into your own and find equal minds to "cut and come again" with—I should LOVE to be there in it all. . . . Well—here we have 3 inches of snow, 15

---

1. Will Stewart was a Bradford-born and -trained artist, craftsman, and teacher. In 1917, he became head of the Technical School in Cairo. He later married Janet's cousin Kathleen Beardshaw and had three children.

degrees of frost, and a hurricane from the N.E.—and as a *bonne bouche* the exhaust pipe of the *furnace* has burst with the frost, so *all* the hot water is pouring onto the Fern Patch, and the *cold water* patiently climbing up into all the radiators. I really could have cried when I found it out. . . . There is nothing so soul-destroying as an imperfect and badly contrived elaborate luxury. (AJ, 22 Mar. 1917)

This letter crossed with one from him describing a visit to the souk of the musical-instrument makers.

They were making the lutes . . . or virginals. . . . The lutes were exquisite pieces in inlayed woods set with ivory ebony and other fretted material. . . . I talked for a long while with the makers. . . . I asked one if he would play. He ceremoniously shut the door of his little shop. Four of us sat down together and with a peacock's feather of which he used the end as quill, he played delightfully. . . .

Then they told me that they had "two kinds of music" the music that was written, and "the other." The "other" I presume being the traditional folksong, in which the majority of the ballads and lyrics and living popular music is cast; doubtless modal music. I wish you were here to put it down and enterpret it. This Syrian promised if you would come to his shop he would give you a lesson and play to you. There is sunlight and leisure, and *all the time there is!* Do come! (AJ, 25 Mar. 1917)

This last remark showed that he had not realized that she was pregnant, and she replied caustically. He had suggested that the Little Mother might come out too, and Janet wrote, "I hope Grannie will go," adding a little unkindly, "[S]he would probably find plenty of bandages and war work to occupy her, and could try her master hand on the Berber servants!" (AJ, Apr. 1917).

Janet must have let Laurence know about her pregnancy, for in May he wrote:

I think Prudence is a ridiculously ill-chosen name for a fourth child, begotten and conceived in war-time. IMprudence is the

149

proper name for its very improper arrival upon the scene. . . .
I suspect it is CRA's *enteté* wish to have a son (while you in-
sist on meeting his absconding fatherhood with an unlimited
supply of daughters), that has brought this upon you; and you
will have him sulky on his return from Egypt, as he was on
his return from the USA at finding that he is still only the father of Women Suffragists. . . .

Ives crept in like a gentle shadow the other day, and spoke
of you as he generally does, as though you were the only
woman he had warmth mingled with respect for. I take you
more in streaks. You have your sufficiencies and even your su-
perlatives in my estimation. But when you mistake literalness
for strength and sane judgement, I want to chop you into
mincemeat and dance on you! . . . I am amused to see, that
CRA whom you MOTHER so much, calls you his "child."
What a mirror to his nature you are! (AJ, May 1917)

In the early summer came a startling letter from CRA saying that there was a possibility he might be offered the vice
principalship of a new college in Cairo.

I suppose it would mean an income of from £800 to £1000 a
year, and a house, and rather pleasant constructive work for a
period of 3 to 5 or 7 years. After which one would return to
England "retired." What do you say? And the children? Life
out here is very pleasant. There is good schooling and they
could get back for the marriageable age; returning to England
if need be for each summer holiday. It would mean of course
cutting all one's English roots, but if a good offer is made,
ought one to refuse it? . . . [W]hat I want from you is an
opinion on the general principle of starting a new creative
"life's work" out here on a good pay in pleasant surroundings
and congenial society. . . . Ask Nevill what he thinks, but best
not consult the 2 Mothers yet, it will disturb them.
(AJ, 11 May 1917)

Probably he was again surprised at the unexpected vehemence
of her reply when it reached him about five weeks later. How
could he not appreciate what it felt like to be in beleaguered
Campden, four months pregnant, with no confidantes near,

and the hint of his not even coming home on leave because of ship shortages?

I have had a good cry over your letter and feel rather better. Is it any good quoting poetry to you—you seem "Years and a thousand leagues away" tonight.

What is love?
'Tis not hereafter
Present mirth hath present laughter.
What's to come is still unsure.

You say "congenial society." Who are they? You have told me nothing. . . . I have no picture of your risings or goings to bed—no idea how you spend your evenings . . . no notion of your mealtimes, all the little homely things seem so unknown. . . . Then again—do you want me to consider *me myself*, apart from THE WORK, I mean the human me, I, with my aspirations (for I too have them, even *for myself*, though you have never asked what they are)—and I have them too for the children, and, separately, for you. Is one to have a legitimate aim for one's own remainder of life? Or ought one to become a shadow cast by the sun of one's children?

What is your "love for us all"—sometimes I want a little tenderness so dreadfully I feel I want to hurt you, and *make* you feel something, if only pain—I don't suppose you know a bit what I mean—I don't mean only now while you're away, but when you are here. Felicity's kisses are wonderful, but with all her capacity for love, she is thank God a baby.

What one pours out to them one must re-draw from elsewhere. I suppose that is why one doesn't have children without a husband. . . . [I]s one real flesh and blood—or merely a pen behind a brain, with an intellect.

Like Richard II with his warrant: ". . . I cannot see." Goodnight. I suppose one ought to conceal all this under a terrible composure. (AJ, 3 June 1917)

Before she had time to send this letter off, her brother, Nevill, had come to stay, and she consulted him as CRA had suggested. She had always felt very close to Nevill, though CRA tended to be dismissive about him, perhaps in some strange way because he was also gay. Nevill was all for doing the positive thing. He thought it would be foolish to turn down eight hundred to one thousand pounds a year, wherever it was, and that Cairo would be as good a place for the children to grow up as Campden. She added his judgment to her letter, ending, "I think I am very honest to tell you all this, and sitting with roses and children climbing everywhere in idyllic peace and calm after the torments of the last fortnight, I think it is very silly of me" (ibid.).

CRA came back to England in late July for six weeks' leave, which was mostly spent dealing with business matters. Phoebe was trying to tie up the ends of his architectural practice and the marketing of his various books.[2] He gave some lectures in Oxford, had visits from guildsmen, and stayed with the Masefields. Then he was gone again in early October, wishing he could stay to see Janet through her time in November. When Prudence was born, he put a good face on it, as it was in him to do. "I am glad that it is all satisfactorily over, but still can't forgive Prudence for putting on the wrong sex as she went through the Ivory Door. Thoughtless of her!" (AJ, Dec. 1917). Meanwhile, no more was heard of the vice principalship.

Janet described Prudence's christening, which was dominated by her increasingly childish and hysterical mother:

[W]e had an uproarious tea in the schoolroom . . . Mother clinking tea cups, and doing everything in threes, and falling on everybody's necks, in between exclamations of "My God, My God, this life of ours! Have some more cake! Mary, put your collar straight" etc. etc. I brutally insisted on Nurse P. carrying her off to, I fear, a cantankerous Xmas at Godden Green yesterday, as Prudence's milk was trembling in the

---

2. Phoebe was CRA's faithful secretary. She had come to Campden as Hilda Pook, played the part of Phoebe in the guild production of *As You Like It,* and was known by that name from then on. She even married Ron Haydon, a Campden man who had played Silvius.

balance (as the Old Man said) and in another 24 hours I
should have used a hatchet on somebody! (AJ, Nov. 1917)

CRA, by contrast, had rather "a *triste* Christmas thinking of
you all at home. I declined an invitation to spend it with 'other
people's children,' however charmingly offered, so Stewart,
Wainwright and I, (three lost dogs!) dined together, drank
portwine, and talked Egyptian archaeology. . . . I wonder how
you all fared" (AJ, Jan. 1918).

Janet's mother came back to Campden not long afterward
and installed herself in the bow window of a house in the High
Street, bowing to passersby.

> On Sunday the house was surrounded by a crowd of what
> Felicity calls "those corner children," all shouting "Grannie,
> Grannie" and waving caps and handkerchiefs to her wild grey
> head at the window. Then . . . she distributed largesse . . . and
> corrected their manners at the same time! Of course it is
> funny written about by my fire in solitude, but when I am
> half drowned in a conversational Niagara mingled as it were
> of beer, lemonade, tea, portwine, gravy, and salad-dressing,
> I could simply scream! And her stay is quite indefinite.
> (AJ, Mar. 1918)

The possibility of the vice principalship seems to have faded,
and with the end of his contract at the training college in view,
CRA had gone back to feeling nostalgic about Campden.
Janet, on the other hand, had been shaken out of her groove by
her brother's views and had begun to think about other places
to bring up her family. Campden seemed increasingly unat-
tractive, especially when the people whom CRA had antago-
nized began to put constructions on the fact that he had a
German mother and had been lecturing in America for the
Bryce Group. She could not face another bitter winter there,
especially when it was set against CRA's descriptions of sun-
drenched Luxor and swimming in the Nile. In February 1918,
she wrote that moving somewhere else "would give your ideas
a jolt and a new pivot and you would thank me the rest of your

life for snatching you from your vampyre-occupation of corpse-munching and maundering over dead ideals. We have our own flesh-and-blood new generation to look to, educate and live for now—and at our age, we have no time to waste vapouring over Might-have-beens" (AJ, 3 Feb. 1918).

The tenancy of the Norman Chapel would have to be renewed in the summer, but it was impossible to deal with it while CRA's future was so uncertain. She wrote again:

> I shall let the Norman Chapel if possible, but if not, such is the power of money and a reckless character, made yet more desperate by local slanders, "Damn the expense!" That is the mood I am in. . . . One thing I am quite clear about as we are on WILL NOTS, I *will not* stay here another winter alone with the children if you are away—but shall simply shut up the house and take a furnished house at Saunton or Oxford for them and myself. Nothing will induce me to go through another winter like the 2 last have been. *You* might like to be isolated here for eight months, shut away from all human intercourse. . . . But if I were not here, I don't believe you would stand it for more than a fortnight. . . . It is making me old and disagreeable, crabby and suspicious, and stale, and you and they will all begin to hate me. IT IS NOT FAIR ON ME! Read this to Mr Stewart and see what he says! Men cannot live by work alone, woman cannot live by children alone, the lives must be blended and interchanged if we are to keep sane, well and happy. . . . I miss your help and steady guidance every hour, and the evenings are simply too awful. (AJ, 11 Feb. 1918)

She took the children down to Saunton, and immediately began to feel much better. It seemed important to encourage CRA to stay where he was until the situation became clearer, and meanwhile she felt more able to carry on on her own.

> I want to hammer in MY views, which seem to be getting a little snowed under by Messrs Furness, Amos and Stewart, (peace be to them). . . . I most reluctantly feel, I ought to urge you to STAY WHERE YOU ARE especially considering the appallingly bad financial prospect, BAD STATE OF THE WAR, and

of your bank (£110 overdraft!!!). . . . Of course, my inference may be wrong, but you WILL wrap your statements up so in— "it would seem then's"—and "We therefore have to understand that's"—instead of "it is," "was," or "is to be's," that one is quite "*confuso.*" . . .

I am now practically a widow, and am getting used to the advantages (as well as the gruesome responsibilities which used to oppress me) of the position. It is all part of the hardening and toughening processes of the war—"stiffening our muscles and purging us all of sentimental dross" as our journalists say! Yes, I assure you, you will not find me the docile, clinging creature you left behind seven months ago! One learns to run the show as the soldiers' wives do, only without any "separation allowance"! And so, one becomes somewhat opinionated, and has to take decisions on one's own, that one might not do if one had a husband sitting in an "upper study," looking rather harressedly patient if one comes to interrupt him! (AJ, Apr. 1918)

"Otherwise," Janet ended, "life slips quietly along here, the mornings and evenings with glowing lights on that wonderful panorama of dune and sea and distant hills are very lovely and refreshing. I feel I have lost my soul and found it again" (ibid.).

Earlier in the year, CRA had mentioned that he had met Col. Ronald Storrs, who had told him that, at Charterhouse School, he had been moved to hear CRA lecture on the guild and the Arts and Crafts movement.[3] Now Storrs, as military governor of Jerusalem, invited CRA "to come and advise as to town planning in Jerusalem. . . . It sounds rather thrilling, but I don't know if anything will come of it; it would be the most interesting thing to do, but of course it might delay my return to England. On the other hand, it would probably lead to other things more in my line" (ibid.). Janet wrote at once: "Your letter

---

3. Ronald (later Sir Ronald) Storrs (1881–1955) was an expert on the Near East, military governor of Jerusalem from 1917 to 1920, and civil governor of Jerusalem and Judaea from 1920 to 1926. He was artistic, musical, and a brilliant linguist.

about Jerusalem made you feel still more remote, and I DO SO HOPE YOU WILL GO. . . . [I]it does seem such a chance. . . . And of course I should say: 'Oh yes, my husband is rebuilding Jerusalem,' it would SOUND so well! . . . How much better to build Jerusalem nearer to the Heart's Desire out there, than in England's Green and Pleasant Land, to mix Omar and Blake!" (AJ, June 1918).

A second letter came saying that he was holding himself ready to go and she should put a notice in the *Evesham Journal*, the *Times*, and professional papers saying that "Mr C. R. Ashbee has been summoned to Jerusalem to make an official Report on the Arts, Crafts and Industries of the Holy City in connection with the new Civic Plan" (ibid.). Janet wired her agreement, sending the little Devonshire post office into convulsions.

At some point in the guild's lifetime, CRA had made Janet a chain—no ordinary chain, for it was made of a series of silver filigree links, of varying lengths, because each one was a word. Each word was joined to the next by a small, round, warm carnelian, pierced by a silver pin. The words made up a verse from the old mad poet, the mystic and genius Blake, and to find the beginning, you had to pull it very gently around her neck until you came to the single letter *I*. Then it read: I WILL GIVE YOU THE END OF A GOLDEN STRING ONLY WIND IT INTO A BALL IT WILL LEAD YOU IN AT HEAVEN'S GATE SET IN JERUSALEM'S WALL. No one knows what has happened to it, nor did we as children, kneeling up on her lap to play with it, guess how prophetic it would be. Now, in the mixed emotions of that summer of 1918, Janet was as yet unaware that the end of the Golden String was already in her hand, and that within the year it would lead her, too, through the gate "built in Jerusalem's wall."

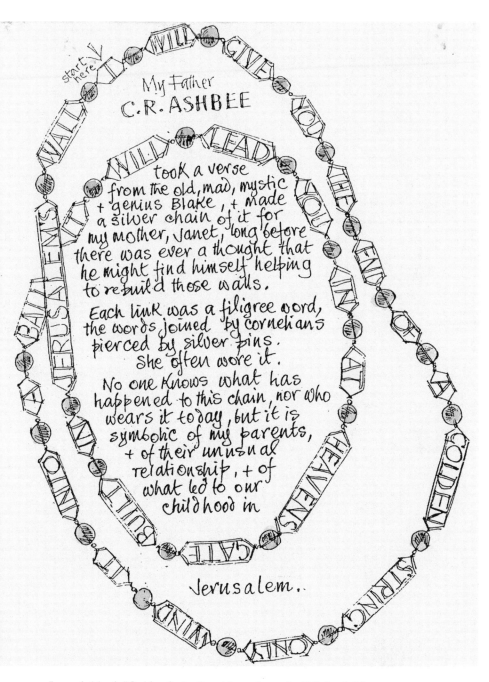

The necklace (reading from "start here"):

start here

I WILL GIVE YOU THE END OF A GOLDEN STRING ONLY WIND IT INTO A BALL IT WILL LEAD YOU IN AT HEAVENS GATE BUILT IN JERUSALEMS WALL

My Father
C.R. ASHBEE

took a verse
from the old, mad, mystic
+ genius Blake, + made
a silver chain of it for
my mother, Janet, long before
there was ever a thought that
he might find himself helping
to rebuild those walls.

Each link was a filigree word,
the words joined by cornelians
pierced by silver pins.
    She often wore it.

No one knows what has
happened to this chain, nor who
wears it today, but it is
symbolic of my parents,
+ of their unusual
relationship, + of
what led to our
    childhood in

Jerusalem..

33. Janet Ashbee's "Golden String" necklace, drawn by Felicity Ashbee

CHAPTER 15
THE GOLDEN BOWL FILLED
WITH SCORPIONS, 1918

CRA was half a Hamburg Jew and half an English Protestant, though he did not accept the dogma of either faith. And he was fresh from a first dose of Islam. The impact of Jerusalem, holy to all three faiths, was powerful and disturbing. "I've never felt so pagan and repelled in my life," he wrote to Janet. "To come back to this mediaevalism after the quiet reverence and sanity of Islam as one has observed it in Egypt, is something of a shock" (AJ, July 1918).

Janet had been down at Saunton again, but now she was back at the Norman Chapel, from which she sent one of her embattled bulletins:

> I am very VERY glad you are there instead of ROTTING HERE as I am. . . . I am very tired and rather fed up and would give simply ANYTHING to hear your policeman's tread waking up Helen and Prue-prue, and feel your calm self-sufficiency as a prop in all this welter of war-food, quarrelling tenants, absconding secretaries, and children with temperatures. . . . Please cable me what you want done about your work, as I CANNOT take on all your creditors, mortgages, tax-gatherers, book sales etc. (ibid.)

Apparently Phoebe, who had agreed to be CRA's secretary when he first went to Egypt, had had a set-to with Grannie, and walked out.

CRA found it hard to think about such things, as Jerusalem began to exercise its fascination over him. He wrote enthusiastically about his colleagues: "My new chief Storrs—the Military Governor—is a delightful person. Oh my dear it's such a relief to work with a sympathetic chief after those dreadful people in the Egyptian Ministry of Public Instruction! He's full of fire, full of vigour . . . mercurial, brainy, with a power of seeing round the Oriental. That means of course that you've got to be a bit of an artist and a bit of a dreamer" (ibid.). Storrs was not the only asset. There was General Money, who had actually read CRA's latest book, *Where the Great City Stands,* and a kindred spirit, Ernest Richmond, who was working on the repair of the Dome of the Rock.[1]

CRA was already running, characteristically, ahead of the report he was supposed to write: "On Monday we ride out to a remote village to engage masons, gather them together, and next week I have to see about getting these wonderful embroideresses to start teaching in the schools, (there are 1000 women out of work), at their native craft, making their own dresses" (AJ, 26 July 1918). He made her jealous by thoughtlessly describing his social life, the Fourth of July celebrations at the American Colony, and coffee with the grand mufti: "[Y]our forecast, that I would be engaged in rebuilding the New or rather the very old Jerusalem . . . is literally coming true" (ibid.).[2] But he was unable to give her any definite idea of his future after the report was handed in.

Janet felt tossed from one emotional extreme to another.

I find it impossible to pick up the threads here. . . . I walk down Campden High Street and think, "Man does not live by Stones alone, but by every word of sympathy that proceedeth out of the mouth of his neighbours, and by every loving touch and smile of those of his own household." The children console me for much cold apathy, they are so warm and so very loving, and so ingenuous. Felicity last night in

1. General (later Major-General Sir Arthur) Money (1866–1951) was the leader of the Egyptian Expeditionary Force, and was in charge in Palestine during the summer of 1918. Ernest Richmond (1874–?), son of the painter William Blake Richmond, was an architect and archaeologist. He became a close friend of CRA and Janet.

2. The American Colony was an unusual American-Swedish religious settlement. See chap. 16.

bed . . . "I must LICK your kiss else I can't taste the sweetness
of it" (quite Oriental and Odalisquey I think!). . . . The descriptions of your parties are thrilling, and of course I should
love to be there. . . . Sometimes I feel awful pangs of jealousy—not passional but intellectual—at missing all you are
going through. . . . Humanly speaking, or if you like, speaking
as a woman, we shall NEVER catch up these separated years—
and shall have to learn each other afresh in the time that re-
mains to us. (AJ, July–Aug. 1918).

In August, she went down to Godden Green for her
mother's seventy-sixth birthday, "very doleful, pouring rain
outside, and masses of damp flowers, and creeper-covered windows inside. . . . I am still uncertainly waiting in mid air like
Mahomet's coffin, to hear WHAT you are going to do, when,
and how" (AJ, Aug. 1918).

By the end of August, the report was being typed and put
together. "I wish I had you to do the pruning," CRA wrote,
"and Mother the gumming" (ibid.). This letter crossed, oddly,
with one from Janet in which she commented on articles he
had written in Egypt that she had just seen:

I'm sorry I didn't have the pruning and punctuating of your
newspaper articles in Cairo. No, no! Too redundant and dou-
ble-negativy. "It would seem, therefore, if we look into the
question, and desire an answer, that we should sooner look to
the answer in formulating our question than we should perhaps have thought possible before we ventured to hope that
such an answer could be made to the question we had formerly hoped to formulate. This may however not be so, but
somewhat after this fashion do I frame the answer to myself.
East and West must, some day interpenetrate and transfuse,
not only each other, but also in less degree, other and outside,
and less tangible points of the compass, and it would seem
hardly possible that this fusion should be as the old men see
in visions, nor do I suggest to you that it might be represented by what has been described as the 'young men's'
dreams. Perhaps one might be nearer the mark in indicating
it to be something in the style our middle-aged and unveiled

wives, free alike from the traumas of education and virginity, have described as—WOOLLEY, not to put too fine a point on it." (AJ, July 1918)

CRA nobly wrote admitting that he had "enjoyed her horrid parody" (AJ, 29 Aug. 1918).

The report was now in, but September came and went, and still there was no decision. "It is a very formidable document," CRA wrote, "(I hear you sniffing! and saying, 'I know the style') in the form of a Blue Book with many photographs I have had specially made, and all bound together, very 'ansom! . . . It's no good being impatient, one cannot hurry these things" (AJ, Sept. 1918). In October, he was working on his proposed park system for Jerusalem "with the old city wall circuit at the centre . . . and the old Guild Bazaar in Jerusalem, which I am to fill with some 40 weavers with looms for cloth, silk and carpets. . . . I wouldn't have missed these 4 months for anything!" (AJ, Oct. 1918).

All Janet could do was go on supplying him with Campden gossip, as much to give vent to her feelings as to keep him in touch. "We have a nice little new curate, just out of Eton collars, with an ebony head and nice eyes. . . . I have been floundering all this week in a sea of insurance payments, rent demands and receipts, letters from vague strangers wanting your book, mortgage duns, etc. (and cursing Phoebe in my heart!)" (AJ, Aug. 1918). She quoted Mary's bedtime prayer: "Let Daddy come home for Christmas," and mine: "Let Daddy come home when he has finished his work in Jerusalem" (AJ, Oct. 1918).

Then everything happened at once. The war ended, and CRA was offered a post in Jerusalem. Storrs was very keen to keep him and see the recommendations of his report carried out. The military government could not provide a salary, so he was attached, with the title of "civic adviser," to the Pro-Jerusalem Society. This body was unique, recently created by Storrs, and embraced notabilities of every race and creed in the

Holy City who were prepared, under Storrs's magnetism, to sink their differences and sit around one table. It was clear that CRA's family would now come out to Jerusalem. He got home leave straightaway, and by the time the Armistice was signed, he was in Cairo waiting for a boat home.

CRA reached Campden just after Christmas, as it turned out, and found himself in a very bleak Norman Chapel, confronted not only with the stark realities of coal rationing, but also with a harassed wife and sick baby. In the sunshine and beauty of Egypt, and in the excitement of the four months in Palestine, he had simply not been able to take in the shift that the war years had made in Janet's attitude and in their circumstances. For him, Campden was still "where we shall spend our old age in peace, with a new creative generation about us," and he still hoped that the Guild of Handicraft might be revived (AJ, 4 Oct. 1918). But now, in five weeks of wintry leave, he had to make his farewells to the Norman Chapel and to Campden. At the end of January, he convened the last meeting of the Guild of Handicraft. Alec Miller wrote to him afterward:

> Seventeen years since I called on you in Cheyne Walk, and how much has happened to us both since! . . . I have so many reasons to have love for you. . . . I love your constant courage, and I felt that last Saturday. You will always keep that I know—though I hate to think how often it has been necessary to call it up in the face of cruel circumstances. Well, you are not beaten. As you reminded us the "Guild" is not in the shops and the tools, but in the ideas and the lives. . . . Well! if the New Jerusalem is not to begin from Campden—in God's name—let it begin from the Old Jerusalem. . . . I shall always be proud to have had a little share with you in the work of preparing for it. (AJ, 2 Feb. 1919)

CRA left for Jerusalem during the second week of February, and Janet began the hectic process of transplanting her ménage: herself, four little girls, Nannie (just out of the hospital), and Kathleen Beardshaw, a young Forbes relation who, in exchange for giving lessons to us older children, was offered the adventure of a passage to Jerusalem. It was Janet who had to deal with Ananda Coomaraswamy and the lease of the Norman Chapel, with the storage of furniture and books to be left behind, and with what should be taken as luggage and what crated and left to follow, heaven knows when. Just before departure, she had a letter from CRA saying that so far no house had been found, and "All things of a household nature, e.g. linen, kitchen utensils, boot brushes, spirit lamp, kettles, towels, are fantastically dear, very bad, and practically unobtainable . . . so if you are still packing when this reaches you, put all such things in as can conveniently be packed" (AJ, Feb. 1919). Could the battered and already bulging black canvas trunks, with their heavy leather corners and flaps protecting the locks, hold any more?

34. Janet Ashbee and her four children, just before departure for Jerusalem, ca. 1919

I can dimly remember a weeping Babushka waving to us from the Gothic porch at Godden Green and, more clearly, the small figure of Grannie, at what must have been an equally emotional but less demonstrative farewell on a London platform. In Liverpool, we boarded the Dutch liner *Princess Juliana,* carrying troops to the Middle East, only to find that the cabin reserved for Nannie and the two youngest had been commandeered by an officer. He stood astride, barring the entrance, and I can see him still. "No gentleman!" Nannie commented. In the end, a friendly clergyman gave up his cabin, whereas Janet and we two big ones were offered the red plush seats of the saloon! It was so exciting that my memory of it is as clear as yesterday. Smoke wreaths hung in the air, the round, brass-bound tables had empty glasses standing on them, and groups of men, still dressed, and smoking cigars, stood around talking. This was LIFE, and a fascinating departure from the rules of the Campden nursery.

The trip held no terrors for us children. One day the cry went up "Mines! Mines!" and the alarm bells started ringing, and everyone went running to their cabins to get their cork jackets, reemerging on deck to take their appointed places by their lifeboats. We were convulsed by Nannie's appearance, cork-jacketed but still white-capped and carrying Prudence, and we clamored to know what the "otters" were, as no sleek black heads could be seen swimming around the ship.

Then came Alexandria, and Cairo, where CRA met us, and finally we set off on the last lap of the journey via Kantara and a long, hot wait at Suez, where, to relieve the boredom, CRA walked Mary and me down to the muddy water's edge. Tall, rickety poles dangling electric lightbulbs at infrequent intervals made the darkness in between darker. He began to recite, "By the wide lake's margin I marked her lie," as we stood each clutching a hand, spellbound. "The wide, weird lake where the alders sigh / A fair young thing with a soft, shy eye. . . ." Ever after, Calverley's "Water-rat"—and we often asked for it— evoked the smelly brown waters of Suez.

35. Street scene in Jerusalem

There followed the corridorless train, with hard wooden seats above which were shelves held up by chains. Spare chains hung from them that jangled with the train's lurching movement. "What are the extra chains for?" I asked, and Mary, with the wisdom of eight years, answered casually, "To fasten prisoners with, of course!" It was on this journey that the Green Bag made its appearance. It was a large cotton bag pulled together at the top with a string. In it was kept the potty, essential on toiletless trains. When need arose, and the train stopped often enough for there to be plenty of occasions, Janet took her brood discreetly onto the sandy track beside the sleepers to do the necessary. I can see the three-year-old Helen now, sitting serenely, fluttering her unfairly long black lashes coquettishly at anyone near while Janet stood, holding the Green Bag and saying persuasively, with an unnatural calm, "Come along Heleny, quickly now, there's a good girl."

It was a great moment when we were finally ushered into the stone-flagged hall of the house, which was to be our first home, and CRA said, "Well, here we are at last!" Then he clapped his hands, and two people appeared, bowing and smiling as in fairy tales. A plump, short woman, the Armenian cook Haani, had crimpy hair and an oily, friendly face, and two eyes of quite different colors. Mary and I soon discovered with fascinated disbelief that one of them was glass, and could be TAKEN OUT! The dark-faced man in a long striped dress with a wide yellow sash around his waist was Hassan. With a flash of white teeth, he seized Janet's hand, kissed it, then pressed it to his forehead. Both Haani and Hassan then vanished into the kitchen, from which unusual smells were already emerging.

The trunks were manhandled upstairs, and as everyone was sorting out where they would be sleeping, CRA turned to Janet and said: "And now, this is your room,—and this is mine." No preamble, no explanation. Years later, she admitted that she had never quite been able to forgive him for the way he did it.

CHAPTER 16

ONCE IN ROYAL DAVID'S CITY

1919

LETTER writing was a necessity to Janet, though, un-
fortunately, most of the people to whom she sent
her graphic descriptions of Jerusalem seem to have read
them, enjoyed them, answered them, and then consigned them
to the wastepaper basket. Her handwriting was increasingly
large and passionate, and covered a great many pages. Ruth
Head, who seems to have been among the destroyers, wrote a
year later, "Your letters make me long to have a whole book
from your pen. 'Domestic Letters from Jerusalem' would sell
like hot cakes" (AJ, Feb. 1920).

She had forgotten to give Laurence Housman any address
and, not hearing from him, had written indignantly. He
replied:

> I wondered and wondered when your High-Mightiness
> would condescend to send me a "change of address" card.

36. The Ashbee family in the garden of their first house in Jerusalem, ca. 1919

At last I wrote to Broad Campden to ask for it. And now I am accused of not answering your letter of January. That "What HAS happened to you?" is good! Nothing has happened to ME, but magnificent upheavals have been happening to YOU. I suppose you expected me to guess. . . . I hope "Jerusalem," which is all the address you give me, will reach you. It sounds spacious. I suppose if CRA is Governor-General of the main drains and sewage works the name itself is sufficient. . . . I am afraid you and CRA are not the right people to be in Jerusalem from the pious, traditional point of view. A friend of mine walked along the Via Dolorosa on his hands and knees with tears streaming down his face, and enjoyed himself thoroughly, believing everything. You won't! It is all thrown away on you. My only idea of CRA is that he keeps repeating Blake's poem to himself with a sort of defiant exhaltation. "As I wasn't allowed to do it in England, I'm doing it here!" It will be rather a wonderful experience for your young to look back on, how they were "Once in Royal David's City." (AJ, June 1919)

Janet set to and learned Arabic. As a natural linguist, it never occurred to her not to try to speak the language of any country she found herself in, though she never attempted to read or write Arabic. She found herself exchanging coal for water rationing, and teenage Cotswold orphan girl helpers for teenage Arab ones; where in Campden she had gone fodder hunting for the pony Kirstie, now it was for George, our stubborn and elderly donkey. All her and Nannie's strict ideas about hygiene and diet went by the board. Meat was rationed, and the nearest butcher served his customers outside, hacking off a chunk of some unspecified animal with a hatchet on the top of a sawed-off tree trunk.

In October 1919, CRA's mother died, without his ever having seen her again. He may not even have realized, in the pressure and fascination of his work, that Grannie was terminally ill, a return of the cancer that had attacked her once before. His sister Agnes had nursed her to the end, and now all he could

learn about it was filtered through the tensions of that household. His sister Elsa wrote aggressively to assure him that his
mother had not needed him: "In fact, I believe she was so completely at rest on THAT POINT, that she, as far as we could
gather, never even asked for you, realising the impossibility of
its fulfilment. . . . I hope your work continues to interest you as
much as formerly, and that Janet and the little girls are well.
My love to those of you who care for it" (AJ, Oct. 1919). Agnes
wrote more gently, sensing the pain that not being there would
cause him, and then turned to Janet to express her own loneli-
ness, "How different the outlook is for you and Charlie—
Good God! The children near you, their arms about you, their
future to plan and be interested in, and the means to do it with!
Well my consolation is of the soul, not the body, and to know
that for one brief month I came into my own!" (AJ, Nov. 1919).
Poor Agnes! This sad phrase, to Janet not to her brother, seems
to sum up her whole rather unfulfilled existence. She was
barely sixty when she died.

It must have been at about this point that the American
Colony first began to play a part in the family's life. For anyone
who has not known Jerusalem during the past hundred years,
the phrase "American Colony" is misleading. It was no ordinary colony, nor were they ordinary Americans. They were a
mixed community of Americans and Swedes whose particular
brand of Christianity had brought them to Jerusalem in 1881 to
"do the Lord's work" and await the Second Coming. They had
learned to live with the Ottoman Empire in its last stages, and
long before the British presence or the eventual Mandate, they
had become an institution for whose help countless people of
every creed, race, or political color had reason to be grateful.
They lived more or less communally, and by the end of World
War I, they had produced some forty or fifty children. Colony
members were known as "Brothers" and "Sisters," or "Uncles"
and "Aunts." No one asked what determined the difference,
and all contributed to the colony according to their skills and

37. House in the Wadi el Jose, ca. 1920

talents. By 1919, many of them were teaching in their school, educating the rising generation "according to the Word."

After we had been in Jerusalem about six months, the clergyman whose house we had borrowed came back, and it was through the American Colony that Janet was able to find a house in the Wadi el Jose, the Arab quarter below Mount Scopus. The house was sealed up and fumigated, to get rid of the bugs, before the Arab plasterers and whitewashers set to work. When we moved in, the bluish white distemper on the walls was fresh and strange smelling, and had long, half-submerged horsehair that held the plaster together and could be surreptitiously picked off when no one was looking.

This new home was a domed, stone-built Arab house tucked into the steep hillside, so at the back there was only one floor, whereas in the front, where the land dropped at a forty-five-degree angle, there were two. No road led to it, and when the plowing season came, the Arabs, with their biblical wooden implements, plowed up the narrow footpath across the

170

field, the only access to the house, and each time we had to spend a lot of time and energy wearing down a new one over the furrows between the olive trees. The house itself was a simple structure, built over and around the cistern, that essential for living in a waterless land. There was an open courtyard in the middle, and the rooms of the nursery—or "harem" as CRA called it—were on two of its sides, the third was the drawing room, and the fourth was merely a wall with the front door in it. So all doors opened into this court. The house, of course, had no bath or bathroom as such. All we had was the six-inch-deep tin "tisht" about twenty inches in diameter, in which we all bathed, that is, had water poured over us to get off the soap. With the move to this house in the Wadi el Jose, and its gradual taming, Janet felt more settled. There was a sense of greater permanence, which her love of system greeted with relief.

As her Arabic improved, she and A'eed (Hassan had gone) would go to the markets just inside the Damascus Gate to buy all the basic foodstuffs, bringing them back on the donkey. When George finally rebelled and refused to respond to any

38. Janet Ashbee in the drawing room of the house in the Wadi el Jose, ca. 1920

more cajolery, Janet part-exchanged him for another with an Arab she had met in the Old City, and the new one was called Georgette, despite his sex, as being the same only different.

The daily milk supply, which was crucial, came in an earthenware pitcher on the head of Ma'azousah, an Arab woman who walked the eight miles from Lifta, a village in a cleft in the hills, way out by the Jaffa road. Like all the Arab women working in the fields, she wore a black, brightly embroidered dress, with a quilted jacket over it to keep off the sun. Her lined, brown face was old before its time. She would set off at first light to make sure "the lady's" milk was in time to be boiled and cooled before the children's seven o'clock breakfast.

On one terrible occasion a little later, all Janet's sense of drama and her now reasonable command of Arabic were called into play. Breakfast was just finished when one of the Health Department inspectors appeared. He had come to say that a case of typhoid had been reported in Ma'azousah's house in Lifta, and we were advised (though he hastened to add that there was no real danger) not to drink her milk until further notice. There was an icy silence. Then Ma'azousah was summoned from the kitchen where she was still innocently resting before the long walk home. Jameelah, the beautiful parlor maid from Bethlehem, was told to bring the jug with what was left undrunk of the morning's milk. Then in an atmosphere electric with emotion, Janet poured the milk out onto the ground in front of us all, with a gesture worthy of Greek tragedy. "Why do you bring me poisoned milk?" she exclaimed. "Do you wish to murder my children?" Ma'azousah burst into loud lamentations. "Bring me a knife! Bring me a knife!" she wailed, rocking herself to and fro. "I will cut off my right hand, if I ever intended to bring poisoned milk to your innocent children, whom Allah bless. My nephew is ill, it is true, but his lips never touched the milk! May Allah strike me dead if I tell anything but the truth!" There was a heavy pause. Fortunately, no one had obeyed Ma'azousah's frenzied demand for a knife. With tears still pouring down her weather-beaten face, Ma'azousah seized Janet's hand and, alternatively covering it with kisses and pressing it to her forehead, begged her forgiveness, and assured her of her unending love and devotion. The inspector coughed and prepared to take his leave, tapping the milk woman on the shoulder to indicate she should go with him. But she would not move until Janet had accepted her protestations as the truth. When Janet told her, "Go in peace," and to come back as soon as her milk was certified as "clean," the tears were gone in a flash, and words of gratitude tumbled from her as she grabbed all our hands in turn, kissing them and pressing them to her forehead. Everyone was purged by this Euripidean drama, and there was an audible sigh of relief. We were all very fond of Ma'azousah!

Janet learned, with advice from the American Colony, about the bulk buying of fruit and other necessities. When the apricots, the golden "mish-mish," ripened, a vast jam-making session was organized. As the smell of cooking apricots rose up the stairs from the kitchen into the court, the women who had brought them would sit cheerfully smashing the fruit stones on the flagged floor with bits of rock, so that the little white kernels could be tossed into the boiling jam to give it extra flavor. And there were several olive trees in the garden, so when the olives were ripe, Arab women vouched for by Janet's servants would come and gather the crop. Tucking their embroidered dresses up into their swathed belts, they rapidly climbed the trees, and their bare, brown legs could soon be seen stamping and jumping among the silver-gray leaves, while shrieks of cheerful laughter echoed around the garden. Meanwhile, a hail of olives showered down, to be picked up and taken off to the public presses.

As winter approached, there was a need for more wood to stoke the stove in the drawing room, as well as the kitchen range. The first time, Janet was caught and innocently bought wood sewn into sacks. But that happened only once! The next time, deaf to the clamorous protestations of the woodmen, she sternly insisted on each sack being cut open. As the wood tumbled onto the scales, a few good-size rocks came rolling out of each sack. The woodmen shrugged their shoulders, and good-naturedly shoveled the logs back into the sacks again, after weighing. When the price had been argued and agreed and the money handed over, Janet, backed by Jameelah, who was now hot in her mistress's defense, asked the chief woodman why he had tried to sell her stones with her wood. The answer came with sublime logic and a winning smile: "And does the lady not expect to buy bones with her meat?"

As quickly as she learned, the demands of this new style of domestic life were a strain on her. The last straw was probably the blizzard of February 1920. Having got used to the summer's heat, she found herself back in Cotswold-type snowdrifts, with the courtyard of the house filled waist-high overnight, so that no doors could be opened into it. Somehow A'eed shoveled out a path so that she could get to her nursery! When this crisis was over, the American Colony stepped in, whisking her off to Jaffa for a rest, from where she wrote:

> I never realised till I had got up this morning how utterly tired out I was, and how thankful to be away from every duty, problem, "scene," and responsibility for a few days. It is LOVELY here! It is just like Sicily—the air full of lemon scent—the sea the bluest blue, and lapping up over its reefs up to the sandy cliff below this house. A blaze of sun all yesterday and today, and the peaceful, orderly kindness and friendly tact of these dear people are better than medicine. Today I have just been lazy—lay on my bed all afternoon with wide open windows, and the good noise of the sea pouring over me. Tomorrow we go to lunch (tell Mary and Fifi) with Meleky and Rushad's father, to meet Colonel Storrs, and also the Governor of Jaffa. . . . After that we are all to be entertained to tea at the Sporting Club, and in the evening we dine with another Arab family. It is all very amusing, and I have a pleasant feeling of playing truant! . . . Love to my four beautifuls, and a kiss each. (AJ, Feb. 1920)

She was recovered enough in March to play the part of administration wife when Herbert Samuel invited her and CRA to accompany him on a fact-finding mission in northern Palestine. They sat in on deputations of Muslim sheikhs and Greek priests, of Maronite Christians and Druzes, and they saw more of the "new agriculture" about which CRA had written in his report of 1918. One afternoon, they slipped out of the official party and, with a good interpreter, had a private session with Abbas the Baha'i.[1] When they dined that evening with their hosts, CRA claimed that they were rather envious; Colonel Stanton, the military governor of the area, said he often went to the Abbas for advice, though he "had to listen for half an hour or so first to the beauty of the flowers and the wings of the mind!" (AJ, Mar. 1920).

At Tiberias they had a surprise encounter with the redoubtable Miss Thomas, president of Bryn Mawr College, whom they had last met on their 1900 trip to America. She was traveling *en princesse,* as Janet described her,

> climbing out of her post-chaise in the darkness at Tiberias, her second carriage having been broken over a rock, saying, as might have Queen Victoria, "We are VERY much displeased! VERY much displeased! The man must go at once into the mountains with FOUR donkeys and bring ALL my luggage— and not forget the coffee-pot. . . ." She then stumped into the hotel and ordered the most expensive rooms and then fell into fresh wrath because it was Saturday, and there was NO BATH because the JEWS pumped the water![2]

As CRA's work developed, crafts were revived or reintroduced into the Old City, and its fabric was repaired where pos-

---

1. After various forms of government service, Herbert (later Sir Herbert) Samuel (1870–1963) was the first civilian high commissioner of Palestine under the Mandate, from 1920 to 1925. Abbas the Baha'i (1844–1921) was the head, or "interpreter," of the Baha'i faith, freed from persecution on the fall of the Ottoman Empire, and lived in Haifa until his death.

2. C. R. Ashbee, *A Palestine Notebook* (London, 1923), 99.

sible. Glassblowers from Hebron were put on a new footing; a distinguished Armenian potter, David Ohanessian, was brought to Jerusalem from Damascus to oversee the production of tiles, plates, jugs, and bowls. Visits to the pottery, either with Janet or with CRA, became treats for us children to look forward to. There in the wonderful cool dampness of potters' clay, Mr. Ohanessian's workmen turned their wheels with bare, skillful feet, and at dusty trestle tables the painters sat, with delicately poised brushes, transforming the dull whitish gray of the first bake into what would be the glories of turquoise and dark blue, yellow and black, on vases and bowls, and on the tiles to replace the shattered ones around the base of the great Dome of the Rock.

And there were other fascinating crafts still alive in the markets, or souks. When the copper began to show through on our

39. C. R. Ashbee in Jerusalem, ca 1920. Courtesy of King's College Library, Cambridge.

176

saucepans, Janet would take us to where the retinning was done, and there, before our very eyes, in the hot street, the miraculous process of renewal took place. First, the simple scrubbing with sand and water, then the darting flame, and strange cake of "tin soap" about the size of the large, evil-smelling kitchen variety, and a saucepan was reborn!

If it was with CRA that we went to any of these places, he stalked ahead, in Semitic—or Islamic—fashion, never bothering to check whether the right number of little girls was at his heels; his womenfolk simply had to follow as best they could. But the porridge-colored corduroy breeches, the white coat, the shining brown gaiters, and his height made it not too difficult to keep him in sight.

Down the middle of each narrow souk was a bright, irregular strip of sunlight, on either side of which were dark caverns with chains hanging from the ceilings to help the Arab vendors heave themselves up when necessary. They sat behind huge piles of vegetables, or figs, or mish-mish, or better still the great flat black tins with little white sugar-dusted cakes looking like tailless mice, or the sesame oil– and honey-soggy triangles, green with squashed pistachio nuts, that smelled so mysteriously.

Best of all, perhaps, was the hellawa (the halvah of today's neat, tinfoil-covered rectangles) sold from huge, oozing mountains in yet other dark souk caverns. It jutted up like a relic from a Herodian quarry, and was of much the same color, stepped and shelved, where slabs had been sawed from it. The Arab shopkeeper would sweep the flies from it with a bunch of fresh leaves, and grab a piece of rough, brownish paper, the bits of straw in its manufacture an integral part of it. Then, clapping it against the side of the monolith, he would hack off as large a slab as he guessed the customer would tolerate, and toss it onto the handheld brass scale. Even if he could be made to disgorge a second piece of paper, the oil would have seeped through in dark patches long before we could get it home to

40. The Souk el Qattanin

41. The walls of Jerusalem

put it in its special dish. The dish was an Arab pewter one, with a filigree lid that rose into an elegant point like Absalom's tomb. But only Janet could be persuaded to buy hellawa. It was too messy for CRA!

And then, of course, there were the city walls of Süleyman the Magnificent. CRA planned, and almost completed, a walk along the ramparts of the walls that would extend right around the Old City (plate 9). Bit by bit, more stretches of the rampart were renovated, crumbling masonry restored, excrescences removed, and small iron handholds cemented in. Whenever a new stretch was completed, we children would have the adventure of exploring it. And it WAS an adventure, with just enough danger to keep the mind on the job, and at every turn or twist of the route another view was to be glimpsed from the slits of the castellations: outward toward the still largely empty, or olive-dotted, hills, inward over the roofs and domes of the

179

Old City. And here you seemed to be literally stepping between trees and houses, for fig trees grew sometimes out of crevices in the masonry, or in yards and tiny spaces between houses, which themselves were stuck, barnacle-like, on the inside of the great wall. Colored washing was strung from window to window, and clucking hens and braying donkeys seemed within touching distance. The warm smells of sunbaked fig trees, a special, heavy scent, of horse manure, and unmistakably of human shit as well are as strong in my memory as is the touch of the burning metal handrails or the warm, rough surface of the centuries-old stone.

For Janet, too, all these things were enthralling. The variety of the problems in the multicultural, multilingual world in which she found herself so surprisingly dropped acted like a tonic. She was rejuvenated. Now in her early forties, and having got over the sheer fatigue of producing four children, and the depression of the war years, she was at her slenderest and most attractive, with the maturity of fulfillment added. The Golden Bowl held for her far more than scorpions.

CHAPTER 17

ADMINISTRATION WIFE

1920–1921

THE summer of 1920 saw the end of military government in Palestine, and the beginning of civilian rule, with Herbert Samuel as high commissioner. CRA was enthusiastic, and hopeful of taking his work further, for Storrs was still governor of Jerusalem, and his post with the Pro-Jerusalem Society seemed secure.

In April, Janet had gone for a few days to Cairo, where she did the rounds of his former colleagues. She wrote:

> I must say it is nice to be in a land of daily postal deliveries, and newspapers, and evening dress, and above all, enough water to cover you in your bath . . . . It is nice to have shade to sit in, and English roses and snap-dragons to look at . . . . Yesterday we had tea at the Amos's. I can form no opinion of him as he did not address a word to me, or notice my presence, except to let me out of the house with apparent relief . . . . It was a bit of a drop to go back to the Russells, who had a great party on, in a completely *"factice"* atmosphere of a sham English country house, everything of the very best and most expensive; two dozen assorted cakes from Groppi, and assorted ladies very like the cakes, and assorted husbands, all with the folds of their trousers where they had been unpacked from the Groppi boxes; you felt in another moment the curtain would go up and the lights go down on a Haymarket Comedy! (AJ, Apr. 1920)

She had also met a woman who said CRA was the most charming man she had ever met. This announcement, reported Janet, "rather put me off her!" (ibid.).

During the last months before she joined him in Jerusalem, CRA and Janet had had a lively correspondence about our education, for though she had never experienced the inside of a school as a pupil, now that she had children of her own, her ideas about governess education were changing. CRA, on the other hand, could think of nothing better for his four daughters than that they should be privately reared as their mother had been.

> Some little association with other children is desirable, but not really necessary. The children have each other, and with careful supervision and guidance at home, I'm sure the individual outlook on the world that is induced by NOT herding and NOT competing, is quite as valuable as that which a school gives. You yourself, my dear, are the best example of what I mean! You wouldn't have had nearly so individual an outlook if you had passed through the school and examination mill. For myself, I regard the exam part of my school and college life as being an almost unmitigated curse.
> (AJ, Sept. 1918)

But Janet, already aware of the enormous differences in temperament, behavior, and needs of her three older children, wasted no time in sweeping into the counterattack:

> [M]uch as one hates exams and any competition, children will always INSTINCTIVELY compete, and as they will certainly want to go to university, they must have teachers who have been there and who teach "somewhat," as you say, after the University standard. I was not educated at all, only brought up to be healthy and ornamental, but then I had only one brother, and £3000 a year at my back, a very different story, even in the 80s and 90s. These four will certainly have to be trained for professions, whether they adopt them or not, and that again postulates entrance exams, etc . . . . I am afraid, my Dear, your head is in the clouds of Islam, and you are thinking of these girls from the Muslim point of view! . . . Another thing you forget when you say, "they have each other" is the terrible feminine outlook which MUST be counteracted at a SMALL co-educational school. They simply cannot go on till their teens never seeing a boy at all!
> (AJ, Oct. 1918)

The question was which of the Jerusalem schools would least conflict with her and CRA's views. They did not want excessive Jewishness, whether of Hebrew-speaking Zionism or rabbinic orthodoxy, nor did they relish narrow Roman Catholic dogma. They decided on the American Colony's almost Quaker-like brand of Christianity, and the school was at least coeducational. Too much religion could be countered at home with Greek and Nordic mythology, the *Arabian Nights*, and Andrew Lang's *Fairy Tales*. So Mary, Helen, and I had our first contact with a real classroom in the stone-built, Turkish-style schoolhouse of the colony. Janet had always been keen on musical drill, and here she was pleased to find that, under Swedish influence, all marching and swinging of clubs and dumbbells were accompanied by music.

At home, of course, there was the *Essex House Song Book*, on which CRA and Janet had lavished so much care. CRA's four little girls gradually became, for him, an acceptable substitute for the young guildsmen of twenty years earlier, and we would sing from it regularly. The pages of the *Song Book* were numbered in roman as well as arabic numerals, and you had to master them if you wanted the privilege of choosing the next song. The first winter in the house in the Wadi el Jose there was no piano, so these sing-alongs were unaccompanied, and we would sit cozily around the stove, the smell of burning olive wood filling the air, the light of the oil lamps casting big shadows in the corners of the room. The wood for the stove was chopped by A'eed, who was handy with an ax and shielded us from rats and scorpions. He too had a glass eye, but it did not have the fascination of Haani's, familiarity breeding contempt.

Jameelah was by far the most attractive of the servants. Her dark hair was twisted in a bun at the nape of her neck, and she wore, on CRA's insistence, her hand-embroidered Bethlehem dress, with the broad sash tucked into itself for fastening. When out, she would wear the white head scarf of the unmarried woman. She constantly complained of being tired, to

42. Janet Ashbee and her four daughters, ca. 1921

which Janet was less than sympathetic when she discovered that Jameelah was in the habit of collecting and eating the snails that clustered on the parched thistles of the Wadi. But she always came to life when it was a matter of looking beautiful to wait on guests in the evenings. The current cook was Waardi—Haani had vanished somewhere en route from the first house—a Nubian from Khartoum, of unspecified age, with a large, battered-looking black face, frequently split open in a grin. She could always find a corner of the kitchen and some kind of tub with soapy water, if dolls' clothes needed washing.

A picture taken that summer by Matson, the great American Colony photographer, shows Janet standing with the four of us, hands on each other's shoulders. We are in the embryo garden of the house in the Wadi el Jose, with the Russian tower on Olivet in the far distance. She sent a copy to Laurence Housman, who replied:

How you do grow, all of you! And with what variety of gesture and character! I could only wish to have had a family, had I also been a man of means, and endowed with a wife given to parthenogenesis. But had that double boon been conferred on me by a god better than the one I have ceased to worship, I would have welcomed just such a stream of progeny, whatever sex it might incline to—as you here display. What will you come to eventually, in your constructive scale of ages and sizes, I can't guess. Have you proposed to yourself a prospective limit, or have you already reached it? The God Malthus I believe allows for four as an outside number, by which I presume, (putting it as delicately as I can) that all further "inside" numbers have to be suppressed. The youngest and littlest is the one that attracts me most, but that is because the ages of four and five are to me the most engagingly provocative in the years that would-be women own to. Could I have wives of that age to live with in chaste concubinage, and with the means commensurate, I would gladly marry a dozen, no—as a matter of fact, three would be enough. (AJ, Sept. 1920)

Janet had to attend official functions as an administration wife, but the occasions she really enjoyed were the unofficial ones, like the marriage of A'eed. Even Helen, now four and one-half, was considered old enough to be included. Dressed in our white cotton frocks with the bands of *broderie anglaise,* and the new straw hats with the rosettes in front, so deftly created by Nannie, we set off across the field to the nearest point where Akhmed's carriage could pick us up. His was the favorite for such expeditions, for his two white horses were less mangy than some, and went faster. They also wore decorative little net ear caps with blue tassels at the tips, which could be tossed with great effect to keep off the flies.

These droshkylike carriages had more character than elegance or comfort. For children there were snags. CRA and Janet sat on the main seat, under the dusty, collapsible hood, with Helen between them. Mary and I sat on a small seat fac-

ing them, and felt the little buttons of its black leather upholstery burning through our cotton frocks and knickers. We bal-
anced as best we could, as the curling iron handrails at the sides
of the seat were too hot to touch. The smell of sweat, and dusty
leather, the rhythmic farting of the horses as they trotted, and
Akhmed's constant cluckings and flickings of his whip were all
essential ingredients.

A'eed was a Christian Arab, and his village, some way out of
Jerusalem, was noisy with excitement when we arrived. The
church was tiny and the service in Aramaic. The bride wore
white, though the bridegroom was merely in a better version of
his usual Western-style jacket, over his galabiah. As we all
came out of the church, A'eed, his beaming face red and glis-
tening with sweat and emotion, suddenly made a grab for
Helen, and amid shouts of applause, he swung her up onto his
shoulders. Then he led the triumphant procession to the house
where the reception was to be held, his bride on his arm, and
Helen perched aloft clutching his headdress with both hands,
and flashing her huge hazel eyes regally at the delighted
spectators.

When the serious business of eating and drinking began,
nursery conventions and health strictures were thrown to the
winds. We sat delightfully on the floor on bits of matting and
quilted bedding, and tucked into our first wedding breakfast of
unleavened bread, goat cheese, golden mish-mish, green and
purple figs bursting with ripeness, and plates of the sugar-
dusty sesame shortbreads, all washed down with murky mul-
berry juice in smudged glasses.

The problem of what to do about 37 Cheyne Walk hung
over CRA all this time. Journal entries of the time give little
hint of who was living there: it certainly was not Agnes, who
had not been able to endure the solitude after her mother's
death. CRA and Janet must have discussed the house, so
closely identified for him not only with the Little Mother, but
also with the moment of its creation, when the guild was at its

zenith and the world was young. Janet had her own problems too, having to do with Godden Green, Babushka, and her brother, Nevill, for the burden of their mother's increasing feebleness was now entirely on his shoulders. By March 1921, a double decision had been reached. CRA would ask for leave and go on his own to deal with Cheyne Walk, and after his return, Janet would go to Godden Green, perhaps taking us two older children with her.

CRA sailed in April, stopping in Cairo for a mixture of business and pleasure. He wrote to Janet, giving her a rhapsodic account of three days spent in the desert with his old donkey boy Hafiz, and a typically equivocal account of a luxurious dinner party, "a trial to both my French and my digestion . . . . Egyptian politics, aspics, ices, cream, champagne, lobster mayonnaise, truffles, silver-gilt spoons and forks . . . . The dinner was followed by a *Soirée,* a dance, and poker for substantial stakes! I wilted into bed at 2.30 and pined for a hard-boiled egg in the desert with Hafiz, though I confess to thoroughly enjoying the flesh-pots on occasion. But I like to share them with YOU!" (AJ, Apr. 1921).

He arrived in London before the end of April, meaning to see Willie Strang, only to hear that he had died. To soften the impact of this blow, Janet wrote him a little note of welcome to greet him at her mother's at Godden Green. It touched him greatly. The translation from Jerusalem to England, where he had not been since that brief, cold winter's leave of 1918–1919, would have been difficult in the best of times. But alone, on a mission, which he must have been trying for ages not to face, he needed more than a little courage. Janet, for all the mixed and bitter associations that 37 Cheyne Walk held for her, half wished she could have been there to stand beside him.

CHAPTER 18
TWO HOUSES
1921

CRA reported back at the beginning of May.

> I felt like a ghost coming back to earth . . . . If any-
> one meeting me in Oakley Street on my way thither
> had offered me a price for the house there and then, I should
> have accepted it . . . . But it was all quite different when I got
> there. If I ever do live in London again, it's the only place I
> want to live in. I don't as you know, my darling, say this be-
> cause you have said the reverse . . . . It's got nothing to do
> with the "nineties," or because I built it, or because it was my
> home and often not a happy one. But I suppose for a com-
> plexity of motives . . . and because the little mother's spirit is
> still watching over the place, and I can't bring myself to sell
> the ashes until I'm absolutely obliged to do so.
> (AJ, 2 May 1921)

As directed in his mother's will, her ashes were buried in the
garden.

He went down to Godden Green and found it lovely in the
spring.

> But that too was full of ghosts, and your dear Mother was
> very, very old . . . . Poor soul! With all her warmth of heart,
> we know she has no philosophy . . . . I wonder what you and I
> will be like when our turn comes, and whether our children
> will suffer us gladly, or be bored, or want to run away and
> hide? . . . Would you like to spend the end of your days at
> G.G? I shouldn't mind if I had my library, and if those dread-
> ful roofs and windows could be reconstructed. I began dream-
> ing plans of it last night. Your father's ghost did not rebuke
> me. (ibid.)

Janet's feelings about the future of 37 Cheyne Walk were
clear. "I have been reading and re-reading your last two letters

of May 2nd and 4th, and yesterday, on receipt of the second, I went straight to the Post Office and wired: 'AUCTION.' . . . It seemed a positive instinct, which you may regard or ignore,— and it may tip the scale in the other direction! But such is my conviction, it is more than an 'opinion' as you know, I have held it all along." She explained that they could not afford to live in such a house:

> Do NOT think me wanting in reverence for the dead; for you know, though Grannie and I were of such opposed TEMPERA-MENTS in SOME things, our OPINIONS and convictions were united on many points . . . . I greatly respected and admired her, and I know she was fond of me, and adored our children. BUT— . . . IF we return in say two or five or seven years, you will then be 60 or 63 or 65, and I think it improbable that a job of a large and highly salaried nature will fall to you AT THAT AGE, in this century of young "blood" and clichés of "too old at 40" etc.:—Ergo, we may quite possibly have to live on our rents, our debts, plus what remains (after my mother's death) of my patrimony, and bring up our children on that . . . .
>
> I wish to keep my strength at the crucial time (I shall then be 45, or 47 or 50) of my life for my children, and to help edu-cate them and launch them, and not waste it going up and down those stairs, and "keeping things nice" as Grannie did, poor soul! For her I suppose it was worth it, as the house stood for her for an IDEA, a complex Vita Nuova from the old terrible life you had freed her from. (AJ, 18 May 1921)

Having shot her bolt for the moment, she went on to tell him about the eruption of violence in Palestine in May. "I wonder how much you have heard of the terrible riots at Jaffa, Jenin and other places? Mr Storrs lives in his uniform, and spends all his time walking about the Old City propitiating and talking to Arabs and Beduins who have been pouring in" (AJ, May 1921).

Prince George was due to visit Palestine, and there must have been anxious discussions as to whether the visit should go ahead. But it would have been confessing to an inability to maintain law and order if the visit had been canceled, and on 20 May the *IREN DUEK*, as Mary spelled it in a letter to CRA, docked at Jaffa with two other ships. Mary's letter continued, "Mummie is going to the Samuels to see the 4th Prince of the King, and then she is going back to Mrs Look who is receiving.[1] Nannie is making her go, would not you?" (ibid.).

The balls and receptions that followed gave scope to the sharpness of Janet's pen. At Mrs. Luke's reception, held in the former German administration building, now Government House, she thought:

> The old Germans must have turned in their graves to sniff the oil lamps blazing in blue and pink globes round the two stories of the cloisters, and coyly hidden in banks of greenery; and to see the naked backs and breasts of Mrs Bramley and Co clasped to the blue and gold breasts of the Officers of the "Iron Duke," whirling to the jazziest Military band ever heard in Jerusalem.[2] . . . Mr Storrs and I sat on the dais and tore everyone to shreds! . . .
>
> The food was bad, and I should say cheap; but you must save on something, and some people prefer spending it on the outside of their tummies (I cannot say backs in this case!). Mrs Heron was WONDERFUL in a creation of majenta satin![3] Very abridged above and below, and very tight in the middle, with an "overflow meeting in front." (ibid.)

The last phrase was borrowed from Monica, Ronald Storrs's sister.

The round of public entertainments went on.

> On Saturday we had a terrible party at Government House, when we had to CURTSY to Prince George (Moi qui vous parle!), and we were all arranged around that enormous room

---

1. Mrs. "Look" was the wife of Harry Luke (1884–1969), the deputy governor of Jerusalem.

2. Mrs. Bramley was the wife of the head of police.

3. Mrs. Heron was the wife of Colonel Heron, the chief public health officer.

like samples of coffee. Mr Cust asked me if I would rather be a Notability of Jerusalem, or an Administration Wife, so I chose the latter! And found myself with the Keith-Roaches, Mrs Richmond etc; instead of with the Vesters, and Sheikh Amin, etc.[4] It was boring, but fairly select, and NOT a Zoo, and quite nice things to eat . . . . Nothing amusing happened.

On Friday Mr Storrs gave a VERY choice, short, and small party (about 45 of the best vintage only) for the Prince—a little music, and a one-act play, all very comfily and nicely done in his best manner. We are all amused and intrigued at Mrs Vester going straight down the Primrose Path, and frequenting EVERY one of these worldly orgies, Anna-Grace in her train, and both looking so pretty—each in a new dress each time, and never a *soupçon* of the Second Coming! I hear Mrs Spafford is very "exercised" about it . . . . You see how worldly I become—you must return and give me a good dose of idealism! (ibid.)

Mrs. Spafford was the matriarch of the American Colony, and Mrs. Vester and Anna-Grace her daughter and granddaughter.

When Janet's long letter finally arrived, he wrote, "I had already decided as to 37 . . . . [T]he auction is planned for October" (AJ, 2 June 1921). She must have sighed with an almost too great relief. Yet it would have been tinged with remorse in case the written word, without the warm sound of her voice, might have made it harder for him to bear.

One thing that made him smile wryly was that both the Victoria and Albert Museum and Chelsea Public Library had asked him for proofs of his Essex House Press books to display "among the finest examples of 19th century typography and craftsmanship! Isn't it amusing, now that it's all over, and one is never likely to produce again, to come back to England, a

---

4. Harry Cust (1896–1962) was aide-de-camp to the high commissioner. Edward Keith-Roach (1885–1954) was an officer in Palestine at the end of World War I, and stayed on to become governor of northern Judaea and then of Jerusalem. He and his wife, Vi, had two boys, Martin and Tony, who were our contemporaries and friends.

sort of Rip Van Winkle, and find oneself regarded as a classic!"
(AJ, 29 May 1921). At the end of June, having "said goodbye,
perhaps for ever, to that beloved spot, the Magpie and Stump,"
he was on his way back to Jerusalem (AJ, 14 May 1921).

Janet wrote once more, hoping to catch him in Athens,
bringing him up-to-date on Jerusalem gossip.

> I dined *tête-à-tête* with Mr Storrs last night (well, I say
> DINED, but it was . . . as he said to Sa'id, a "damnable din-
> ner"!). But he was really delightful, and I appreciated the
> compliment of being asked by myself . . . . I think he really
> misses you . . . .
>
> It is a most anxious and worrying time politically, and of
> course he gets pelted by both—or all—parties. We discussed
> Heaven and Hell, divorce, intrigues (*à propos* Harry Cust and
> the Duchess of Rutland and, subsequently, Mrs Rubens (now
> Lord Sackville's OPEN MISTRESS), Faust, Dante, Homer,
> Jerusalem,—etc. etc.; and then he sat down and played most
> deliciously before his car swirled me home. (AJ, June 1921)

CRA and Janet had hoped to have at least a fortnight together on his return, but just as they were about to enjoy this
too brief moment, the telegram announcing Babushka's stroke
must have come. Booking for trains and boats was thrown to
the winds, and with a small suitcase each, an incorrectly remembered hotel address in Port Said, and an overoptimistic
hope of picking up a ship once there, Janet, Mary, and I left
Jerusalem.

What with anxiety about her mother, and about leaving
Helen and Prue, the whole thing must have been a nightmare
for Janet. An added complication was that all four of us were
suffering from whooping cough, so that Janet ought not really
to have been traveling with us. For Mary and myself, it was all
excitement, one of the great moments being hanging our heads
out of the train window and not whooping, while Janet felo-
niously signed documents to say we were not suffering from
any infectious disease. We had never consciously been a party

to adult deception before, and it made us feel deliciously grown-up and wicked!

When we got to Port Said, there was no boat, and nothing to be done except wait. After several days, an enormous liner majestically made its appearance. Janet impulsively dashed down to the quayside and, with us trailing behind her, summoned a willing dinghy to row us straight out to the ship. Having climbed up the longest-ever series of steps slung at her side, she demanded to be taken straight to the captain. Her manner was so imperious that no one demurred, and we were soon standing in the captain's incredibly elegant quarters, shining with polished woodwork, brass rails, and crimson plush. Behind an enormous desk stood a white-uniformed figure with eyes as blue as the Mediterranean. Janet came straight out with an urgent request for berths for the three of us. The captain seemed to think he could oblige, and asked politely where it was she wanted to go. "We're bound for Australia," he added. Janet's consternation was comic!

The other thing that made the trip memorable for us children was "the Diamond Star." Its existence was disclosed to us only in the privacy of our cabin, on the first night after we had managed to get passages on a French boat bound for Marseilles. Janet had never been known to wear it, its Victorian design being anathema to CRA, but when she undressed for bed, she disclosed the exciting fact that the mysterious swelling in her stays (she had gone back to these hated garments after the last of us was born, as a protection against total loss of figure) was the Diamond Star, wrapped in tissue paper and sewn into the stays' reinforced pink cotton lining. She put her finger on her lips to make the occasion more impressive, and explained in a hushed voice that it was in case of Dire Emergency—for there was no doubt about it, they were real diamonds!

Janet's homecoming to Godden Green was not much less complicated than CRA's had been to 37 Cheyne Walk. But at least Nevill was there on and off, and the two slipped easily into

43. Nevill Forbes at the piano, Godden Green

their old close relationship. What was to happen if Babushka were to remain bedridden for years? How well should—or indeed could—things be kept up, with Janet in Jerusalem and Nevill increasingly involved in his Oxford academic life? In between such discussions, Nevill would sit down at the piano

194

and just play. In 1921, the piano was still the standard grand on which Janet had accompanied her father and his musical friends before her marriage. Nevill would settle down at it in the curved bay of the three Gothic windows, and play marvelously, always from memory: Debussy, César Franck, Poulenc, Fauré, Du Parc, Palmgren, Milhaud, Renaldo Hahn, as well as Rachmaninoff and Tchaikovsky and, probably for the benefit of Babushka in the room above, Glinka and Mussorgsky.

The Godden Green we came back to that summer seemed much the same as the one we remembered from earlier visits. In fact, the house itself had changed little since Janet's childhood. The creepers had become more luxuriant, and the mauve wisteria now surrounded the bedroom window. We spent long hours in the garden, and were not much impressed, after Jerusalem, by what was said to be one of England's hottest summers. Outside, we were free as air. Indoors, we had to be quiet so as not to disturb Babushka, and perhaps even more the two formidable nurses who had established themselves in an anteroom, playing cards.

When summoned to the sickroom, we would go in to see Babushka without undue distress. Long, glazed chintz curtains framed the big windows. Within them hung others, soft and frilly-edged. And inside them again, biscuit-colored blinds, usually half pulled down by a cord tipped with an ivory acorn. Near one of the windows stood a huge dressing table, swathed in frilled white muslin, with a fascinating collection of silver-topped bottles and pots, and hand mirrors and brushes of polished, yellowing ivory, inlaid with ebony or silver initials. In the big bed lay Babushka, her white hair done up in leather curlers, to be released only for the doctor's visit. She just lay there, her soft old hands flecked with brown marks and still covered with rings, straying at times over the bedclothes.

"Good evening, Babushka," we would say. And if I was in her line of vision, she would usually respond with: "And how is

Dr. Carrick today?" I took this question to be some curious adult joke best ignored. Only years later, when albums of old photographs of her Russian youth were found, did I discover how much I, with my cropped hair, was like her doctor-brother, George, when a boy. He had died in St. Petersburg in 1908.

By September, it seemed fairly clear that Babushka's state had stabilized, and Janet began to worry less about her than about the other half of her family in Jerusalem. By the end of the month, our return trip was fixed, at least as far as Trieste, where it was thought we could more easily pick up a boat. We went in to say good-bye to Babushka, who had said she had something she wanted to give to each of us. We stood dutifully while the old ringed fingers fumbled in the bedclothes. Then, into our hands, she pressed a tiny flat object, matchbox-size and biscuit-thin. "Here's an icon for each of you—to remember your Babushka by," she said. And we were pulled down into the old-age-smelling flannel nightgown for a good-bye kiss.

We had in the first instance no idea what they were, but their mauvish gray velvet backs lay softly in our palms. Once home in the Wadi el Jose, several boring rest-time hours were spent with spit and a hanky cleaning them, until at last their shining brass- and silver-engraved surfaces disclosed on Mary's a tiny Virgin and child, and on mine a Christ with hand raised in blessing. They are surely of no great antiquity or value, but a small link with the Russia of 130 years ago.

CHAPTER 19

IF I FORGET THEE, O
JERUSALEM, 1922

CRA was not good at writing the newsy letters that Janet longed for while she was away, and he gave an insufficient account of how the little ones were getting on without her. But in September, a letter arrived for Mary and myself, full of his rhyming in the style of Southey that we loved so much:

> Last night, tell your dear Mother, Mr Richmond and I went for a Dog Hunt in the Wadi el Jose. We went with pistols and a posse of Police, six of us all together. We rounded up 40 dogs! Pariahs! In a Bedouin camp. They had been keeping us awake for a week. We shot three. Then there was a great baying and praying and gainsaying, and a kneeling and an appealing and a squealing, and a mighty denying, and a replying and lying and a crying, with explanations, and hesitations and declamations and prevarications, ending at last with a general Kalaaming and becalming and disarming. Bedouin women in draperies and painted faces came out and kissed our hands, and called on Allah. (AJ, Sept. 1921)

And a great deal more in the same vein!

Janet, Mary, and I arrived back at the beginning of October to face the biggest problem of all our time in Jerusalem: the Drainage Scheme. During 1921, the British administration had built a waterborne sewage system for the mainly Jewish suburbs around Me'a She'arim, with money given by the Zionist Commission. The system broke down, and the sewage was deposited in the mainly Arab district where we lived. As CRA put it in his *Palestine Notebook*:

> The drainage *débacle* in the Wadi el Jose is for us, and many others, very serious. The administration is of course responsi-

ble. It accepted the money from the Zionist Commission and failed to carry out the work effectively . . . . The best Moslem residential area in the city has now been flooded with the drainage of Measchoerim, and a pool of liquid sewage lies, at the moment of writing, in the lovely valley between the Grand Mufti's house and ours . . . . The property owners, all Moslem, are very angry. They have sent in petition after petition, and all have been ignored . . . . Had the situation been reversed, and the drains of a Moslem slum voided into the best Jewish quarter, there would have been an outcry in Israel as would have moved Wall Street and Park Lane . . . . Meantime I have told the Administration that unless another house is found me, and within a certain time,—I go.[1]

So, just as the garden in the Wadi el Jose was beginning to take shape, and the house itself had finally become home, with the books, dolls' prams, and even the piano from 37 Cheyne Walk, we were stunk out, as CRA put it.

Feelers were put out to find another house, even a temporary one, and when Ernest Richmond and his family went on home leave, we moved into their house in Katamun. To start with, it was hoped that our departure from the Wadi el Jose might be for only a short time, until the matter of the Drainage Scheme was dealt with, so we did not vacate the house there completely. It merely became known as "the Wreck" because, like Robinson Crusoe, we were constantly going back to fetch something. When the Richmonds came back, the Keith-Roaches went away, and their extraordinary house up on the Mount of Olives became, though we did not yet know it, our last home in Palestine.

Jerusalem has always attracted more than its share of eccentrics, whether prophets or kings, soldiers or administrators—or architects. One of this last group, of Swiss or Bavarian extraction, had built the Red House, so-called because of its high-pitched vermilion roof. It had an enormous, space-wasting

---

1. Ashbee, *A Palestine Notebook,* 205.

central hall, like a castle keep, with a staircase to the upper floor clinging to its inside wall. Its position on the crest of the Mount of Olives added to its keeplike character, and the views it commanded, except to the west, which was blocked by the Böcklin glories of the old German administration building, were breathtaking in every light. We moved into this remarkable house with at least some of our paraphernalia. Living as we now were, up on the Mount of Olives, meant other changes in our lifestyle as well. Miles from our old haunts, there were no more donkey rides to Herod's Gate, no more casual shopping in the Old City, no more chance walks around the walls, and, of course, no more American Colony school, which was now too far away for the daily walk.

It is difficult to guess how much of the final decision to hand in his resignation was CRA's and how much had to do with Janet's reactions to frequent house-moving and the general uncertainty. They would have discussed it endlessly. She knew too well how much he had been enjoying the work of recent years to think of trying to sway him, and her own lifestyle had been nothing if not stimulating! There were, almost certainly, other forces at play behind the scenes, and the famous—or infamous—Drainage Scheme was only the last straw.

Foremost among the things that CRA felt were changing the nature of his work was the Zionism of increasing numbers of the civilian administration, of men such as Wyndham Deedes and Norman Bentwich, even of Herbert Samuel himself.[2] CRA's Arab sympathies, too, must have been becoming ever more apparent, and his opinion, which he made no effort to conceal, that everything beautiful in Palestine, apart from nature, was Islamic cannot have endeared him to some of his colleagues. Perhaps too, the affinity between CRA and Storrs

---

2. Wyndham Deedes (1883–1956) was a civil secretary. Though a Gentile, he was an ardent Zionist and a friend of Chaim Weizmann. Norman Bentwich (1883–1971) was a barrister and the first attorney general in Mandate Palestine.

was beginning to wear thin. If there were signs that he was thinking of abandoning his post before his contract was up, then his Drainage Scheme protest must have been greeted as heaven-sent by the people who wanted to be rid of this turbulent priest of the Arts and Crafts.

He resigned in March 1922, giving as his sole reason the fact that he had been driven from his house by the failure of the Scheme. His resignation was accepted with alacrity. Storrs wrote:

Dear Ashbee

I have received your letter of yesterday in which you place your resignation in my hands. Your reasons, which I fear you consider sufficient and final, leave me no alternative but to accept it. In presenting it to the Council, I shall not fail to convey to them the gist of your message, but I would like to place on record now my keen regret at the step you have found it necessary to take, together with the debt of gratitude I owe you for the remarkable work you have accomplished for the Council, for the Society, and so for the City of Jerusalem. Both in the work actually done, and in the principles of future work that you have established, you will have left upon the City an ineffaceable and most honourable sign of the care, skill and the imaginative insight and foresight which you have lavished upon it. From the personal point of view, I need hardly say how much I feel the severance of a connection and an intimacy, and the departure of a colleague whose friendship I greatly prize.

Believe me, yours sincerely.
(AJ, 11 Mar. 1922)

The letter was impossible to fault, and difficult to accept as other than genuine. If CRA was bluffing, then this flat acceptance of his bluff must have left him near tears. If, on the other hand, he was driven to resign by frustration and hopelessness, then he would have read Storrs's honeyed words with a mixture of cynical rage, admiration for the turn of phrase, and bitter regret.

We did not leave for another six months or so, and life continued, apparently unchanged. In May, we all went to a great send-off at the American Colony for Mrs. Vester, who was going to the United States to try to get American citizenship for her German husband. The garden parties in which Janet took part, and in which we children roamed among the official guests, continued, with Herbert Samuel moving about, as CRA always said, "in his best bronze mask." And all the while, forever and forever, between the trunks of the tall pines, there stretched the Judaean desert, not green and pleasant, but infinitely and subtly beautiful. But the Golden String that had led us in at the gate "built in Jerusalem's wall" had almost unwound itself.

Janet was soon to be faced, again, with removal to an uncertain destination, with no prospect of income other than her father's railway investments. The two of them must have talked about it after we children were all in bed, sitting outside in the early-evening dark, looking out over the few lights of Bethany and the other distant and scattered Arab villages. First stopgap thinking for CRA was another lecture trip to the United States, though his heart was not greatly in it. For Janet and us four, it was perhaps winter in some modest hotel in the south of France, where postwar inflation was making living, for the moment, very cheap for the British. Ultimately, the only home that could at least temporarily receive such a collection of family and possessions was Godden Green, which at least had enough bedrooms, even with Babushka and her hospital ménage in one wing. Provence too, would be a good transition from the warmth of Palestine to the rigors of England, and learning some French would be a bonus. It would give a breathing space to sort out the tangled emotions that would follow from leaving official life and the stimulating, exasperating, beautiful "El Khuds." They must both have known (though Storrs had not yet coined the phrase) that "[t]here is no promotion after Jerusalem."

I remember nothing except the actual moment of farewell, as starkly as if it were now, and as awful as only the partings of childhood, and perhaps very old age, can be. How COULD we leave Jerusalem? The walls and the golden onions of the Russian church in the Garden of Gethsemane—the best place ever for hide-and-seek! The Arab cemetery where we used illicitly to play house in the cradlelike tombs ("All those tiny dead people digged in," as Prue once said). The scents of pepper tree and eucalyptus, of piles of figs and mish-mish; the fly-twitching flanks of mangy donkeys, the scarlet underwings of startled grasshoppers, the blinding forecourt of the Dome of the Rock; the incense-smelling, candlelit interior of the Holy Sepulchre; the sad mutter of the mourning Jews; the jackal hosts of Midian howling in the velvet dark of the Wadi el Jose.

HOW COULD WE LEAVE JERUSALEM? But the old cars were waiting; everything and everybody was stuffed in or tied on, and the good-byes were being said.

And then I looked at Waardi. The checked scarf tied around her crizzly, graying hair was a little crooked, her hands twisted in her crumpled blue apron, the tears poured down her lined black face.[3] My own misery welled up, and I flung myself at her and was enveloped in a great wet, noisy embrace of grief.

The car doors banged, a last wave, and the strange cortege moved off.

Jerusalem-the-Golden, with boiled, watered-down milk, and almond-butter blessed, the "City on a hill which cannot be hid," the Golden Bowl filled with Scorpions, to which Blake's string had led us, blurred through tears into the September dust.

---

3. *Crizzly* is an Ashbee family word, meaning "crimped and curly."

CHAPTER 20
RESHUFFLING THE PACK
1922–1929

A SOLITARY journal entry by CRA in October 1922 reads: "Leaving Jerusalem after four and a half years is rather like, as Janet says, waking up from a rather pleasant dream out of 'Alice in Wonderland.' 'Why, they're only a pack of cards after all!' And look at the house we were trying to build!" (AJ, Oct. 1922).

Now he seemed outside it all, and from the moment we arrived in Provence he was engrossed in writing *A Palestine Notebook,* in which he edited the journal entries of the past four years into a vivid and idiosyncratic account of his experiences in Jerusalem. By November, he had sent the first draft to Ernest Richmond, the only member of the administration whose ideas were close to his own, and then started recasting it in less libellous form!

In December, he left for England to take a ship for his lecture tour of America, while our destination was the planned cheap hotel in Provence. This time, CRA's lectures included "Old and New Egypt," "The Survival of the Arts and Crafts" (with a Jerusalem slant), and, much more daring, Zionism. There is a brief note from me in January: "My Lovely Daddsey, I hope very much that you do like America, and that you do not have to bear Mr Store's company on the boat" (AJ, Jan. 1923). (Richmond had written that Storrs was also going to the United States, for fund-raising.) "I had it in my power," CRA wrote to Janet from New York, "to try to arrange a lunch of influential New Yorkers for him, but declined the questionable distinction" (ibid.).

In the wintry solitude of Bandol, Provence, Janet was left to organize what she could by way of schooling for her brood. We

44. The Ashbee children with Hélène Giadoux on the beach at Bandol, Provence, ca. 1923

did our daily piano practicing among the palms of the echoing salon, and once a week we went to Toulon by train for Dalcrose dancing classes, which made a break. And we spent enjoyable hours playing with new French friends on the huge springtide deposits of seaweed on the deserted beach. Janet had constant battles with the pompous and autocratic maître d'hôtel, who obviously resented his winter respite being interrupted by a horde of children, and who was stingy with the butter. But the empty hotel and the advantageous exchange rates brought visiting friends: Nevill and Nurse Parsons came, and a car was hired for a week's tour of Arles, Nîmes, and Avignon. We became fond of our only real uncle, even if we older ones laughed a little, secretly, at his old-Bettyishness. He was almost timorously gentle, and very generous.

Janet pondered the future. With Godden Green as the starting point, schools would have to be in nearby Sevenoaks. A
French one run by two sisters, the Mademoiselles Honorée,
had been suggested, and CRA was deputed to go and look it
over on his way to America. As usual, his information was
sketchy, "a mere note," Janet complained. "I can see you are getting thoroughly spoilt, and the antiquated boilers and absence
of cream at Godden Green will be a sore blow!" (AJ, Mar.
1923). In a later letter, she said that she thought "100 dollars
doesn't sound very flourishing if net result of tour. I am laying
in some clothes and all the children's school uniforms, which
are fabulously cheap here, both stuff and making" (ibid.). But
CRA could report that his last lecture, "Modern Light on
Ancient Egypt," had been broadcast: "The little black receiver
with holes round is just in front of my table." He added that he
felt this "tapping of the sound-waves" seemed to contain "wonderful possibilities" (AJ, Apr. 1923).

Janet set off for England in mid-April 1923. Her "harrowing
letter" describing the event caught up with him in
Philadelphia, but has not survived. "You poor dear, I do see you
in the midst of all your worries with Cooks, and passports, and
French officials . . . and luggage and tickets, and four little girls
all feverishly excited, and Miss Hands laying down the law . . . .
I wish I could turn over to you some of the many motor cars
and travelling facilities that my numerous friends here shower
on me" (ibid.).

At the end of April, he was back from what Laurence
Housman called "his dip into the good-hearted, optimistic
crudities of American life," and later that year *A Palestine
Notebook* appeared (ibid.). Ernest Richmond sent him reports
of reactions in Jerusalem: "The *Palestine Weekly* gave it two
columns of abuse. The High Commissioner with twinkling eye
used the word 'malicious' in speaking of it, but his eye still
twinkled. Ronald Storrs can't smile about it, he is furiously
angry" (AJ, Feb. 1924).

45. Janet Ashbee with Mary and Felicity at Godden Green, ca. 1924

As for us children, an elderly hired car took Mary, Helen, and myself daily to the French ladies' school, resplendent in our purple blazers, striped cotton frocks, and white socks, carrying our unfamiliar tennis rackets. We learned horseback riding, though we never had our own ponies. We went to art classes, where another gentle, arty woman in seaweed-colored weaves, amber beads, and pewter brooches had taken over the same Lime Tree Studio where Janet had been initiated thirty-odd years before. And there were dancing classes at Sevenoak's Crown Hotel, to which we carried our pom-pommed bronze dancing pumps in embroidered linen shoe bags. We trekked down to Seal church on Sundays, rain or shine, and there was a good deal of reading aloud—long narrative poems from

CRA (not many children have heard ALL of William Morris's *Earthly Paradise*!) and classical novels from Janet—while we darned innumerable stockings.

In February 1924, Babushka died. Only now did the whole question of where we should put down real roots come to a head. CRA had now practically no regular income, so Janet was in the stronger bargaining position, though that was not really the way she looked at it. Godden Green had to be sold, at least on paper, to somebody, and it seemed that an advantageous arrangement could be made among Janet, her brother, Nevill, and the trustees of various settlements. CRA's architectural expertise would be available to reduce this Victorian gem—unrecognized as such in the pre-Betjeman era—to something more manageable. A deal was struck, and as soon as the house became legally theirs, CRA threw himself into the attack on what he had always felt was a monstrosity. As he had hoped, Janet's father did not rebuke him, nor haunt or hamper the demolition of the grouped and coruscated mock-Tudor chimneys, nor the slicing off of the steep-pitched purple-and-green-striped roof. Bathrooms were added, the servants' wing and

46. The Godden Green house as transformed in 1924–1925

dairy were swept away, and the coach house and stables were converted into cottages for the gardener and for renting out.

Then a school crisis loomed. During the summer of 1924, the Mademoiselles Honorée, who were more faded than had at first been suspected, sold out. The new head was English, and wore an artificial silk jersey adorned with a long string of artificial pearls. Real or nothing was Janet's criterion of breeding. We must have brought home reports of undesirable aspects of school life, for Janet asked for an interview, during which the headmistress said, unguardedly, "If I'd known running a girls' school was going to be so difficult, I'd have opened a kennels instead." We were removed forthwith!

47. C. R. Ashbee with Helen and Prue at Godden Green, ca. 1924

Two other schools were settled on. Prue and Helen went to an open-air school, because Prue had developed bovine tuberculosis glands, and they did most of their lessons outdoors in a breezy atmosphere of brown overalls, woolly caps, rabbits, and guinea pigs. Mary and I moved to what was almost a dame school, with a born teacher as headmistress. Something about her governess-like appearance probably made Janet feel at home with Miss de Ville. She was barely five feet tall, ageless, and wore a pince-nez. Her slightly graying brown hair was pegged up with tortoiseshell combs into a collapsing bun. She wore a pewter brooch on a black velvet band around her throat, and was always dressed in a brown alpaca frock liberally dusted with chalk. She taught the Top Class—there were only two— everything except maths and geography; science of any sort was nonexistent. We loved it, and were sublimely unaware of how much our poetry-based home culture irritated her. She must have let fly to someone, who maliciously told Janet "how perfectly sickening those Ashbee children are! Whenever I say, 'Now I don't suppose any of you children know a poem called so and so,' Mary and Felicity ALWAYS SAY 'Oh yes, we do! Daddy read it to us last night.' or 'Mummie was telling us about it at breakfast.' It is absolutely maddening." "She can console herself," Janet remarked, "with their rotten arithmetic!" (AJ, July 1925).

For Janet, once she was again installed in her childhood home, a feeling of almost feudal responsibility for "the Green" began to assert itself. Godden Green was still no more than a hamlet, with a pub, a sub–post office, and some two dozen laborers' cottages, most of them attached to the great Sackville estate of Knole. There were also about six gentry-owned houses. But as none of the residents of them seemed interested in doing anything for their immediate neighborhood, Janet took on the duty herself, with particular reference to the thirty-five or more "cottage children." She started her own little Sunday school, a nondenominational mix of Bible stories, child-geared hymns, and Negro spirituals. She wrote to CRA, "I am having a little tea-party here on Wednesday for all the mothers on the Green with babies under Sunday School age, and am going to start a tiny clinic like the Broad Campden one. They are all thrilled as no one does anything."

She also went further afield in her effort to teach us children that even our modest privileges entailed some duties. In the last two years before her marriage, she had had some connection with the Shaftesbury Society, and now she found that one of her younger Forbes cousins was doing voluntary work there in connection with what were then known as cripple parlors. Through her, each of us was put in touch with a disabled child, whom from then on we wrote to and knitted scarves or socks for. Several of our school friends were even roped in to do likewise. Today, it would smack of do-goodism, an echo of the Victorian theme of *Ministering Children.*

But the thing grew. To letters and socks was added a summer day's outing for each mother and her disabled child, with rail tickets sent in advance, and a taxi to meet them at our local railway station. Then a coach was hired that brought the crippled children's entire families to Godden Green, to be waited on and entertained by us and sent home to Battersea in the evening with boxes of vegetables from the garden, and huge bunches of flowers from the herbaceous border, Janet's pride.

My charge, Jimmy, was a four year old in leg irons, only about seven years younger than me, who had been abandoned and taken in by a childless and penniless couple as their own. When his adoptive mother died four or five years later, his father, a gas case from World War I, could no longer cope, and Janet got Jimmy into an orphanage and maintained him there. With better feeding he soon abandoned his leg irons, and went happily on to train as a carpenter. As a pastime, he joined the Territorials, was called up at the start of World War II, and was at Dunkirk. He told me afterward that, as he lay on the beach hoping against hope for one of the little ships to pick him up, there were only two thoughts in his mind, "Me ole Dad and Godden Green." He was killed on the Anzio beachhead, to Janet's rage and grief.

Once CRA had finished altering the house at Godden Green, he was so restive that Janet encouraged him to join his American headmistress-friend Caroline Ruutz-Rees in Venice.[1] She wrote to him there, saying that there were "no maids in sight . . . so don't come rushing back and want huge house-parties . . . . I am so very glad you are having a perfect orgy of your favourite old white-haired ladies! I shall expect to see you back very refreshed and full of information and beautiful visions, and memories of hot sunshine and sea water, and architecture, and endless discussions about Rabelais and Aristotle and all those worthies" (AJ, Aug. 1925).

After Venice he went to Berlin to see Arthur Wauchope, who was now heading the Army of Occupation there. Janet had urged him to take this opportunity of renewing their twenty-five-year-old friendship, and wrote to him there, "Of course I shall never believe that you and Arthur have met until I get a joint letter to that effect signed together. I must say I envy you that part of your holiday. I should like to see Berlin again after 32 years, and in such a very changed guise" (AJ, Sept. 1925). In the autumn of 1926, she was able to.

She spent ten days with Arthur Wauchope, and they were a relaxation and a joy—apart from one extraordinary and unexplained explosion on his part, apparently referring in some way to my birth. Janet nearly packed her bags and left. But a long walk through the woods alone with him put things right, and it was never mentioned again.

> The great General apologised for his brutality so fully, I had
> to forgive him! . . . I have learnt many things, and guessed

---

1. Caroline Ruutz-Rees (1865–1954) was the potent, brilliant, unmarried founder and headmistress of the high-powered private school Rosemary Hall in Greenwich, Connecticut. She was a friend of Janet as well as CRA.

many others . . . . You are absolutely wrong about the "unconsciously homogenic." Ten days spent with him almost alone have convinced me of this. You know I can generally tell. There is something very wonderful about him—unique, compelling. I am told here, though he is so gentle, he is the "sternest, most feared, and best obeyed English General they have ever had here"; I can well believe it. His steel grey eyes can command as well as soften under music or poetry, and his enchanting humour can turn a double-edged dagger when roused. Well! You will say it is a good thing I am coming back on Saturday! *Demnoch,* my love to you, my dear . . . . P.S. Thank you for making me come. It has been a wonderful experience, and I have been SO happy. (AJ, Oct. 1926)

In spite of all she had been through, there remained something almost innocent about Janet. Over the years, she should have got used to the effect she had on people, yet it often seemed to come as a surprise.

In her commonplace book there is an extra page stuck in at a later date, between two other pages of pictures, poems, and letters to do with Arthur Wauchope. It is headed "Two Strange Scenes" and dated 1926. The first scene is about Nora Tomlin, whom Janet had first met at Porthgwidden in 1901, when she met Arthur. Nora married soon afterward, but the marriage had failed: "Nora, mortally ill in bed . . . I said to her, 'Oh Nora, why did YOU not marry Arthur?' With her lovely smile she said: 'I? But of course it was YOU he was in love with!'"

The second scene: "In Berlin, Arthur and I standing by the big log fire one evening, I said: 'Arthur, you know Nora married the wrong man. Why didn't YOU marry her?' 'Oh my dear, that is plunging into very deep waters,' said Arthur, and changed the subject." CRA and Janet were already three years married when she and Arthur first met. He was too sensitive, too shrewd a judge of character, not to know that to declare his love, if he ever let his fantasies range that far, would be to destroy what became a rare and lifelong friendship.

Janet was only forty-five when we came back from Jerusalem. She threw herself into the education and emergence of her four children, but there was no getting away from the fact that life at Godden Green could never be as stimulating as the three and one-half challenging, amusing, though at times alarming years in Jerusalem. Apart from anything else, she was almost immobilized in the country. Carriages and horses, with the attendant paraphernalia of coachman, footman, and groom, had vanished with World War I, and cars were as yet mainly for the older rich with their chauffeurs, or the young rich who daringly drove themselves. There was no bus service until the 1930s. Something of the helplessness engendered by this situation perhaps lies behind a passage in a letter she wrote to CRA in March 1927, having spent a day in London and lunched at the Army and Navy Stores in a "wilderness of battered English, country house ladies, embittered looking old parsons, ferocious colonels, and meeching, dim ladies who form the central block of Eaters and Shoppers" (AJ, Mar. 1927).[2] She went on to tell him how she had just "wandered right along the river front, a prey to that extraordinary malaise that used to attend me in 1898 to 1902—a mixture of fear of the unknown, of not living up to something, and not knowing one's way about life; and a curious emptiness, as of having strayed down a wrong turning in a dream . . . . I prowled past our door. That block of houses really look awfully well still, and not the least 'dated' ('Thank you!')" (ibid.). She did not allow herself to dwell on such thoughts for long.

Janet's fiftieth birthday was in December 1927. If the thought depressed her, then she should have been cheered by three letters she received, all within a month of the event. Francis Bennett, a former soldier still in touch since a first meeting in Jerusalem, wrote, "You are the only woman I know to whom I want to TELL anything" (AJ, Jan. 1928).[3] Laurence

---

2. *Meeching* roughly means "skulking."

3. E. K. "Francis" Bennett (1887–1958) was a fellow and later president of

Housman, regretting the briefness of a stay with her, wrote, "It was so NICE seeing you again, and as always, amusing! Under your sober sensibleness, you are one of the people who amuses me not scornfully, benevolently!!" (ibid.). And Frank Taylor from Philadelphia reminisced: "I gloried in seeing your astonishing beauty. I still carry a picture of the doorway in your old home in the street, framing that beauty, when I got my first thrilling sight of you at Chipping Campden. Do you mind, if I say that your strength of character and joy of living, which I realised later, made a happier and a better man of me?" (ibid.). Only a year later she was to need all such moral support and more.

In February 1929, without anything that could have been seen as a warning, Janet's brother, Nevill, committed suicide. He was not quite forty-six. The shock was the greater because she had always believed that they were close enough for her to have known if he were in any state of anxiety. A feeling of guilt was thus mixed with her sense of isolation and loss. The thought would not leave her that her too great involvement in her own family had held him back from sending her, his much loved and only sister, a cry for help.

Three years earlier, after staying with him in Oxford, she had written to CRA that, if there was any doubt in her mind, it was that Nevill ought perhaps to have got further. But, she wrote, he seemed "so happy in his lot and content, that one forgets to lament his ineffectualness, or rather, his NOT *'sich geltend machen,'* for I don't think he does really put his talent enough out to interest. But it is evident wherever he goes, he is liked and welcomed, and that, I dare say, is better than a title or the headship of a college—cosmically better, I mean" (AJ, ca. Apr. 1926). Later, she said she had always believed Nevill's suicide was due not only to a tendency to hypochondria, but also to an

---

Gonville and Caius College, Cambridge, and one of the founders of German studies at Cambridge. He was a lifelong correspondent of Janet.

unreasoning anxiety about the possibility of blackmail. The law as regards homosexuality was still unchanged, and repressive.

Nor was that the only law to be feared then. Another cruelly archaic one was still current. If you failed in a suicide attempt, unless found insane, with the prospects that that entailed, you could be tried for your own attempted murder. Nevill only partially succeeded in killing himself, but in Janet's words, his doctor, knowing what could follow, "let him go."

There was another unexplained and macabre detail that Janet spoke of only much later. On the fatal morning, some little sprigs of yew, formed into rough crosses, had been laid by an unidentified hand on the doorstep of Nevill's Oxford house. At a time perhaps nearer to superstition than we think we are today, it was taken as a sign of approaching death.

Janet must have been in a state of shock when she reached Oxford, but at least she was in time to cradle Nevill's poor, bandaged body in her arms until he died. All of us four children wrote at once from our scattered places of learning—Mary was already living with a family in Hamburg, the rest of us in various boarding schools. These loving letters, too treasured to go into the journals, were some small solace. She kept them folded in the almost shrinelike privacy of the pages about her brother in her commonplace book.

Nevill's death was a kind of watershed for Janet, another milestone passed, a gap that could never be filled. Suddenly she felt older.

I did too. I was not quite sixteen when Uncle Nevill died, and though I still had a little girl's pigtails—childhood lasted longer then—I sensed that my own childhood was already over, for it was the first time I saw my mother cry.

CHAPTER 21
DOVES ESCAPING
1929–1939

AFTER Nevill's death, Janet felt responsible for Willy, his cook and companion, so she took him on to cook at Godden Green, which he did for some years. She also employed a succession of boys, who were supposed to divide their time between the house and the garden and who, as a result, were never quite sure when to slick down their hair, or how to get the dirt out of their fingernails before hastily donning a starched cotton jacket to wait at table.

By this time, Mary had outgrown our "dame school" and had been sent, because both CRA and Janet were so concerned that our education not be competitive, to a small, intellectually unambitious girls' boarding school called Crofton Grange, near Orpington. To the extent that the school offered any education at all, her butterfly progress through it left her happy but untouched. We all followed her. Because she was happy, it was assumed that I would be too. I was not. I was constantly in trouble, wrongly (I was convinced) accused of every sin in the calendar, but stubbornly refusing to bedew the study carpet with the contrite tears that were expected. Helen, after a delayed concussion caused by a blow on the head by a lacrosse ball, developed a teenage depression that took the form of sitting whenever possible at the piano, with the pedal full down, awash with Debussy, Rachmaninoff, and Ravel; no one knew how to handle it. Prue, who was heavily dyslexic, showed every sign of wanting to get on as soon as possible with the business of living in the heterosexual world outside.

After Prue had left, Janet could not resist writing the headmistress a valedictory letter. She would like, she said, to disclose the qualities the four Ashbee girls had been labeled with, judging from their school reports over the years:

Mary: Frivolity
Felicity: Mutiny
Helen: Egocentricity
Prudence: Depravity

As she licked the envelope and put it out for the post, she must have felt considerable satisfaction. She may even have been secretly pleased that her children were so different from the norm. For my part, I wish we had been able to say, as one of Freud's sons is alleged to have said in a similar situation, "Take me away from here. I waste my precious youth!"

48. Laurence Housman, photographed by Howard Coster. Courtesy of the National Portrait Gallery, London.

The handling of teenagers was much more complicated, Janet found, than the early upbringing of the "four little girls straight from the Rue de la Paix," as Ronald Storrs had described us, walking up the aisle of St. George's Cathedral in Jerusalem. CRA was less help now than he had been when we were younger, turning what she called "a deaf nose" to the business of our puberty. And her own experience, from the 1880s and 1890s, was not much help to her. She had, in the early days of her marriage, been notably liberal and open to experiment, as this story has shown over and over again. But motherhood brought out a strength in her that was also, increasingly, conservative. After a visit to Godden Green, Laurence Housman wrote a poem about her, taking his title from Robert Louis Stevenson's story "Thrawn Janet." The old word *thrawn* means "perverse" or "cross-grained."

> *When dear Janet, on this planet*
> *Started for a life of action,*
> *Quick conclusions, rash confusions*
> *Mixed to form her chief attraction.*
> *So, of course, when she began it,*
> *Jerky was the life of Janet;*
> *Forward movements found her plastic,*
> *Novelties—enthusiastic.*
>
> *But when Janet, reproductive,*
> *Got a family and ran it,*
> *Then to all things reconstructive*
> *She opposed a face of granite.*
> *And with her four lovely daughters*
> *In the Ark took up her quarters.*
> *There she sits, to watch the shaping*
> *Of her Fate—four doves escaping!*

(dated 1930; in the possession of the Ashbee family)

The doves had not yet started to escape, but Janet hoped she was preparing them adequately for their independence.

218

Janet and CRA had always planned that we should have a year or so after school living with families in Germany or France, which is what happened, though there was always a worry about where the money would come from. In 1927, she sold some violins and the Diamond Star that she had stitched into her stays six years earlier, but for the most part she depended on investments. Whenever the post brought the fat envelopes from the bank that contained handwritten "pass books," she would clasp them unopened to her bosom in a dramatic gesture, before daring to see whether some obscure railway had ceased to pay a dividend.

Mary went to Hamburg in 1929, and Janet and I went to see her there. Janet wrote back to CRA that Mary was in her element, "'Ach-Ja-ing' and 'Herrlich-ing' with the best of them . . . though she cannot quite get over having to use four sorts of cloths to clean her wash-stand daily, and five on cleaning days!" (AJ, Jan. 1929). Then Mary went on to Paris, and I went to Hamburg, before which CRA and Janet took me to Florence in February. CRA must have been in a difficult mood, and I can remember how cold the hotels were; anyway, Janet must have reacted badly, and she wrote to him later with an apology. He apologized in his turn, though he was never one to admit to feeling guilty. His letter made her ponder over their relationship to us.

> Of course none of us two (you and I) ever will know the "side of the moon's face turned" to the other one! I often wonder what each of the children is like when I am not there. I tried several times to arrange for F. and you to go off together, and I LOVE to think of you having her to yourself, but she would not . . . . I daresay it was, as you say, her *"Feingefühl,"* . . . which made her THINK I would feel left out; a sort of point of honour. I know that she is really DEVOTED to you, and most sweetly and understandingly devoted.
>
> I am so glad . . . that you love in Felicity a trait of me. Of course I have never known what you love in me, or why, or in fact, even that you did at all, for you have kept it so very well

concealed for 32 years! But it is awfully nice to know it via Felicity! (AJ, Mar. 1930)

While I was in Hamburg, Janet and Helen came to see me. We went to one of the weekly "family evenings" of CRA's cousins, and Janet sent home a horrified account of their self-absorbed dullness: "No one suggested music or general conversation . . . . I was firmly dug in on the *Sofa-platz* with Tante Mary and a barrage of Alida's and Esther's baby-talk across us. Fifi and Helen embroidered and knitted and it got more and more Ibsen-y and dreadful!" (AJ, Apr. 1931).

In 1933, Helen went to Germany to a school for landowners' daughters, based on a farm. It was a misguided attempt to shake her out of a state of postdepression, and, because the school was in Berchtesgarten near the Austrian border, she was induced by the prospect of a half day per week of musical study in Salzburg. Janet was reassured when she delivered her there and saw "the very buxom and normal Ja-Ja maidens," but it did not work (AJ, Jan. 1933). Helen did not stay the course—the pig-slaughtering sessions were more than she had bargained for. She did, however, set up an innocent little trade-smuggling currency between Salzburg and Berchtesgarten, taking advantage of her huge hazel eyes, peachlike skin, and British passport at the frontier. And she did shake hands with Hitler, giving him *"Gruß aus England."* He had such compelling eyes, she wrote, which so appalled me when I heard—I was moving to the left at the time—that I wrote her a sisterly letter of disgust and stern reproof!

In 1931, Arthur Wauchope was appointed high commissioner in Mandate Palestine, and in 1935 he invited Janet and CRA to come and stay with him. CRA went first, stopping off in Cairo for a get-together with as many of his old students as could be mustered. Arriving in Jerusalem, he wrote, "For me the happiest moments of the day are the last few, after 11 at night, when Arthur sends 'the boys' to bed, and gives me just a little of himself. . . . I wonder how it will strike you and Fifi" (AJ, Mar. 1935). As Arthur's goddaughter, I had been included in the invitation. Janet and I set off before CRA was back, and she wrote to him from the boat, "I can't tell you how much I am enjoying this fallow and lovely time, and only wishing it were twice as long before we have to pull up our socks and 'act pretty.'" Then she gave him the home news: Mary had got into the chorus at Glyndebourne, and a portrait of mine had been in the Summer Exhibition at Burlington House—"You will really have something to go to the Academy for, now!" (AJ, May 1935).

In Jerusalem we stayed at first at the American Colony, which made Janet feel as if she had never been away, and then at Government House. "Arthur is looking very well," she wrote, "fit and spry, very comic, (his hair longer than ever, in curls and wisps), and the best company as ever, most amusing, scurrilous and naughty" (ibid.). I was, she wrote, a great success partly because I was such an "entire contrast to all the be-painted, twig-insect-like, lounging, attenuated girls here, and the hard-bitten, sterilised women who haunt the vast (*Zauber-flöte*–like) cocktail bar of the King David Hotel, a horrid place" (AJ, June 1935).

One of the highlights of the stay was the visit to our old milk woman, Ma'asouzah, whom Arthur's officials had found still living in the village of Lifta.

> F and I drove to the edge of the Lifta valley where we found Ma'asouzah, her nephew and a small son, and two donkeys waiting at 4.0 P.M. We got out and mounted astride on the two minute and wobbling creatures, who then picked their way down watercourses filled with boulders for about 1½ miles, up precipices and over moraines of stones (houses shaken down by the earthquake and never rebuilt) till we got to Ma'asouzah's new house (and her new husband's) side by side with the New Husband's Newer Wife's house! Each of them has four children by him, besides accumulations of other wives and husbands! Anyway, by 4.30 a whole army of peasants surrounded us, and all came into her lovely big room

... oranges cut into sections ... sesame-sprinkled little breads and greenish shortbread fingers; and four vast, platter-shaped breads, a bowl of olives, and four large cups of sweat tea!!! The delicacy and charm of their attentions was so remarkable in that bare, vaulted, entirely naked and unfurnished room! Plus their savage though beautiful aspect .... We were there two hours, which simply fled by in amiable chat, my Arabic returning in full force ... quite long, coherent speeches. (AJ, May 1935)

As a final honor, Janet was offered Ma'asouzah's new husband's chestnut mare to ride back to the road on, while I ambled along behind on one of the donkeys. At parting, Janet wrote, Ma'asouzah "burst into tears, kissed us all over saying we were more than her mother to her, (and even Daddy more than her father . . .)" (AJ, ibid.).

Prue chose dancing as a career. It made sense in the light of her dyslexia, and none of her sisters had chosen it—Mary trained as a singer, I was learning to paint, and Helen went to the Royal College of Music after the pig-farm episode. But it did not help Prue's difficult relationship with CRA who, in his longing for "David," had always seen her as one disappointment too many. And now she had chosen the one art form that he viewed with real distaste. He had always drawn back from dancing as a Jezebel-like activity, flaunting the emotions and tearing down defenses. After a year with the Mary Wigman Dance Group in London, she persuaded Janet that she should complete her training at the group's Dresden school. And so Janet made yet another journey to Germany to find a safe family for Prue to lodge with, safe not only in terms of respectability, but also in a wider sense, for by the summer of 1936 the Nazi shadow was beginning to lengthen across Europe.

Two months later, Prue wrote to say that she was engaged. She quoted Lao-tzu in her letter, which set the alarm bells ringing at Godden Green, as it was so out of character. And it was an unusual situation. She was underage. And Horst

Nessler was a twenty-four-year-old penniless German artist who did not know his own father, and was already at risk with the Nazi authorities because of some outspoken political cartoons. CRA advised waiting for a second letter before Janet packed her bag, and she did so. In the end, she went by train to Dresden toward the end of February 1937 (she did not attempt an airplane until she was more than seventy), planning to meet not only Horst, but also both his parents.

She wrote to CRA at once. "I am to meet first the father and then the mother early next week. Meantime, I am busy getting impressions." She went on to give a vivid description of Horst and his studio, bare of everything except minimal and "monastic" furniture, and his paintings. She found them "remarkable, influenced by Jan Breughel, Friederich, and the 18th century German landscapists; rather fairy landscape and villages, some small figures, marvellous colour and a queer light that never was on land or sea" (AJ, Mar. 1937).

She was soon fairly sure that it was "the real thing," which, coupled with the atmosphere of rising political tension, settled things. Within weeks of Janet's visit, Horst and Prue left for England. To start with, CRA put up a surprisingly Victorian obstruction to his youngest daughter's union, but the rest of the family rallied behind her, and she and Horst were married at Seal church on 28 July 1937. (Prue thereby automatically surrendered her British passport.) They then went to Zurich, where Horst thought he could best start a new artistic life.

After only six months, a passport crisis overtook them, caused by the Austrian *Anschluss*. The Third Reich was beginning to call in all the *Auslands Deutsche*. CRA was on a ship traveling to Australia, happily editing the journals into a six-volume typescript called "The Ashbee Memoirs," so Janet was cut off from his usual calm reaction. She started at once pulling what strings she had to get her "sparrows," as she called them, back to England. One who gave considerable moral support in the struggle to get reentry visas for the young couple was the

Rhodes scholar Thornton Page, and the "sparrows" had not long safely landed at Croydon airport before he and Helen announced their engagement.

Seal church thus saw a second Ashbee wedding, and Janet watched another dove escaping, this time for Chicago. At the wedding, Laurence Housman made the speech in honor of the bride's parents:

> I have at least this qualification for the entertaining task before me. I have known Janet Ashbee and CRA a good deal longer than they have known themselves. That statement I see causes some surprise. But when I first met them they did not know themselves for the good old crusted conservative characters that they really are. CRA in those days, wore the fancy dress (intellectual and sartorial) of the William Morris period of Socialism. Today, you see him sitting clothed, and in his right mind, in the conventional garb of ceremony, which enables him to qualify for the invocation of the Hymeneal anthem which begins: "Be present, awful Father, to give away the Bride." The black coat of respectability has descended on him, and he wears it as to the manner born. Yes, CRA always was a conservative, but he did not know it. I did.
>
> Janet also. The first time I saw her on her own territory, she stood like a Madonna enthroned, in a very decorative costume, with two acolytes on either side of her carrying candles. She was then CRA's best show-piece. It was a beautiful pose, but it was a pose all the same. She too has now become, either herself at last, or a changed character. Of that change, real or apparent, I composed a few years ago, the following poem. (AJ, 27 Aug. 1938)

He then recited "Thrawn Janet," and went on:

> We are here today to watch the escape of Dove no. 2. To my retrospective gaze Janet is as decorative as ever she was, but more herself: she has settled down, and become, like CRA, a good conservative. I say it with regret, for I am still myself a Socialist.
>
> But I still like Janet so much that there is only one thing

missing from this feast that I regret. In a certain African tribe it is (or was) the tribal custom (before it was tyrannously interfered with by predatory Imperialism), it was the good established custom that at the Bridal Feast the Bride's mother should be eaten.

I am so sorry that here in England we cannot be allowed that pleasure. It would have made a perfect finish to a delightful entertainment. (ibid.)

In the winter of 1938–39, CRA and Janet made their last trip to the United States, on the pretext of seeing Helen in her new life. CRA went first, in November, and Janet followed a month later, bewailing her "extreme shabbiness . . . . I shan't be able to compete at all in the well-dressed society of Greenwich and Newhaven" (AJ, Nov. 1938). But it did not stop her, when she was in Chicago with Helen and Thornton, from going to an "opulent diamond and fur-sprinkled lunch" to hear Jan Masaryk.[1] "A galaxy of 3000 or 4000 bright women, and a few men . . . ," she wrote to CRA, "a room about as big as Olympia, you would NOT have liked it, nor the ice-cream clattering that went on" (AJ, Jan. 1939). She and CRA followed each other home, and both were back well before the escape of Dove no. 3.

Mary and Ted Lewis, a lawyer, had met while she was living and studying in London, drawn together by their passion for music. They were married in July, as Helen and Prue had been, in Seal church.

---

1. Jan G. Masaryk (1886–1938) was the leader of the Czech delegation to the Paris Peace Conference and Czech minister to Great Britain from 1925 to 1938.

CHAPTER 22
WIFE TO WIDOW
1939–1942

DURING the weeks preceding the outbreak of war, Janet and CRA had had a hurried visit from the billeting officer to see what accommodation could be called upon in an emergency. "Ashbees, Godden Green," was listed as having ten bedrooms, only three of which were occupied. At this point, Mary had been evacuated with Ted's office to the north of England, I had joined the Women's Auxiliary Air Force, and Helen was in Chicago. The only child at home was Prue, with Horst and their baby, born in the middle of August, the first grandchild. CRA and Janet were elderly and had no form of domestic help; they might reasonably have refused. But in the patriotic fervor of the moment, it never occurred to them to do so. In the first week of September, they had a phone call to say that a dozen evacuee children, aged between three and thirteen, would be arriving in the next few days.

Mrs. Orford, the mother of one of our Battersea cripple families, came to help, and it was almost a reversion to a previous epoch. After tea, with hands washed and hair brushed and combed, the older children trooped into the library where, in the hushed atmosphere of oak paneling and Morris hangings, CRA read aloud to them from *Huckleberry Finn*. This regime lasted for several months, roughly during the "phony war" as it came to be known. But then Janet and CRA fell ill, she with nervous prostration, he with the onset of what proved to be cancer of the prostate gland, which was inoperable. The evacuees had to be dispersed.

CRA was in a nursing home in Sevenoaks. Janet wrote to him, recalling Abbas the Baha'i whom they had met in

Palestine twenty years earlier. "Do you remember the Old Baha and his watchword, 'Radiant Acquiescence'? I think you are most marvellously carrying out his idea, as so expressed, and I do admire and envy your power of ACCEPTANCE, as you are now, in your captivity, not kicking, but helping your recovery by philosophy and co-operation. I takes me hat off to you!" (AJ, Mar. 1940).

Janet had been told that he probably did not have more than about two years to live. She did not tell him, feeling sure that he would react no better for knowing the number of his days. Pragmatist that he was, he might simply not have taken the information in anyway. And he was not a total invalid, at least to start with, having mastered the distasteful equipment he had to use. Janet found an unofficial caregiver, Mary Murphy, who was in need of a home, to help look after him.

CRA and Janet had not long been back at Godden Green when Germany invaded the Netherlands. In the sudden panic about the possibility of a fifth column among the refugees who had been given asylum in Britain, there was a swoop by the authorities. One who vanished into an unnamed internment camp was Horst Nessler. Janet at once went into action. He was her and CRA's son-in-law, the father of their first grandchild! German or no German, they had pledged their good name for him as well as giving financial guarantees. She used what contacts in high places she still had to find out where he was and what the future held for him. It took six weeks of letter writing, phone calls, and waiting, while news bulletins told of the little ships bringing back the Dunkirk survivors, and the dogfights of the Battle of Britain crisscrossed the blue skies over Godden Green during that heartbreakingly beautiful summer of 1940.

Sometime in August, Janet heard that Horst was in Huyton camp, near Liverpool, and she went up to seek him out. In September, he was released, having volunteered for the non-combatant Pioneer Corps, and was soon chopping down trees in the Forest of Dean. Prue and their one-year-old, Conrad, left Godden Green to find a billet in a miner's cottage nearby. When there was talk of their coming home again for Christmas, and of Mary and Ted Lewis, with their new baby, Olivia, possibly coming too, Janet wrote, "A semblance of Old Times in 'Deadlock Hall.' With two grandchildren, it would be grand. Ha! ha! . . . What a star in the morning a baby in the house is" (AJ, Sept. 1940).

All these comings and goings helped to buoy her up in the face of CRA's depression about the war and the way the world was going. In May 1941, a land mine demolished four of CRA's houses on Cheyne Walk, including no. 74, the House with the Copper Door. And at the end of June, a German bomber, hurrying to escape, jettisoned its load in the garden at Godden Green. So to the depression at the loss of his architectural work was added rage at the sight of the uprooted silver-birch and tulip trees, lying broken beside the giant crater. Janet read a great deal to him, to try to counter his dark mood, and I blew in from time to time on a twenty-four- or forty-eight-hour pass. CRA could still be taken out of himself by tales of life in the WAAF, and of the people I had hitched with to get home, or tempted into an argument about the "isms" that might follow the war.

It was a strain for Janet to watch CRA's slow decline, and she had two more bouts of illness that year, and went into a local nursing home. They wrote to each other daily during these separations, mostly about the books both were reading, and the discussions they would have on her return. In her last letter—the last entry, as it happens, in the "Ashbee Journals"—she almost regretted that their being together again soon would mean an end to this enjoyable exchange!

Did she think back, now that his life was coming to an end, over their years together? Laurence Housman had seen how complex their marriage was when he had noticed that CRA, "whom you MOTHER so much, calls you his 'CHILD'" (AJ, May 1917). Through what "ages of woman" had she passed during

228

the forty-three years of their subtly changing relationship? First, the almost-schoolgirl Janet. Then the vital, clear-thinking, but unawakened "comrade-wife." Then the maturer Janet, no longer quite so easily deferring to her older husband's opinion, the sounding board for his ideas on whom he so much depended, whose sense of humor could puncture any pomposity with gentle derision. Then the bruised but not broken Janet, who had chosen "amputation" and was stubbornly going to see it through. At last, the radiantly fulfilled, childbearing Janet whose joy in motherhood put "comrade-wife" temporarily into eclipse. And then the Janet of middle age and older, who could be the sharpest critic of his writing—"dipping his pen in cotton-wool"—yet who would rise at once to his defense if she thought he had been unjustly dealt with. Despite frustrations and suppressed longings, she retained an extraordinary yet unsubservient loyalty. I remember, perhaps because the words surprised me at the time, his saying to me a week or so before he died that his marriage had been "made in heaven."

It was May 1942, and the mauve wisteria was rampaging all over the south side of the house, pushing its tendrils in at CRA's bedroom window. Perhaps, in the upsurge of emotion in that moment just before dawn, Janet's thoughts went back to their early Whitmanesque days, and the color and smell of the wisteria mingled and merged with that of lilac. As Whitman wrote in his elegy for President Lincoln,

When lilacs last in the dooryard bloomed
And the great star early drooped in the Western sky at night,
I mourned,
And yet shall mourn with ever returning spring.

She went out and gathered great armfuls of the blooms and spread them all over his body and around the room.

He looked surprisingly small in his coffin, I thought, and the heavy scent of the wisteria, forever now associated with that image, stayed with me for a long, long time.

CHAPTER 23
COMRADE-GRANDMOTHER
1942–1961

THE house at Godden Green was handed over to the army after CRA's death, and after the complications were all sorted out, Janet went to a quiet little family hotel on the north Yorkshire moors by herself to try to get adjusted. Goathland was an unsophisticated and peaceful spot, which she came to think of as a very special place. It gave her a new perspective, and a new feeling for the North, and in spite of her first insistence that she did not want to move from Kent and its family associations, she did not cling to them.

For the first three years after CRA's death, she lived in Wiltshire, first near and then with Mary who, with her growing family, was in rented accommodation near Ted's current Royal Air Force station. Toward the end of the war, Ted was moved to Morecambe, and Janet bought a small house nearby at Hest Bank. When Ted was "demobbed" (that is, demobilized), his office moved back to London, but Janet decided to stay on in this little north Lancashire seaside town.

By an incredibly lucky chance, I was able to find a cook-housekeeper for her, a woman of country stock who had worked in that capacity before the war, and was thinking of going back to it. We were both serving on the same RAF station during the last months of hostilities. A meeting between Janet and Sergeant Bond, as she then was, was arranged, and in spite of her square-pocketed, grenadier appearance, they understood each other from the first. Each recognized in the other, without the need for many words, a quality that seemed to offer the possibility of an unconventional, almost feudal relationship. In the easier democracy of the North, they always went out together as Mrs. Ashbee and Miss Bond, but at home she was, at her own request, just Dorothy. Janet would read aloud to her as she did her embroidery or sewing.

By this time, Prue's marriage to Horst, and Helen's to Thornton Page, had come apart. Helen came back to Europe with her six-year-old daughter, Tanya, in the winter of 1945–46, and from then on lived in France and Italy. Prue was living in London with her child, Conrad; Horst, who had at last acquired British citizenship, was also in London. It took Janet some time to come to terms with the breakup of two of her children's marriages. After the adjustments and sacrifices she had had to make to keep her marriage with CRA together, her first reaction was that they should have tried harder, and then that the failure was somehow also hers. She never lost touch with her two former sons-in-law. Prue's second husband was part Indian, and Helen's was Italian; I once made the flippant suggestion that she write a book called *Sons-in-Law I Have Known*. She had a good laugh over the idea, but never attempted it.

Living as she did now so much farther from previous friends, and increasingly immobile because of arthritis, she came to depend more than ever on her correspondence. The local postman was soon used to taking away sheaves of letters addressed to all corners of the globe when he delivered the equally varied morning mail. She was very reluctant to use new envelopes, if used ones could make a second trip, and as these missives were usually stuffed with clippings and letters from others, to be read and returned, they often bulged. In those days, glue was more primitive; finding that envelopes stuck down with Gloy needed prolonged pressure to keep them shut, Janet used to sit on them. It took Dorothy some time to identify the strange, silvery, sluglike tracks on her mistress's skirts, until she actually caught her at it!

Keeping in touch was thus Janet's main occupation, and foremost among the people to whom she wrote regularly were the ones who had been stalwarts since Campden years: Gerald

49. Janet Ashbee writing letters on her eightieth birthday, 28 December 1957

Bishop, Laurence Housman, and John Masefield. But it was not until 1950, when she was seventy-two, that she could bring herself to revisit Campden itself.

It was probably Keith-Roach who persuaded her to overcome her reluctance, in honor of CRA. He had retired to Cheltenham, and had been invited to give a lecture in Campden on CRA's life and work. Having at last made up her mind, Janet decided to do the trip in style, renting a car for the weekend. She wrote a long account of it, labeled "Campden Saga," to be passed around to all her "Dearest Family." Her first call was on George and Edith Hart, he looking "more red Indian than ever . . . she almost unchanged (though with six grandchildren) from the schoolgirl farmer's daughter whom, she reminded me, I had taken to Dr Dewhurst's house . . . to have six stitches put in her forehead from a blow by a hockey ball in the match in which we were both playing" (Mar. 1950; in the possession of the Ashbee family).

She had little time to hunt up the "labouring folk" except for the

> handsome Hopes (do you remember the baby Dr Withers and I saved from pneumonia death with whisky?). Now a beautiful girl, happy wife and mother. The two old folk SWEET. Sam Hope DELICATELY inquiring if I had married again!!! We re-lived the awful story of her lost wedding-ring, and he recalled how Daddy had come to see him when he was ill, and had said: "What can I give you?" (perhaps thinking a few flowers, or a poem read aloud?). Sam said "Wull, 'alf a crown wud be very noice, Sir" and Daddy produced one, and with it Sam got his first clutch of eggs, and started his hens, which LED TO A PIG! They had THEN, 10 children, and 13 shillings a week—1904! They are now in a council house, "with a lavatory," blissfully happy. (ibid.)

Keith-Roach's lecture went very well:

> People were spellbound, I think as much by Keith-Roach's non-blind affectionateness, as by the real interest of the

233

matter. At the end, to my horror, Will Hart got up and said, "We are very fortunate in having Mrs Ashbee with us tonight, so I will ask her to say a few words," so I had to rise, and I am sure looking murderous, uttered a few grateful sentences. I did SO wish ONE of you COULD have been there, it was such a very real, spontaneous reaction to evidently deeply cherished memories. (ibid.)

It had taken her more than thirty years to lay to rest her particular and private ghost, but it was fitting that she should have done so. She was a believer in not letting "the sun go down on your wrath."

CRA had made Janet and Alec Miller, his favorite guildsman, his literary executors, and as soon as postwar conditions allowed, Alec had come over from the United States, where he now lived, to help her sort things out. Now, in the spring of 1961, he came again, with a few days at Hest Bank high on the agenda. Both were looking forward to it, though with some trepidation, for they recognized that it might well be an emotional meeting and, perhaps, their last. But it never took place. Janet died suddenly on 8 May, having just finished a letter to me in which she wrote with excitement, if a little fearfully, of Gargarin's first orbit in space.

She had characteristically taken the trouble to write her own obituary, on condition that her anonymity was respected, and it appeared, short and expressive, in the *Lancaster Guardian and Observer:* "A woman of wide reading and culture, and a competent pianist (especially in accompanying) she had rather a boisterous sense of humour, and a racy manner of narrating, which made her company amusing and even exhilarating . . . . She realised she had had 'a good run for her money' as she phrased it, in a most interesting and adventurous life; and especially desired there should be no long faces or mourning at her departure" (19 May 1961). One of her young friends from the local drama group came to the funeral with a tearstained face, but in her brightest spring suit, saying that she could never have worn black because it was knowing Janet that had taught her not to be afraid of old age.

Janet had left strict instructions to the local builder-cum-undertaker that she wanted just a plain coffin, no oak or brass handles. And her instructions to us were that, if it was not "too much trouble," she would like her ashes to be put in the family grave in Seal churchyard, with CRA, Nevill, and her parents. The day fixed for us to take the casket of ashes down to Seal was, by a strange chance, 17 May, CRA's birthday, and we had expected to see Alec Miller there. But he did not come. We learned only afterward that he had died the day before, as if wishing to mark the date and to leave his bones in England, near the friends whom he had loved so much, and who had so profoundly influenced his life.

It was a lovely spring day, with blue sky and flying clouds and the little fourteenth-century church looking out benignly over the meadows toward the Pilgrim's Way. And then there was a hitch. Someone had forgotten to see that the grave was opened. While the village was combed to find the grave digger, the assembled mourners stood around waiting. Gradually, the tension eased. "No long faces," she had said. Finally, a panting Shakespearean figure with a spade appeared. And as the earth flew upward, we held our breaths, half expecting a sudden exclamation of "Alas, poor Yorick!" CRA would have greatly appreciated the Elizabethan overtones—and HOW Janet would have laughed.

Suggested Reading

Index

SUGGESTED READING

Crawford, Alan. *C. R. Ashbee: Architect, Designer, and Romantic Socialist.* New Haven and London: Yale Univ. Press, 1985.

Greensted, Mary, ed. *The Arts and Crafts Movement in the Cotswolds.* Stroud, England: Alan Sutton Publishing, 1993.

MacCarthy, Fiona. *The Simple Life: C. R. Ashbee in the Cotswolds.* London: Lund Humphries, 1981.

INDEX

Page number in italic denotes illustration.

Abbas the Baha'i, 175, 226–27
Addams, Jane, 56
A'eed, 171, 174, 183; marriage of, 185–86
Alfriston, Sussex, Clergy House, 34
Archer-Houblon, George Bramston, 72
Arts and Crafts Exhibition (October 1896), 20–21
Arts and Crafts Exhibition Society, the, xxvii
Arts and Crafts Movement, xx–xxiv, xxvii, 2, 41
Art Workers' Guild, xxiv, 41
Ashbee, Agnes, 18, 20, 30, 42, 168–69, 186
Ashbee, Charles Robert (CRA), xix, *14, 176, 208;* affair with Chris Robson of, xxiii, 133–36; architectural training of, 16; in Berlin, 211; birth of, 14; in Cairo, 146–48, 187; at Cambridge, 16; and Edward Carpenter, 135; and comradeship, 25; death of, 229; depressions of, 108–9, 113, 228; design work of, xxv; doubts about marriage to Janet of, 28–30; engagement to Janet of, 30; with evacuee children, 226; fact-finding mission in northern Palestine of, 175; at Godden Green, 13–14, 17; in Hamburg, 101; homosexuality of, 16; honeymoon of, 34–35; and Jerusalem, 155, 158, 220–22; journal of, 1; marriage of, xxii, 1; and Alec Miller, 113–14; onset of cancer of, 226; *A Palestine Notebook,* 175, 197–98, 203, 205; proposal of marriage of, xx–xxii, 22–24; "Report on the Arts, Crafts and Industries of the Holy City," 156, 159–61, 175; resignation of Jerusalem post of, 199–200; return to

London of, 187–92; in Sicily, 116–17, 124; slow decline of, 228; and Tollemache family, 132; in United States, 53, 120, 124, 138, 203, 205, 225; in Venice, 211; wedding of, 31; at Wellington College 16; *Where the Great City Stands,* 159
Ashbee, Elizabeth (née Lavy; a.k.a. "the Little Mother"), *15,* 31, 35, *57,* 60, 73, 149, 164, 186; death of, 168; Janet's jealousy of, 55, 108
Ashbee, Elsa, 18, 20, 169
Ashbee, Frances (later Langham), 31
Ashbee, Helen Christabel, 216; birth of, 142; engagement and marriage of, 224, 231; visit to Germany of, 220
Ashbee, Henry Spencer, 15, 31
Ashbee, (Jane) Felicity, 216; birth of, 135; and disabled child, Jimmy, 210–11; joins the WAAF, 226; visit to Florence and Hamburg of, 219–20; visit to Jerusalem of, 220–22
Ashbee, Janet (née Forbes), xix, *9, 39, 47, 57, 89, 124, 130, 163, 167, 171, 184, 206, 232;* alphabet of the guildsmen of, 51–53; in Berlin, 7–8, 211–12; in Birmingham, 101–3; birth of, 1; and Gerald Bishop, xxii, xxvii, 106–7, 109–10, 111–18, 119; on Gwendolen Bishop, 40; in Boston, 65–66; breakdown of, 118–20; "bulging red book" of, xxviii, 105–8; in Cairo, 181; and Edward Carpenter, 34; and 37 Cheyne Walk, 19–20; and Chicago, 56–57; childhood of, 6; in Chipping Campden, 81–86, 233–34; command of Arabic of, 168, 171–72; as "comrade wife," xxi–xxii, 23; connections with the Shaftesbury Society of, 210; at Court House, Long Crendon, 67–70, *68;* CRA's proposal of

marriage to, 22–24; death of (1961), 234–35; diptheria of, 114; in Dresden, 223; dress of, 40; description of CRA of, 17–18; description of mother by, 4; descriptions of Mary and Felicity by, 143–44; description of Miss Thomas by, 175; description of wedding night by, 32–33, doubts about marriage to CRA of, 27–30; editing for Essex House Press, 43–44; education of, 7; engagement to CRA of, 30; fiftieth birthday of, 213; in Germany, 22; and Godden Green, 213, 230; golden string necklace of, 156, 157, 201; Guild of Handicraft "river expedition" on, 48–50; in Hamburg, 101; in Hest Bank, Lancashire, 230; holiday in Oxford of, 98–100; and homosexuality, xxi–xxii, 1; honeymoon of, 34–35; and George Ives, 37–38; in Jerusalem, 220–22; journal of, 12; as Lady of the Guild, 45–47; last poem of, 126; letters to CRA of, 138–40, 141–45, 150–56, 159–61, 174; marriage of, xxii, 2; as mother, xxiii, 218–19; and mother-in-law, 108; in New York, 59–65, 121; obituary of, 234; and parents, 5; in Paris, 8–10; poem for CRA of, 112, 116; portrait by Harriet Halhed of, 99–100; at Poynetts, 46–47; in Provence, 203–5; "Rachel," xxviii, 2, 31, 67, 120, 125–26; relationship with CRA of, 105–7, 120, 125–27, 132–33, 228–29; return to England of, 192–96; in South Africa, 88, 90–91; in United States, xxvii, 54–66, 225; in Washington D.C., 58–59; wedding of, 31; writings of, xxviii–xxix
Ashbee, Mary Elizabeth, 216; birth of, xxii–xxiii, 128–29, 131; marriage of, 225; visit to Hamburg and Paris of, 219
Ashbee, Prudence, 216, 226; birth and

christening of, 152–53; engagement of, 222–23; marriage of, 223, 231; relationship with CRA of, 222
Ashbee daughters, 205–6; education of, 181–83, 205, 208–9, 216–17; letter from CRA to, 197; voyage to Jerusalem of, 164–66
Ashbee Journals, the, xix, 1
"Ashbee Memoirs, The," 223

Balfour, Max, 34, 37–38, 53
Barnett, Reverend Samuel, 16–17
Beardshaw, Kathleen, 148, 162
Beauty's Awakening, xxvi, 41
Bennett, E. K. (Francis), 213–14
Bentwich, Norman, 199
Bishop, Gerald, xxviii, 77, 86–88, *87*, 99, 132, 232–33; poems to Janet of, 107–8, 111; relationship with Janet of, xxii, 106, 113
Bishop, Gwendolen, 40–42, 72, 86–87, 91, 107; poem of, 112–13
Bodley, G. F., 16
Bond, Dorothy, 230–31
Borwick, Leonard, 22, 28, 74
Bryce Group, 138–39, 153
Buckley, Wilfred, 60

Cambridge, King's College, 1, 133
Campbell, Mrs Patrick, 92–94
Carrington, Reverend Thomas and Mrs, 81, 83
Carpenter, Edward, 16–17, 27, 34, 135
Carrick, Valery, 27
Caterson-Smith, Robert and Mrs, 102–3
Cellini, Benvenuto: *Treatises*, 27, 30
Charteris, Mary, Lady Elcho, 92–93
Cheyne Walk, Chelsea, London, no. 37 (the Magpie and Stump), *18*–19, 186–89, 191
Cheyne Walk, Chelsea, London, no. 74: *35*, 36, 41, 67, 73; destruction of, 228; music room or studio of, *74*; planning for, 26, 30

Chipping Campden, Gloucestershire, xxv, *76;* bathing lake at, *97;* silk mill in, 76, *80;* Woolstapler's Hall, 81, *82*

Cobden-Sanderson, T. J. and Annie, xxvi

Colverd, George, 49, 96

Coomaraswamy, Ananda and Ethel, 129–30, 163

Cotton, Sid, 71, 81, 113; death of, 140–41

Crane, Lionel, 42–43

Crane, Walter, 40, 41, 44, 85

Creighton, Beatrice, 69

Criminal Law Amendment Act 1885, xxi

Curtis, Lionel, 28, 34, 37–38, 53

Cust, Harry, 191

Dalmas, Philip, 28

Davis, Louis, 43

Dease, Louis, 82

Deedes, Wyndham, 199

De Morgan, William, 85

Dixon, Arthur, 101

Downer, Charlie, 49, 70, 103

Drayton St. Leonard's, Oxfordshire, Waterside, 71, 77

Essex House, Bow, London, 26, *33*

Essex House Press, 27, 30, 43; books of, 191; closing of, 113

Essex House Song Book, 75, 79, 183

Forbes, Frank, 2, 4–5, 99, 131; patronage of the Guild of Handicraft of, 13

Forbes, Jessie (Carrick, a.k.a. "Babushka"), 4, 142, 153, 164, 187, 194–96; death of, 207; stroke of, 192

Forbes, Nevill, 7, 90, 151–52, 187, 193–95,*194,* 204, 207; suicide of, 214–16

Forbes family, *11;* visit to St. Petersburg (1897), 27

Fuller-Maitland, J. A., 75

Gainsborough, Earl of, 82

Gainsborough, Lady, 98

Godden Green, Sevenoaks, Kent, 209–10; house at, xix, xx, 2, *3,* 187–88, 193, 195, 230; return to, 201, 205; transformation of house at, *207*–8, 211

Granville Barker, Harley, 95

Guild of Handicraft, xxii, xxv–xxvii, 13, 20, 30, 98, 142, craftwork of, xxix; difficulties of, 103–4; establishment of, 17; furniture for Grand duke of Hesse at Darmstadt, 27; last meeting of, 162; liquidation of limited company, 114, 131; metalworkers of, *45;* move to Chipping Campden of, 78–80, 84; piano made by, 74–75; plays of, 40, 50–51, 86, 96, 103; river expeditions of, 40, 48–50, 71–72; workshops at Essex House, 25–26

Haani (Armenian cook), 166

Halhed, Harriet, 21; portrait of Janet by, 99–100

Hallingbury Place, Essex, 72

Hart, George, 89, 233

Hassan, 166, 171

Head, Henry (later Sir), 2, 119–20

Head, Ruth, 167

Hill, Octavia, 71

Holland-Martin, Rob. *See* Martin Holland, Rob

homosexuality, xxi

Housman, Laurence, xxviii, 37, 88, 205, *217,* 233; comment on marriage of Janet and CRA of, 228; first meeting with Janet of, 44; letters from, 94–95, 131, 136–37, 149–50, 167–68, 185, 213–14; limerick about the Little Mother of, 55; poem about Janet of, xxiii, 218; poem for Mary Ashbee by, 128; speech at Helen Ashbee's wedding of, 224–25

Hubbard, Elbert, 61–65; *Philistine,* 61, 64–65

Hubbard family, *16*

Hughes, Lewis ("Jacko"), 49, 69, 77, 96, 113

Ives, George, 37, 150

Jameelah, 172, 174, 183
Jerusalem: American Colony in, *165*, 169–70, 174, 183, 201, 221; city walls and ramparts of, *179*–80; Drainage Scheme in, 197–200; house in the Wadi el Jose in, *170*–71, 183–84, 198; Red House in, 198–99; revival of crafts in, 175–77; souks in, 177, *178*; violence in, 189; visit of Prince George to, 189–91

Keith-Roach, Edward and Vi, 191, 198, 233–34
Kelmscott Press, 30
Kelsey, Cyril, 48, 84, 86, 96–97

Leipzig, international exhibition (1914), 136
Lewis, Ted, 225
Lodge, Sir Oliver, 102
London, Jack, 85
Long Crendon, Buckinghamshire, Court House, 67, *68*, 71
Lowes Dickinson, Goldsworthy ("Goldy"), 28, 37, 86, 138

Ma'azousah, 172–73, 221–22
MacCarthy, Fiona, xxviii
marriage, xix–xx
Martin Holland (later Holland-Martin), Rob, 98, 108
Masaryk, Jan, 225
Masefield, John, 2, 86, 110, 233; comment on "Rachel" of, 127; poem about Chipping Campden of, 79
Mead, George, 56
Mile End, London, xxv
Miller, Alec, *84*, 85, 113–14, 234; death of, 235; letter to CRA, 162
Moira, Gerald, 42–43

Money, Arthur (later Sir), 159
Morris, Jane, xxvi
Morris, May, 42–43
Morris, William, xxv, xxvii, 30; *Earthly Paradise* of, 207
Murphy, Mary, 227

Nessler, Horst, 222–23, 227, 231
Noel, Mrs. Miriam, 143
Norman Chapel, Broad Campden, Gloucestershire, *129*–30, 137–38, 158, 162; lease of, 154, 163
Norton, Charles Eliot, 54

Ohanessian, David, 176

Page, Thornton, 224, 231
Paris, international exhibition (1914), 136
Parsons, Nurse, 119–20, 204
Partridge, Fred, 84, 129
Pauncefote, Julian, Lord, 58–59
Phoebe (Hilda Pook), 152, 158
Pilkington, Alf, 96
Pinsent, Ellen, 102–3
Pro-Jerusalem Society, 161, 181

Raper, Robert W., 99–100
Rawnsley, Canon, 38
Richmond, Ernest, 159, 198, 203, 205
Robson, Chris, xxiii, 133–36, *137*, 141; death of, 145–46
Rolfe, Henry Winchester, 53–54, *122*–*23*
Ruskin, John, xxiv, xxvii
Ruutz-Rees, Caroline, 211

Samuel, Herbert (later Sir), 175, 181, 199, 201
Samuels, Simeon, 49, 96–97
Saunton, Devon, 154, 158
Savage, Reginald, 44
Seal Church, 27, 31, 223–25
Shaw-Hellier, Colonel, 35, 116, 124
Somervell, Arthur, 75
South Kensington Museum, the, xxiv

Spottiswood, Sylvia, 73–74
Stewart, Will, 148
Storrs, Ronald (later Sir), 155, 158–59, 161–62, 181, 199–200, 203, 205, 218
Stoy, Miss Hedda, 5, 7, 43
Strang, William, 44, 86, 187

Taylor, Frank, and Mrs, 121, 214
Terwilliger, Mabel, 61, 121
Thornton, Bill, 77
Thorp, Joseph, 95
Tollemache family, 132
Tomlin, Nora, 212
Toynbee Hall, Whitechapel, London, 16,

Varley, Fleetwood, 48
Victoria and Albert Museum, xxiv, 191
Victoria, Queen, 66
Ville, Miss de, 209

Waardi, 184, 201
Walton, E. A., 78
Watts, Mary, 40
Wauchope, Arthur, 73–74, 114, 131, 145, 220–21; feelings toward Janet of, 211–12
Webb, Sidney and Beatrice, 85, 92–94
Whall, Christopher, 41
Whistler, James Abbott McNeill, 78
Whitman, Walt, 229
Whitney, Henry Melville, 65
Wilde, Oscar, xxi
Wilson, Henry, 41
Woodroffe, Paul, 42–43
World War I, 136–37
World War II, 226
Wright, Catherine, 122, 143
Wright, Frank Lloyd, 57, 121–22, 143–44; photographs by, *14, 15, 57*

Printed and bound by Thomson-Shore, Dexter, Michigan
Composed in Adobe Caslon text with Big Caslon display from Carter & Cone
Book design by Christopher Kuntze